SEALS AND SEA LIONS
OF THE
WORLD

SEALS AND SEA LIONS
OF THE
WORLD

Nigel Bonner

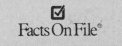

Facts On File®

AN INFOBASE HOLDINGS COMPANY

SEALS AND SEA LIONS OF THE WORLD

First published in the UK 1994
by Blandford, an imprint of Cassell plc

Text copyright © 1994 W. Nigel Bonner

Facts On File, Inc.
460 Park Avenue South
New York NY 10016

Library of Congress Cataloging-in-Publication Data
Bonner, W. Nigel (William Nigel)
    Seals and sea lions of the world/Nigel Bonner.
        p.   cm.
    Includes bibiliographical references (p.   ) and index.
    ISBN 0-8160-2955-5
    1. Seals (Animals)   2. Sea lions.   I. Title.
QL737.P64B662 1994   92-46594
599.74'5--dc20   CIP

Facts On File books are available at special discounts when purchased in bulk quantities for businesses, associations, institutions or sales promotions. Please call our Special Sales Department in New York at 212/683-2244 or 800/322/8755.

Typeset by Litho Link Ltd, Welshpool, Powys.
Printed and bound in Slovenia by Printing house DELO Tiskarna by arrangement with Korotan Italiana, Ljubljana

10 9 8 7 6 5 4 3 2 1

Contents

Acknowledgements

In writing this book I have drawn heavily on the published work of others. I am deeply grateful to a lifetime's accumulation of colleagues who were ready to answer questions, provide material or read parts of the manuscript, point out errors and suggest improvements. In particular, I would like to thank Ian Boyd, Bud Fay, Kathy Frost, Bill Gillmartin, John Harwood, and Bernie McConnell.

I am grateful also to those of my friends who looked out photographs of seals for me, especially Kathy Frost and Kit Kovacs, for whom nothing seemed too much trouble. I am sorry I was not able to use more of the many excellent pictures that were lent to me.

Finally, like so many authors, I have to acknowledge a great debt to my wife. Studying seals in various quarters of the globe has meant more than the usual number of separations in our life, but she has unfailingly given me support and encouragement. And, in more practical terms, she has read the drafts and the proofs, and prepared the index. Thank you, Jennifer.

Illustration Credits

All the photographs were taken by the author, who also drew the line illustrations, except for the following:
Doug Allan, pp. 14, 18, 106, 148
Ricardo Bastida/Diego Rodriguez, p. 73
Márthan Bester, p. 46 (bottom)
British Antarctic Survey, pp. 142 (top), 168 (bottom)
Martin Cawthorne, p. 64
Audrey Cornall, p. 51 (top)
Randall Davis, p. 213 (bottom)
Bud Fay, p. 76
Kathy Frost, pp. 101, 109 (bottom)
William Gilmartin, US National Marine Fisheries Service, p. 113
John Henderson, US National Marine Fisheries Service, p. 114
Lex Hiby, Sea Mammal Research Unit, p. 119
Brendan P. Kelly, p. 103
Kit Kovacs, pp. 77, 89, 91, 109 (top), 107, 181
Dick Laws, pp. 142 (bottom), 144, 149
Ole Mathiesen, p. 83
Bernie McConnell, Sea Mammal Research Unit, pp. 129, 130
Paul Thompson, p. 96
Daniel Torres, p. 42 (bottom)
Fritz Trillmich, pp. 43, 166 (bottom)
Bobby Tulloch, pp. 12, 65, 87
US National Marine Fisheries Service, pp. 51 (bottom), 184, 186
Bob Warneke, pp. 49, 62

Preface

I first remember seeing seals in the wild from the cliffs of Cornwall, sometime in the early 1940s. They were little more than black specks in the sea to me then. My main interest at that time was in beetles, particularly those associated with carrion.

However, in 1953, a fortunate opportunity was offered to me to go to South Georgia as part of a two-man expedition. My companion, Bernard Stonehouse, was planning to study penguins. That left me to work on the elephant seals.

This started an enthusiasm which still stays with me, 40 years later. After nine years with the elephant and fur seals at South Georgia, I turned to British seals, as the head of the Natural Environment Research Council's Seals Research Unit. Here, with the support of some stalwart colleagues, I got to grips with seal – fishery interactions. Seven years later, I joined the British Antarctic Survey and returned to my original seal studies in South Georgia.

My various posts have given me the opportunity to watch seals in every continent of the world. Their attraction has not waned, though I have never become as emotionally attached to them as some people do. I have viewed with dismay some attitudes to seals, which seem to be based solely on sentiment and with little understanding of the seal's place in nature.

Seals, because of their aquatic habit and the remoteness of their haunts, are not easy animals to study, but through the years they have exerted a fascination on people who have encountered them. I hope this book will give interested people the opportunity to understand a little more about the way seals have evolved and live today in a world where interactions with our own species are inevitable. If it arouses further interest – as I hope it will – the books listed at the end will lead the reader further into the subject and perhaps engender an enthusiasm to study these fascinating animals in the field.

Nigel Bonner
Godmanchester

A Note on Scientific Names

Some people have difficulty in dealing with the Latin names (they are often Greek!) of animals, so a note on the rules and conventions may be helpful. It was the Swedish naturalist, Carolus Linnaeus, who in the middle of the eighteenth century devised the system used today. All animal (and plant) species were to have a unique name made up of two parts, the generic name, which would be common to similar species, and the trivial, or specific name, which would be unique as an identifier of that species. The system starts from the tenth edition of Linnaeus' great book *Systema Natura* (1758) and the valid name for any species is that first published, provided it was accompanied by a proper description (and follows certain rules).

The Linnaean system avoids the use of common or vernacular names, which can give rise to confusion. What is called *"havert"* in Norway is often known as 'horse-head' in Newfoundland; both are what I usually call the Grey seal, but it could be identified as *Halichoerus grypus* throughout the world.

One often sees a Linnaean name written with a person's name and perhaps a date after it, thus *Phoca vitulina* Linnaeus 1758. This tells us that we are dealing with the common seal (Harbour seal) described by Linnaeus in 1758. (He would have called it *'kobbe'* in Swedish. Sometimes the name is in brackets: *Halichorus grypus* (Fabricius 1791). This tells us that the Grey seal was first described by Fabricius in 1791, but under a different generic name – *Phoca*. Later it was decided that Grey seals were so different from the seal described by Linnaeus as *Phoca* that they were put in a different genus. These 'author's names' are helpful in some groups but they are not much needed for seals, where there is usually little doubt about which species is being referred to.

And finally, I should justify my capitalization of seal names. Where the first part of a seal's vernacular name is an adjective, like 'Grey seal' or 'Southern elephant seal', it is capitalized to show that I am not writing about seals that are necessarily grey in colour, or elephant seals which occur further south than some others. If I write about monk seals as a group, I do not capitalize it, but if I refer to a specific monk seal, say the Hawaiian monk seal, then that gets a capital.

Chapter 1

The World of Seals

SEALS AS MARINE MAMMALS

Seals are familiar animals to most people and everyone can recognize a 'seal', though in fact there is not just one kind of seal, but thirty-three species in three groups (Fig. 1.1). Seals in the broad sense are often referred to as 'pinnipeds'. This name is derived from the Latin for wing- (or fin-) footed, a reference to their flippers, and as we shall see, the structure of their limbs is basic to their way of life.

The first of these groups, seals in the strict sense, comprises the Family Phocidae, with 18 species. These phocid seals are often referred to as 'true seals' or 'earless seals' because the outer opening of the ear possesses no cartilaginous flap, or pinna, visible on the surface. However, some of the 'earless' seals can erect a small ear cartilage beneath the surface of the skin to reveal quite a wide ear orifice, and there is no doubt that all phocid seals possess and make use of fully functional ears.

The second group, the Family Odobenidae, contains only the walrus. The walrus is quite unmistakable. Like phocid seals, it lacks an external pinna to its ear, but in most other respects it resembles the members of the third group, the Family Otariidae, the fur seals and sea lions. The 14 species in this family all have ears with little scroll-like pinnae and hence are often known as 'eared seals'. The three families together constitute the Order Pinnipedia.

The two main groups of pinnipeds – otariids and phocids. California sea lions and Northern elephant seals bask on a rock on Año Nuevo Island, California.

PINNIPEDIA

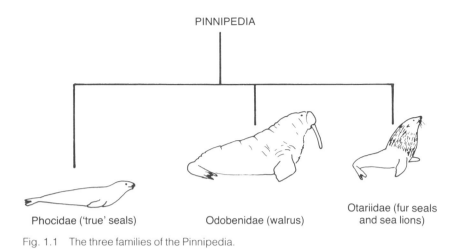

Phocidae ('true' seals)   Odobenidae (walrus)   Otariidae (fur seals and sea lions)

Fig. 1.1   The three families of the Pinnipedia.

Phocid, or earless, seals sometimes show a trace of the cartilage of the external ear. Here a Pacific Harbour seal cranes out of the water.

Otariid seals are often called eared seals because of the small scroll-like external ear, shown here on a bull Antarctic fur seal.

WATER AS AN ENVIRONMENT

We can recognize seals as seals because of certain basic similarities that they share. These result mainly from the fact that they are all aquatic mammals. Mammals originated as small terrestrial forms living much as shrews do today, but in the course of the evolution of the class, three groups have entered the sea: the whales, sea-cows, and seals. The whales are the most successful and highly adapted of these, with representatives in every ocean. Whales – and their smaller and more numerous relatives, the dolphins – are typically denizens of the deep oceans, rarely approaching the shores and living out their whole lives from birth to death at sea. The sea-cows, the dugongs and manatees, are estuarine or coastal. They too never leave the water, but they are a much less successful group, with only a handful of living (or recently extinct) species. Seals have not become as completely aquatic as the whales or sea-cows; they must return to land (or to ice) to bear and rear their young. Nevertheless, they have undergone extensive adaptations to render them supremely well fitted to aquatic life, and it is mainly these features of aquatic adaption that give the seals their characteristic appearance and make them so easily recognizable.

All animals are, to a great extent, a product of their environment. A typical mammal is the result of a series of selective pressures that acted on its ancestors and these, back through the reptiles of the Cretaceous and even earlier amphibian forebears, had evolved to live on land. On land, the mammal's ancestors were living in a medium of air; on taking to the sea the air was replaced with water, and this was a very profound change.

The only member of the Odobenidae, the walrus, is unmistakable.

Obviously, air is a very different substance from water, but it is worth examining some of these differences. Firstly, water is very much denser than air. Sea water is, in fact, over a thousand times as dense as air. Associated with this is the fact that water is 1,700 times more viscous than air. This means that a body moving through water has to do 1,700 times as much work to push through the water as it would through air. Water is about 16 times as good a conductor of heat as is air, and it has a much higher specific heat (that is, the amount of heat required by unit mass to raise the temperature by the same amount). The specific heat of water is 4,200 times that of air. Combining the specific heat with the density of water means that the heat capacity per unit volume for water is over four million times that of air.

There are other differences also: for example, water conducts sound much better than air, and it contains much less oxygen. However, let us first look at how the differences between water and air have affected the evolution of the seal's body.

BODY SHAPE OF SEALS

The body shape of any seal is noticeably sleek. It is elongated and roughly spindle-shaped, tapering more markedly to the rear. The head fares smoothly into the trunk with no abrupt constriction at the neck and projecting appendages are reduced. The small ear flaps of the otariids, and their absence in the other two families, have been noted already. In phocids and the walrus, the testes are internal and in all male seals the penis normally lies in an internal sheath so there is no projection on the outside. In female seals the

Seals are essentially torpedo-shaped, creating a streamlined body-shape that can slip through the water with minimal resistance. This is a Crabeater seal in the Antarctic.

mammary glands form a smooth sheet of tissue under the skin of the ventral surface and up the flanks, while the nipples are normally retracted so that they lie flat against the body surface. Even at the peak of lactation, the mammary glands cause no projection of the body surface, as in most mammals. The general contours of the body are smoothed by a layer of subcutaneous fat, the blubber, though as we shall see later, this has other functions as well.

All these modifications add up to a body that is streamlined, and so it presents the least resistance when it is propelled through the comparatively viscous water. The projections that remain are the limbs, and these have been profoundly modified.

Many mammals have modified their limbs – the mole for digging, the sloth for hanging and the bat for flying – but typically mammalian limbs have a fairly uniform structure. Consider a mammal in the same size range as many seals, the deer for example. The legs of a deer form four supporting pillars, one at each corner of the trunk, that keep its body clear of the ground and form a system of levers, with which force can be exerted by the muscles to push against the ground, and so propel the animal in locomotion. When the animal is walking slowly, the muscles that propel it are mainly those in the upper segments of the limb but when startled, another set of muscles, those situated in the back in the lumbar region, come into play and the animal arches its back as it bounds away.

A seal is quite different. Because water is so much denser than air (indeed, about the same density as the tissues that make up a mammal's body), when the seal is immersed in the water it is effectively weightless. The buoyancy of

A Leopard seal floats weightlessly in the water. Its limbs have no supporting function.

the water suspends the seal in the water column and there is no need at all for any supporting function from the limbs. While this gives the seal a three-dimensional freedom of movement in the water, locomotion by the usual mammalian method is impossible, because the limbs do not bear on the ground. For the seal, what is needed is a limb that can exert force against the medium surrounding it, and we see that the limbs have been modified to do just that.

LIMBS AND LOCOMOTION

Pinniped limbs are relatively much shorter than those of most mammals. This shortening has taken place in the bones of the arm and leg, which are short and sturdy and wholly contained within the general contour of the body. What appear to be the armpit and crotch of a seal are, in fact, at the level of the wrist and ankle respectively. On the other hand, the bones of the hand and foot are relatively elongated. The fingers and toes are bound together in a web of skin and connective tissue to produce a surface that can, like the blade of an oar, push against the resistance of the water and so propel the seal along.

Birds and bats have done very much the same thing in modifying their fore limbs, but because the viscosity of air is so much less than that of water, the wing of a bird or bat has to be relatively much larger than the flipper of a

The fore flippers of a fur seal are broad paddles. There are cartilaginous extensions to the finger bones, to increase the width of the flipper, which leave the rudimentary finger nails set back from the edge. The three main claws on the folded hind flipper are flanked by two rudimentary ones.

seal. A penguin, which is a bird that 'flies' through water, has flippers that are much more like those of a seal than the wings of its flying bird relatives.

The method of swimming is different in phocids and otariids, with the walrus intermediate between the other two groups, and this is reflected in the structure of their limbs. In otariids, it is the fore flippers that are the source of power. They form broad blades, the elongated fingers decreasing serially in size from the first to the fifth. (All seals have the full complement of five fingers or toes in each limb.) Besides the elongation of the digits, the flipper is further lengthened by cartilaginous extensions beyond the end of the digits. As a consequence, the nails are set back on the upper surface of the flipper, where they are of no use in grooming and have become rudimentary nodules.

The otariid hind flipper is composed of similarly elongated digits joined by a web and provided with cartilaginous extensions. Here, the first and fifth digit are much longer than the inner three toes. The nails of the outer toes, with the stiffest cartilaginous extensions, are reduced, but those on the inner toes are developed into strong nails, which otariids use to groom their coats. The under surface of the heel of the hind flippers, like the sole of the fore flippers, is free of hair and covered with thickened skin with a pattern similar to that on the human palm, and which increases grip when the fur seal or sea lion moves on land.

In phocids, the fore flipper is more variable than in otariids. In northern phocids it has a short, blunt outline with the first digit not much longer than the fifth. Each digit is equipped with a strong claw. Some seals, like the Grey seal, use these claws to exert a traction grip on the ground, for example when a seal is hauling out on a rock or ice. In the Ringed seal, the claws are used to scrape snow and ice to construct a breeding lair or to keep a breathing-hole open. In Antarctic phocids, the fore flipper is long and pointed, with the first digit markedly longer than the others. Some Antarctic phocids have reduced claws, others quite well-developed claws, but these never reach the size seen in northern phocids. All phocids use their fore flippers for grooming and show dexterity in reaching all parts of their bodies.

The phocid hind flippers, like those of otariids, form broad fans with the outermost toes longest. They are comparatively widely spaced, for despite the tapering of the hinder part of the body, the thigh bones are set almost at right angles to the hip girdle, widening the separation of the flippers. Northern phocids have strong claws on each toe, but in southern phocids these are reduced or absent. Both sides of fore flippers and hind flippers in all phocids are covered with hair and no definite sole can be distinguished on the foot.

These differences in structure reflect the different ways of swimming in the phocids and otariids. A sea lion or fur seal swims very much in the same manner that a penguin does, with long simultaneous sweeps of the fore limbs. The flipper is held perpendicular to the direction of movement on the power-stroke and then rotated about its long axis at the wrist so that it is feathered for the recovery-stroke. The hind flippers play no part in sustained swimming and simply trail behind, but in confined quarters otariids can occasionally be seen to paddle with them.

Quite the reverse applies to phocids. When swimming, they hold their fore flippers pressed against their sides (there is a recess in the blubber coating, so that the flippers fit into the body contour), and swim with their hind flippers. Swimming is by alternate, inwardly directed strokes of the flippers, the toes being spread to the full extent of the web on the power-stroke, and relaxed with the web furled on recovery. The movements of the flippers are accompanied by lateral waves of the hindquarters, which like those of a fish, help to propel the body through the water. As in otariids, when manoeuvring slowly, phocids may swim differently. Often the fore flippers are held out from the body as stabilizers and the seal moves solely by slow almost imperceptible sweeps of the hinder end of the body.

These different methods of swimming are reflected in the anatomy of the two groups. Otariids need their main muscle mass around their shoulders, since it is by movements of their fore flippers that they swim. In consequence, the shoulder-blade and the neural processes of the thoracic vertebrae – where the muscles involved in moving the flippers are attached – are enlarged. The neck is very massive in fur seals and sea lions, and it helps to balance the body against the source of power, as a man rowing a dinghy will choose to sit more or less in the middle of the craft.

In phocids, the power output comes mostly from the long muscles in the lumbar region of the back (the longissimus dorsi and iliocostalis), which are very well developed, with a corresponding development of the transverse processes of the lumbar vertebrae and the back of the pelvic girdle, where these muscles are attached. The muscles of the limb itself control the position of the flipper relative to the body and the spreading or closing of the web. Three hamstring muscles secure the shank (which is internal to the general

The well-developed claws on the fore flippers of this Grey seal can exert a strong traction grip when hauling out of the sea or moving on land.

The hind flippers of this Weddell seal form a broad fan, haired on both surfaces.

In the water, these Crabeater seals swim by sweeps of their expanded hind flippers. The fore flippers are held passively but provide stability.

body contour) close to the pelvis and nearly parallel to the long axis of the body. This facilitates the transmission of power from the lumbar muscles to the flipper, but at the same time makes it impossible for the seal to bring its hind flippers forward under the body.

An animal which drives itself along in the water from a power source at the hinder end of the body cannot afford to have a long, mobile neck, though it needs to retain flexibility at the forward end of its body to be able to grasp prey. Phocid seals have no obvious neck, as we mentioned above, yet they retain the standard mammalian complement of seven cervical vertebrae. When swimming, the heavily muscled neck is retracted in a downwardly directed U-curve. This conserves the dynamically advantageous streamlining but allows the seal to extend its neck suddenly when it strikes at prey. Seals can do the same thing on land, as many a seal researcher has discovered to his or her cost.

These modifications for aquatic locomotion have been made at the cost of mobility on land. Otariids are the most agile of the pinnipeds when ashore. They can walk by moving their fore flippers alternately, usually bringing the hind flippers up together, the belly being carried clear of the ground. The weight of the body is balanced about the insertion of the fore flippers, with the head and neck extended forward. The hind flippers are used mainly to provide the third leg of the tripod that ensures stability. Only the 'heels' are brought in contact with the ground, the fan formed by the toes and web being held clear. Because of the shortness of the free segment of the hind limb, the 'steps' taken are very short and the sea lion or fur seal progresses slowly. If it needs to move faster, it can break into a gallop, moving the fore flippers simultaneously, followed by an abrupt arching of the back and bringing up the hind flippers

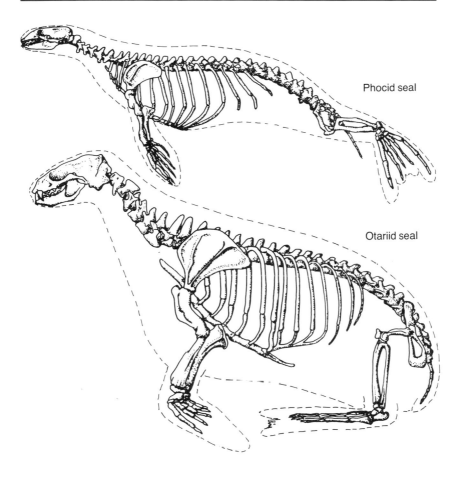

Fig. 1.2 Skeletons of a phocid seal and an otariid. In the otariid, the main muscular development (indicated by the enlarged cervical and thoracic vertebrae and shoulder-blade) is in the region of the neck and shoulders; in the phocid, it is the muscles of the trunk, particularly the lumbar region, that are most developed.

together, progressing in a series of bounds. Antarctic fur seals can make about 19 kph (12 mph) over a smooth surface and over rough ground they can progress nearly as fast as a person can run. The roughened callus on their palms and heels provides a sure grip even on very slippery surfaces, which gives them a very definite advantage in a chase.

On land phocid seals crawl on their bellies, heaving themselves forward with a 'humping action'. The seal first takes it weight on its chest, then flexes its back to bring its pelvic region forward. The weight is then transferred here, while the back is extended, thrusting the chest forward. In this way the seal hitches itself along. The seal may hold its fore flippers passively against the sides as it moves, or it may take some of its weight on them, particularly but not exclusively, in the case of larger seals.

Otariids can lift the body clear of the ground and walk on four legs when ashore. Here a female Antarctic fur seal returns from a foraging trip to find her pup and suckle it.

These Harbour seals, typical phocids, crawl over the mud of the Wash in East Anglia. Their tracks show clearly how they use their fore flippers to drag themselves along.

The clumsy and energy-intensive form of terrestrial locomotion has severely restricted the mobility of seals on land, particularly phocids, with consequences for their breeding behaviour which will be discussed in Chapter 7. On ice, however, phocid seals can travel much more economically. Ribbon seals are said to be able to slide over ice as fast as a person can run and crabeater seals in the Antarctic have been estimated to travel at 25 kph (16 mph), progressing with a sinuous movement involving alternate backward strokes of the fore flippers and vigorous side-to-side flailing of the hindquarters that recall the swimming movements.

KEEPING WARM

Not only is sea water colder than the approximately 37°C (98.6°F) which is the core temperature for most mammals, but because water has a much greater heat conductivity and capacity than air, a terrestrial mammal immersed in water loses heat rapidly across its surface. To avoid loss of energy in this way, seals have developed adaptations to reduce heat transfer to the surrounding water.

Since heat is lost across a surface, one way of doing this is to reduce the amount of body surface. The streamlining and reduction of projecting appendages that helped to reduce drag when moving through the water has simultaneously gone some way to achieving this. Another way of reducing surface area is to take advantage of the geometrical relationship between surface and volume. Since the surface of a solid body increases as the square of the linear dimension, but the volume increases as the cube, it follows that for bodies of the same shape, large ones will have relatively less surface area than small ones. This is most easily understood in the case of a very simple shape, like a cube, though these are not very like seals (Fig. 1.3). However, a seal may be regarded more or less as an ellipsoid, with the major axis about four times as long as the minor axis, and the same relationship applies.

Seals have exploited this strategy to conserve heat, and seals are all large mammals in the literal sense. There are no small seals, as there are small rodents like mice, or small carnivores like weasels. The smallest seals are probably Ringed seal females, which may weigh only about 45 kg (99 lb), but this is huge compared with 30 g (1 oz) for a male Least weasel (*Mustela nivalis rixosa*).

Once surface has been reduced, the other way to conserve heat is to insulate what surface remains. The conventional way of doing this in mammals is the provision of a hairy coat. The hair traps a layer of still air around its roots and this air, with its low heat conductivity and capacity, soon warms up and reduces the loss of heat to moving air outside the hair boundary. Such a hair coat is a very effective insulator in air, particularly when a layer of much finer and more numerous fur fibres are developed beneath the coarser hairs of the coat. However, in water a hair coat is much less effective. If water penetrates the pelage, then heat is lost to it at a much greater rate than in the case of the air layer. Even so, retaining a stationary layer of water trapped in the hair has by no means a negligible effect on heat balance.

Sea lions and true seals have hair coats (very sparse ones in the case of elephant seals), but one group, the fur seals, has developed this method of

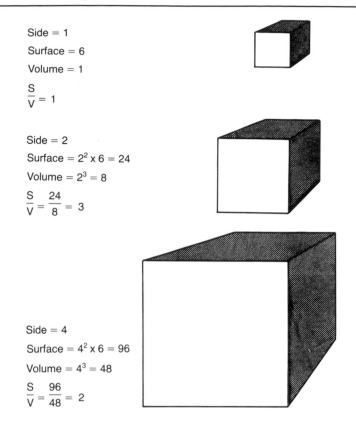

Side = 1
Surface = 6
Volume = 1
$$\frac{S}{V} = 1$$

Side = 2
Surface = 2^2 x 6 = 24
Volume = 2^3 = 8
$$\frac{S}{V} = \frac{24}{8} = 3$$

Side = 4
Surface = 4^2 x 6 = 96
Volume = 4^3 = 48
$$\frac{S}{V} = \frac{96}{48} = 2$$

Fig. 1.3   The surface–volume relationship. As the linear dimension of a solid increases, so the ratio of surface to volume grows less, so that larger bodies have relatively less surface area.

insulation to a very high degree. In most mammals the hair grows from little groups of follicles, emerging from a common hair canal. The follicle towards the front end of the mammal produces a stout, backwardly directed guard hair, and it is followed by a series of three or four finer secondary fibres (Fig. 1.4). In fur-bearing mammals (mink, for example), the number of secondary fibres is greatly increased and they are much finer, forming a definite underfur. Fur seals have done the same thing, but they have carried it further. The guard hairs are very stiff and bristly and the tuft of fur fibres that lies behind each guard hair has increased in number to 50 or so. This can result in total densities of up to 57,000 fibres per cm^2 (370,000 per sq in). The stiff guard hairs support this dense mat of underfur fibres and sebaceous glands in the skin produce oily secretions which make the fine tips of the underfur water-repellent. As a result, when the seal is in the water, the water penetrates only as far as the surface of the underfur layer; although the guard hairs are wetted, a stationary layer of air is trapped against the skin, minimizing heat loss.

Fur is an effective insulator, but it has the disadvantage that when the seal

Seals are often in water that is very much colder than their body temperature. This Weddell seal, off Adelaide Island in the Antarctic, keeps warm with its blubber layer.

This section through the pelt of a fur seal shows the stiff guard hairs supporting the very fine cinnamon-coloured underfur. When submerged, the water penetrates only as far as the tips of the underfur fibres.

dives, the increasing pressure of the water compresses the layer of trapped air. For each 10 m (33 ft) the seal descends, the air layer is reduced by half. In an Antarctic fur seal, the fur layer is about 15 mm (0.6 in) deep, so at 30 m (98 ft) this will be reduced to only about 4 mm (0.16 in), not a very effective insulation. For this reason, fur seals tend to remain and feed near the surface of the water, though they certainly can dive to considerable depths. Other seals regularly forage at greater depths; some, like elephant seals, feeding many hundred metres beneath the surface. Another form of insulation is required for these seals.

This is provided by the blubber. Blubber is a layer of fatty tissue beneath the deeper layer (dermis) of the skin. Fat is a poor conductor of heat and when in air, blubber is about half as effective as an equal layer of stationary air.

Fig. 1.4   The basic 'pilosebaceous unit' of a mammal. From each unit grows a stout guard hair, which overlies a group of fine underfur fibres. A sebaceous gland, to waterproof the hair, and a sweat gland are associated with each unit. In fur seals, the number of underfur fibres is greatly increased.

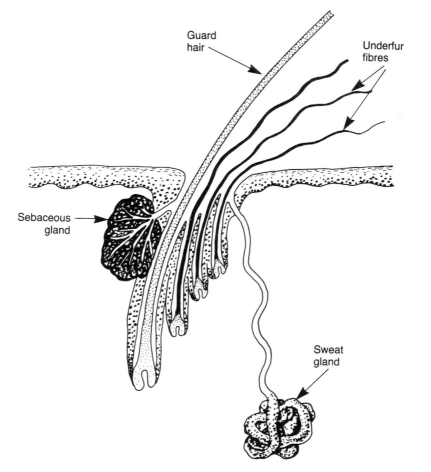

The blubber layer on this Harbour seal wraps the body in a heat-retaining blanket. A Harbour seal may have blubber 7 to 10 cm (2¾ to 4 in) thick.

When immersed in water, the insulative value of blubber is reduced to about a quarter of its value in air, but since blubber is incompressible, this is unaffected by how deep the seal dives. Seals commonly have in excess of 7 to 10 cm (2.8 to 3.9 in) of blubber over their bodies, which effectively prevents loss of heat from the core.

Blubber has other functions besides insulation. As already mentioned, it helps to smooth out the contours of the body, assisting in the streamlining, but it also acts as a very important food store. Seals must come ashore to breed and to moult and at these times it is common for males to spend a long time without food or drink, living on the stored resources of their blubber. Females are generally ashore for shorter periods, but they have the responsibility of producing great quantities of milk to feed their young, the fat for which is derived from their blubber. Nearly all the fat in a seal's body (apart from a fatty pad behind the eyeball) is contained in the blubber. There is no visceral fat around the kidneys or in the mesentery as in most other mammals.

The blubber is not continuous over the whole surface of the body. It is lacking over the head and the flippers, thus these present a potential site for heat loss. However, seals can reduce the flow of blood to these areas (and, of course, to the skin over the blubber layer covering the rest of the body) so that the surface transfers heat from the core very slowly.

If a seal can keep warm in water, it will be able to cope in air no matter how low the temperature drops. A Weddell seal on the surface of the ice in the Antarctic may be in air at $-40°C$ but will not be distressed by it. In fact, if the sun is shining, the seal may be acquiring heat from the sun and it is truly basking. On the other hand, some seals seem to be distressed when it rains. As they are presumably not affected by the wetness of the rain, it may be the percussion of the raindrops on their sensitive skin that they dislike.

Because seals can tolerate cold climates, they are characteristic animals of polar regions and the largest populations of seals occur there. However, seals are by no means confined to cold climates and one species, the Galapagos fur seal, lives exclusively on the Equator. For seals in temperate or tropical regions, avoiding overheating may be a problem. Elephant seals breeding on the beaches of Año Nuevo Island, off California, may flip damp sand on to their backs; monk seals on Hawaii seek shelter beneath vegetation and the fur seals on the Galapagos Islands resort to caves in the lava. Even in areas as cool as South Georgia, on a sunny day fur seals ashore can be distressed by the heat. They then spread their deeply pigmented flippers out on the ground and lose body heat by radiation from them.

MOULTING

Like any other mammal, a seal has to replace its hair from time to time. The moult is more striking in phocids than in otariids. The latter tend to lose the old coat rather gradually, so that there is no question of all the hair and fur being replaced at one time. This is not the case with phocids, which grow a new crop of hair each season. During this process, the blood supply to the skin, where the new hair is developing, has to be greatly increased and this inevitably means heat losses are increased too. Because of this, many phocids spend more time out of the water at the moult. Some, such as elephant seals, come ashore for several weeks during the moult and congregate in large heaps where, by lying in contact with their neighbours, they reduce the surface exposed to the air. Moult in elephant seals is a catastrophic process, the superficial layer of the skin being shed together with the hair. This comes away in rags and tatters, leaving the seal with a very decrepit appearance. The seals often choose to wallow in peat bogs at this time, which seems to indicate that moulting causes considerable irritation.

SENSES

Seals share with other mammals the basic sensory equipment that allows them to gather information about their environment. Mammals generally are highly visual animals and seals are no exception. Water absorbs light much more than air does. Because of this, it is always twilight beneath the surface, so it comes as no surprise to find that seals have large eyes. A large eye, like a large aperture on a camera lens, has greater light-gathering power and seals commonly have eyeballs about 40 mm (1.6 in) in diameter, the Ross and elephant seals having especially large eyes, about 60 mm (2.4 in) in diameter. To give light entering the eye a better chance of stimulating the sensory cells of the retina, seals' eyes are backed by a reflective layer, the tapetum, that reflects any light passing through the retina back to the sensory cells. (It is the tapetum that gives a cat's eyes that greenish glow when illuminated in a car's headlamps.) The seal's retina is adapted to low-light vision. Under the microscope, the sensory cells are seen to be rods, which are more sensitive than cones, though the absence of cones implies that seals do not have colour vision. In fact, some studies show that some visual pigments associated with cones are present, but these may be used for vision in bright light or when

The head of a pinniped is equipped with sense organs to receive stimuli from its environment. In this young Antarctic fur seal, the whiskers (tactile sense), nose (olfactory sense), eyes (visual sense) and ear flaps (auditory sense) can be seen clearly.

ashore, rather than for enabling the seal to distinguish colours.

To see at all, a lens system is needed to refract, or bend, light rays to focus an image on the retina. In a terrestrial mammal most of this refraction is done at the interface between the air and the cornea, the transparent covering of the eye. Minor adjustments are made by the eye lens to accommodate objects at different distances. In a submerged seal, much less refraction occurs at the surface of the cornea, since there is little difference of refractive index between the water and the cornea. This means that the lens has to be more powerful to compensate and a seal's lens is almost spherical.

This system produces a sharp image underwater, but an eye designed to operate at low light intensities beneath the surface needs modification if it is to operate satisfactorily in bright sunlight at the surface. Seals protect their eyes from bright light by closing the pupil, with its very deeply brown-pigmented iris, first to a vertical slit and then to a tiny pin-hole. This compensates for the increase in light intensity, but it does not affect the refraction. With its near-spherical lens, the seal might be expected to be very short-sighted in air. However, the surface of a seal's cornea is not spherical: it has different curvatures in the horizontal and vertical axes. This might be expected to result in the seal being not only short-sighted, but astigmatic as well. In fact, the combination of the vertical-slit pupil parallel to the astigmatic axis has the effect in bright light of focusing to a sharp image on the retina. Contraction of the pupil (like decreasing the aperture on a camera lens) will also increase the depth of focus and minimize the short- sightedness.

As a result, seals can see clearly in air as well as in water. Their sense of sight is probably more important to them in air. Seals use visual cues for many purposes. In a herd of Harbour seals hauled out on a rocky shore, individuals are constantly raising their heads to look about for signs of danger. A breeding bull elephant seal judges the intentions of an intruder at least partly from his attitude; a seal lying prone is ignored, while one that rears up is interpreted as a challenger.

Hearing is another important sense for seals. Water transmits sound much better than air does. Sound travels faster in water and it is less attenuated, so it travels further. In terrestrial mammals there is a great difference in the acoustic impedance between the air and the tissues of the head. This results in most of the sound being reflected away from the head. In order to gather sound vibrations, the ears are equipped with the familiar external flaps, or pinnae. These funnel sound down the orifice of the ear to the ear-drum, from which a series of tiny bones (the ossicles) transmits the vibrations to the inner ear, where they are received by the sensory cells in the cochlea. This system allows sensitive discrimination of the origin of sounds: everyone is familiar with the way a cat pricks up and swivels its ears to locate a rustling mouse.

This does not work in water. Any diver knows how difficult it is to locate the origin of a sound once submerged. This is because there is now very little difference between the impedance of the medium transmitting the sound, the water, and the tissues of the head. Consequently, sound vibrations, instead of being reflected, are absorbed by the bones of the skull and transmitted direct to the inner ear and cochlea. The sound, which appears louder, seems to come from all directions.

Despite this, seals have developed modifications of their skulls so that they can localize sounds underwater. One of the bones of the skull associated with the ear (the squamosal) has an enlarged flattened surface, facing upwards and to the front, in the same direction as the eyes face. Sound vibrations arriving perpendicularly to this surface are absorbed by it and transmitted to the inner ear. Vibrations which arrive obliquely are reflected and do not reach the cochlea. By making scanning movements with its head, a seal can locate the origin of a sound very precisely. A Harbour seal, for instance, can separate two sound sources only three degrees apart. The bones of the middle ear, the ossicles, are much more massive in seals than in terrestrial mammals and it is believed that this too is an adaptation to underwater hearing. Sound-waves in water cause the whole of the skull of the seal to vibrate, but it may be the inertia of the loosely attached ossicles that creates the vibrations that actually stimulate the sensory cells of the cochlea.

These specializations are more marked in phocids than in otariids, and all phocids are more sensitive to sound in water than they are to sound in air. Even in air, however, they seem to hear as well as humans and most can probably detect higher frequency sounds than can humans (though this is true of many, if not most, mammals – humans are rather insensitive to high frequencies).

Seals are very vocal animals and clearly communicate with each other: elephant seal bulls roar to express their dominance, fur seals call to their pups, Harbour seals grunt and bark, and walrus produce eerie bell-like tones. There is no question of a 'language', however, as has been suggested (wrongly, I think) for dolphins.

Do seals echo-locate, as do dolphins? Some, like the Weddell seal in the Antarctic, produce surprisingly loud underwater sounds: they can be heard 30 km (19 miles) away. The sounds consist of trills, each composed of a series of pulses of decreasing frequency which are believed to function as dominance signals; chirps, which sweep through a range of frequencies; and growls, which probably function as threats. The chirps are similar to the sound pulses that are used in echo-location by dolphins and may function in the same way, though the structure of the seal's brain (which is comparatively simple) does not appear very suitable for processing the data produced by echo-location. Other seals, Harbour seals, Leopard seals and sea lions, have been recorded as producing clicks or trills that could function as echo-locating signals, and some biologists believe that this function does exist, though this view is not generally accepted.

Whether or not seals can echo-locate is debatable. What is not in question is that seals can find food underwater without using their sense of sight. Many seals feed in muddy estuarine waters where visibility is very restricted. I knew a Grey seal cow in the Farne Islands which was blind in both eyes, yet maintained good condition and reared pups in three successive years. Clearly, she was able to find food not only for herself, but also for the foetus she was gestating. It seems likely that seals use their very well-developed whiskers for detecting vibrations underwater. The whiskers, or vibrissae, are arranged in definite groups. There are the mystacial vibrissae (growing from a pad on either side of the snout), the superciliary vibrissae (which sprout from above the eye), and the rhinal vibrissae (usually only a single pair of whiskers on top of the nose). Each of these whiskers is inserted in a fibrous pouch, or follicle. This follicle is very richly supplied with nerve fibres; a single whisker of a Ringed seal was found to contain about ten times the number of fibres found in the vibrissal follicle of a typical land mammal.

These whiskers probably function to detect the vibrations set up by prey in the water. Their structure suggests that they would be most useful in receiving large amplitude displacements produced by objects vibrating at low frequencies, such as the movements of a swimming fish. Watching seals in captivity chasing fish in their tank, it can be seen that the whiskers are pushed forward as they chase and capture their prey. Harbour seals with their whiskers clipped take longer in captivity to capture fish than those with their whiskers intact. Experiments on a Spotted seal showed that if it were blindfolded, it could still surface in the centre of its breathing-hole in the ice. However, if it were blindfolded and its whiskers were taped down, it bumped into the ice several times before locating the hole.

Seals use their whiskers on land when socially interacting with each other. The mystacial whiskers may be held back against the sides of the muzzle, or held erected forwards, the latter usually indicating aggressiveness. Antarctic fur seals, in particular, make much use of the whiskers in female–male interactions. A cow wishing to drive off the attentions of the much larger bull will erect her own whiskers and snap at the muzzle of the bull. This stimulates the bull's whiskers and causes it to withdraw. Biologists working with the fur seals can take advantage of this response: to drive off the attentions of an aggressive seal, it is necessary only to tickle its whiskers with a slender pole, whereupon it retreats.

The sense of smell is usually of great importance in mammals and for some it may be more important even than sight. It is difficult to measure the sense of smell in seals. Underwater, smelling in the usual sense cannot be used. Sea water irritates the olfactory epithelium that covers the scroll-like turbinal bones in the nose, so the nostrils close underwater to prevent this. But it is clear that in air, smell is an important sense to many seals. The turbinal bones of seals are complex and large, indicating that they have an extensive olfactory epithelium. Many seals have a strong and characteristic scent. The Ringed seal was once known as the 'stinking' seal, on account of the very strong smell produced by the breeding males. Similarly, male South American sea lions produce a strong odour when in breeding condition. If these scents are apparent to humans, it seems certain that they will be detected by the seals that produce them and have a role in social interactions. But the strongest evidence that seals make use of their sense of smell comes from the relations between a seal mother and her pup. In all seals studied, it has been found that the mothers recognize their pups by their smell. The mother–pup bond is established in the few minutes after birth and thereafter, if the pup is separated from the mother, on coming together again she will always sniff at it to identify it as her own.

ORIGINS AND EVOLUTION OF SEALS

I have discussed above some of the modifications that fitted seals to their life in the sea. Obviously, there must have been some transitional forms from whatever mammalian stock it was that gave rise to the seals.

Our understanding of the origins and relations of animal groups comes from a variety of sources: the study of anatomy (often the anatomy of fossilized remains of extinct forms), comparisons of the numbers and arrangements of chromosomes or of biochemical features, and analogies between different groups.

Fossils are a particularly good source of evidence, because they can be accurately located, giving an indication of the geographical distribution of potential ancestors, and they can be dated, putting a suggested evolutionary line into a time context. Most importantly, they can often show directly the links between one group and its successors.

The earliest fossils found which may be related to seals come from California, from the beginning of the Miocene period, about 22.5 million years ago. The first finds consisted only of two incomplete skull fragments, some teeth and a couple of intercranial casts. The fossils were named *Enaliarctos*, 'the bear of the sea'. Although *Enaliarctos* had many characteristics of the terrestrial bears, including the typical shearing, or carnassial teeth, it also showed aquatic modifications. However, the incomplete nature of the specimens did not allow much further speculation.

This was changed when a nearly complete skeleton of *Enaliarctos mealsi* was

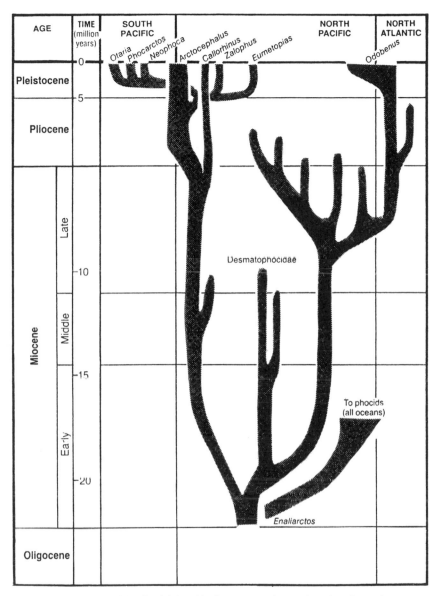

Fig. 1.5   The origins of the Otarioidea. *Enaliarctos* may have given rise also to the phocid seals.

discovered at Pyramid Hill, near Bakersfield, California. *Enaliarctos* was about the size of a Harbour seal, about 1.4 to 1.5 m (4½ to 5 ft) long and probably weighing about 80 kg (176 lb). This protoseal was already modified for an aquatic existence: it had converted its limbs into flippers and developed a seal-like vertebral column. The terminal finger bones appeared to have attachments for cartilaginous extensions, as in otariids. However, the shank bones of the

31

leg (the tibia and fibula) were long, so that the hind limb was longer than the fore limb, a feature of phocid seals. It appears from the skeleton that *Enaliarctos* swam by using both its fore and hind limbs (as well as by undulating its body), but at the same time it was probably fairly active on land. *Enaliarctos* presents many characters that are intermediate between a bear-like (arctoid) carnivore and modern seals, both phocid and otariid.

Three groups of fossils have been found from the middle of the Miocene period, about 14 million years ago. One, the Desmatophocidae, became extinct by the end of the Miocene, but the two others continued to the present, one giving rise to the walrus (Odobenidae) and the other to the sea lions and fur seals (Otariidae).

All these fossils come from the North Pacific. On the other side of the American continent, fossils that represent the earliest phocid seals have been found in Maryland and Virginia, and dated to about 14 million years ago. Because these fossils represent well-differentiated phocids, it is supposed that the origin of the family took place a good deal earlier, about 20 million years ago.

Before the discovery of the nearly complete *Enaliarctos* skeleton, these fossil groups, from two quite different areas, had led many seal biologists to believe that the Pinnipedia was not a true biological group with a single ancestor, but an artificial grouping derived from two ancestral lines – a diphyletic group. One of these was from a bear-like carnivore, which gave rise to the otariids (fur seals and sea lions) and the odobenids (walruses), while the other gave rise to the true seals, the phocids. The features that make these two links are fine details of the ear region of the skull and some other detailed osteological features.

This view had been contested even before the discovery at Pyramid Hill. Molecular biologists studying the structure of various proteins (albumens and eye lens alpha-crystalline protein) found that the proteins of phocids and otariids were more similar to each other than to the proteins of modern arctoid carnivores. More significantly, comparisons of the DNA of phocids and otariids found a closer resemblance between these groups than that between either of them and other mammals. Close similarities were found in some of the bones of the flippers of pinnipeds of all three groups: elongation and enlargement of both the major elements of the first digit of the hand; progressive decrease in emphasis of the fingers; the reduction of the fifth intermediate finger-bone; the strong development and elongation of the first wrist-(and ankle-) bone and proximal finger-(and toe-) bones; and the elongation of the fifth toe.

These findings, reinforced by the discovery of the nearly complete *Enaliarctos* skeleton, supported the single-origin, or monophyletic, theory. However, I am not convinced. Many of the similarities between the two groups (otarioids and phocids) could have arisen by convergence – similar responses to similar selective pressures from the environment. Although phocids and otariids usually swim by very different methods, it seems to me very likely that in their early ancestors there might have been less distinction (as was certainly the case with *Enaliarctos*) and hence an opportunity to acquire common characters like those noted in the flippers. The biochemical data are more difficult to explain in this way, but it is a striking feature that

32

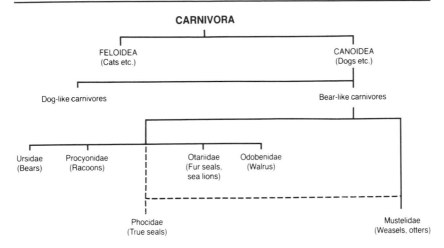

Fig. 1.6   The relationship of pinnipeds to other carnivores. Whether the phocids are derived from a common ancestor with the walrus, fur seals and sea lions, or whether they had a separate origin from an otter-like ancestor, is still debated.

conclusions reached by the molecular biologists about evolutionary courses seem often to be at variance with those drawn from the study of fossils.

At this stage, I feel it is impossible to be certain whether the Pinnipedia are a mono- or di-phyletic group, but while this is of considerable interest to students of evolution, it may not matter so much to those who are more interested in living seals.

CLASSIFICATION OF SEALS

Zoologists can rarely agree on the higher groupings of animal classification, and this is the case with seals. At the top, there are discussions on whether the Pinnipedia constitute an order in their own right, equivalent to the Carnivora Fissipedia (i.e., the 'Split-footed' carnivores), or whether they are a suborder within the other carnivores. Of course, those who believe the seals are a diphyletic group, with two lines of carnivore ancestor, have to abandon the idea of a single order for them, but they often still use the term 'Pinnipedia' because of its convenience to describe a similar group, the members of which are all clearly distinct from any other mammal.

There is most agreement on the nature of the pinniped families, the Otariidae, the Odobenidae and the Phocidae. These do seem to be natural groupings, and there is little doubt that each sprang from a different and single ancestral line. Usually the Odobenidae are placed together with the Otariidae in a suborder, the Otarioidea, but some people maintain that the walruses are more closely related to the true seals than to the fur seals.

Within the three families there is most diversity in the phocids. The walruses need no further subdivision, since only one species survives, though around the early Pliocene, four or five million years ago, there was a great

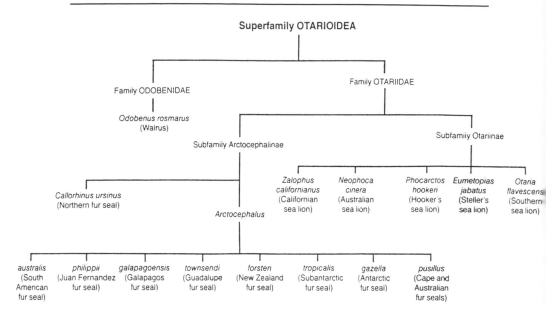

Fig. 1.7   The classification of the otarioid pinnipeds.

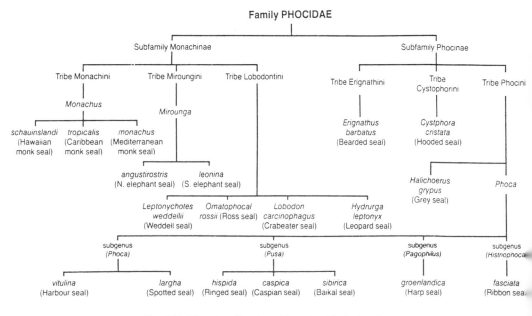

Fig. 1.8   The classification of the phocid pinnipeds.

diversity. The otariids are sometimes split into two subfamilies, the fur seals in the Arctocephalinae, and the sea lions in the Otariinae. This is a convenient and apparently sensible arrangement. The fur seals, *Arctocephalus* in the south and *Callorhinus* in the north, all have fur and rather pointed noses, while the sea lions, in both the north and south, have predominantly hair coats and blunt noses. But there is fossil evidence that *Callorhinus* split off from the *Arctocephalus* stock right at the beginning of the Pliocene, five million years ago, while the sea lions did not separate until about two and a half million years later. I shall treat the fur seals and sea lions separately in this book, but they are perhaps better regarded as forming one family with no further subdivision above the generic level.

The true seals, the Phocidae, are clearly different. The family splits into two: the southern phocids (subfamily Monachinae) and the northern phocids (subfamily Phocinae). In the first of these groups are the monk seals, the elephant seals and the Antarctic seals, while in the second subfamily are the Bearded seal, the Hooded seal, the Grey seal and seven species all closely related to the Harbour seal.

Chapter 2

The Fur Seals

INTRODUCTION

The nine species of fur seals, as is evident from their name, share the characteristic of having an abundant underfur layer in their pelage. This made them attractive to hunters and at one time or another, each species has been reduced, some to mere remnants. Hunting has now been abandoned or controlled and some stocks of fur seals have made spectacular recoveries, a striking contrast with most other endangered species. I shall return to this subject later.

Like all the otariids, the fur seals have scrotal testes (in contrast to the phocids and the walrus) and two pairs of abdominal nipples. There are three pairs of incisor teeth in the upper jaw (only two in the lower jaw), one pair of canines, and six pairs of cheek teeth, or post-canines (there is no obvious distinction between premolars and molars in seals, apart from the developmental one that the premolars are preceded by milk-teeth). The first two upper incisors on each side of the mouth have a deep transverse groove across their biting surfaces and the outer pair are enlarged to look like canines. Like all other otariids they have a karyotype of $2n = 36$ chromosomes (32 in the walrus and 32 or 34 in the phocids).

The fur seals comprise two genera, *Arctocephalus* and *Callorhinus*. Originally these were all classed together as 'sea-bears' (*Arctocephalus* comes from two Greek words meaning bear-headed), but the northern fur seal was put in a

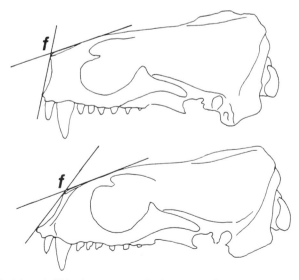

Fig. 2.1   The facial angle (f) is always greater in *Callorhinus* (top) than in fur seals of the genus *Arctocephalus*.

Nose-to-tail lengths and body weights for the 9 species of fur seals

	Males	Females
South American *A. australis*	200 cm (79 in) 120 to 150 kg (265 to 331 lb)	150 cm (59 in) 40 to 50 kg (88 to 110 lb)
Juan Fernandez *A. philippii*	200 cm (79 in) ?140 kg (?309 lb)	140 cm (55 in) ?40 kg (?88 lb)
Galapagos *A. galapagoensis*	154 cm (61 in) 60-70 kg (132-154 lb)	130 cm (51 in) 20-35 kg (44-77 lb)
Guadalupe *A. townsendi*	180 cm (71 in) 160-170 kg (352-375 lb)	120 cm (47 in 40-50 kg (88-110 lb)
New Zealand *A. forsteri*	145-200 cm (57-79 in 120-155 kg (265-342 lb)	125-150 cm (49-59 in) 40-50 kg (88-110 lb)
Subantarctic *A. tropicalis*	180 cm (71 in) 70-160 kg (157-352 lb)	145 cm (57 in) 24-45 kg (53-99 lb)
Antarctic *A. gazella*	165-200 cm (65-79 in) 110-200 kg (242-441 lb)	115-140 cm (45-55 in) 22-50 kg (49-110 lb)
Cape and Australian *A. pusillus*	230-273 cm (91-107 in) 200-360 kg (441-794 lb)	120-160 cm (47-63 in) 40-110 kg (88-243 lb)
Northern *Callorhinus ursinus*	210 cm (83 in) 120-270 kg (265-595 lb)	100-140 cm (39-55 in) 30-50 kg (66-110 lb)

separate genus, *Callorhinus* (Greek, beautiful-hide), by the nineteenth-century zoologist, James Gray. The differences between these two genera are rather trivial; the most obvious ones being that in the northern fur seal, the fur on the fore flipper extends only to the wrist, where it terminates in a sharp, straight line, whereas in the others the fur extends past the wrist on to the dorsal surface of the flipper. There is also a distinct difference in the appearance of the face in these two groups. The northern fur seal has a blunter snout, the angle made between a line drawn from the top of the head and another line between the nasal bone and the tip of the muzzle always being less than 125 degrees. *Arctocephalus* fur seals have more pointed snouts, with this facial angle being more than 125 degrees. *Arctocephalus* seals, with one exception, are found in the Southern Hemisphere and hence they are often called southern fur seals.

SOUTHERN FUR SEALS

All the southern fur seals look rather similar. They range in size from the relatively enormous Cape fur seal, in which males may attain a nose-to-tail length of as much as 2.73 m, (9 ft) to the small Galapagos fur seal, with males reaching only 1.54 m (5 ft). Males in all species are larger than the females, an adult Antarctic fur seal bull being almost four times as heavy as an adult cow. Southern fur seals are generally coloured a grizzled dark grey-brown on the back, shading to lighter beneath. It is difficult to describe their colour accurately in the field, as it varies considerably depending on whether the hair is wet or dry, clean or dirty, or fresh or faded. The difficulty is complicated by the fact that in the adult males many of the outer guard hairs – the ones that are actually visible to an observer – are white-tipped. As these tips wear away, the seal appears darker, or less grizzled.

Only in the Subantarctic fur seal is there a clear colour pattern. In this seal, the chest and the face to behind the ears is a bright nicotine-yellow, or a pale creamy colour. There is also a conspicuous tuft of black hair, or crest, on the forehead of the adult males, formed by extra long guard hairs.

Pups of all species are born in a black or very dark brown natal coat through which white-tipped hairs gradually grow, to give a grizzled appearance. Towards the end of their first summer, the pups moult the natal coat to reveal their yearling pelage, which is typically more silvery than that of the adults.

Exceptionally, in the Antarctic fur seal about one or two in a thousand pups are born in white coats. When they moult, the replacement guard hairs are also white and these white animals are very conspicuous in the rookeries. They are not albinos: pigment is present in the skin; the flippers, for example, are a milk-chocolate colour instead of the normal intense black, and the

Southern fur seals have a grizzled appearance. The white tips of the dark guard hairs of this Antarctic fur seal bull can be seen in the photograph.

A rare aberration in Antarctic fur seals is this white coat coloration. The animals are not albinos, as pigment can be seen clearly in the exposed skin.

underfur is pigmented, although less so than usually. More significantly, from the point of view of the animal's survival, the eyes have the usual quota of pigment, rather than the pale-pink eyes of true albinos. These seals are in this condition because the guard hairs are completely devoid of melanin, the pigment responsible for their normal coloration. These guard hairs are deeper-rooted than the underfur fibres, and it seems that the pigment does not develop in the deeper layers of the skin, which may also account for the paler shade of the skin on the flippers.

DISTRIBUTION AND STATUS OF FUR SEALS

The current distribution of the fur seals may represent in many cases relic populations, following near extermination of the original populations in the intense hunting that was carried on in the nineteenth century. In some cases, the seals that we find today may not be the same species that inhabited the location prior to hunting. Fur seals are found in greatest abundance where cool, nutrient-rich water currents promote high plankton production to support stocks of fish or invertebrates on which the seals feed. Their other requirement, of course, is a secluded spot in which to produce their young. Because fur seals breed in very large colonies (or at any rate did so before the arrival of the hunters), there is normally a very extensive dispersion area around the focus of the breeding site in which the seals feed, although in general, we have rather little information of the fur seals' whereabouts at sea.

South American fur seal

The South American fur seal (*Arctocephalus australis*), as its name implies, is the fur seal that occurs on the coasts of the South American continent. Mainland colonies are now very rare (except in Peru) and most seals breed on offshore islands. The northernmost colonies on the Atlantic side are at Recife dos Torres, in southern Brazil, and in Uruguay, where there is a major breeding colony on Islas de Lobos in the estuary of the River Plate. Remnants of colonies are found around Isla de los Estados and on islands off the west coast of Tierra del Fuego. There are some seals on the Chilean coast, particularly around the Chonos Archipelago; while further north, on the Peruvian coast, this species has seen an astonishing increase; from as few as 40 in the early 1950s, the South American fur seal in Peru had increased to more than 20,000 by 1980. Most of this increase has occurred in the three main colonies at San Juan, Paracas and San Fernando, south of Lima.

Another group of South American fur seals are found on the Falkland Islands. They breed mainly on islands in the west – the Jasons and New Island. At one time there were many more colonies but intensive sealing, which lasted into this century, greatly depleted them. The Falkland Island fur seals are perhaps a little larger than those on the mainland, and they have been assigned to a separate subspecies, *A. australis australis*, the mainland animals being *A. australis gracilis*. There is little justification for this distinction on the basis of present knowledge and it seems more sensible to drop the subspecific epithets.

Three other species are found on islands off the Pacific coast of the Americas.

Juan Fernandez fur seal

The Juan Fernandez fur seal, *Arctocephalus philippii*, is found, as its name suggests, on the Juan Fernandez Islands off the coast of Chile at latitude 34°S, longitude 80°W and on Isla San Felix, about seven degrees further north on the same longitude. Most of the seals are on what used to be called Isla Mas Afuera, now renamed Isla Alejandro Selkirk (since this is the island on which the model of Defoe's hero actually spent his lonely sojourn), with another flourishing population on Isla Mas a Tierra (now officially called Isla Robinson Crusoe). These seals were once astonishingly abundant. Daniel Torres, a Chilean seal-worker, has estimated from recorded catches that the population towards the end of the seventeenth century probably exceeded four million animals. Despite this, the seals were hunted to such an extent that they were considered to be extinct for nearly a hundred years until, in 1966, about 200 were photographed on Alejandro Selkirk Island. The most recent estimate (1984) is 6,000 seals, and increasing. There is some hunting by the local fishermen who live on the Juan Fernandez Islands, but the seals are divided between a number of colonies (31 on the two main islands) and this does not seem to be a major threat.

Galapagos fur seal

Further north, among the Galapagos Islands (on the Equator at longitude 90° to 92°W), the Galapagos fur seal, *A. galapgoensis*, is found on the islands of Fernandina, Isabela, Pinta, Marchena, San Salvador, Santa Cruz and

Distribution of southern fur seal (1).

Genovesa. Following nineteenth-century hunting, the population reached an all-time low around the beginning of this century. However, recovery has taken place and by the 1940s Galapagos fishermen knew about sizeable colonies on Pinta and Marchena. Recent censuses indicate a total population of about 30,000 seals, which are rigorously protected by the Galapagos National Park authorities. These seals seem very susceptible to food shortages caused by the El Niño phenomenon, where a change in the current circulation in the Southern Hemisphere radically reduces the productivity of the surface waters in which the seals feed. Despite this, it seems likely that the population is continuing to increase and may now be close to its pre-exploitation total.

South American fur seals, on New Island, Falkland Islands.

Juan Fernandez fur seals at a breeding site on Isla Alejandro Selkirk.

Galapagos fur seals.

Guadalupe fur seal

The next of these island fur seals is the Guadalupe fur seal, *A. townsendi*, found on the island of the same name off the western coast of Mexico at latitude 29°N, longitude 118°W. This is the only member of the genus *Arctocephalus* to be found substantially north of the Equator. The Guadalupe fur seal and the Juan Fernandez fur seal have certain characteristics in common: in particular, a long nose with an inflated rhinarium (the dark, hairless area around the nostrils) and downward-facing nostrils that have been described as giving the appearance of a shark-like muzzle. At one time they were placed in a separate genus, *Arctophoca*, but there seems little support for that practice now. Guadalupe fur seals once had a wider distribution, being found on the Santa Barbara Channel Islands, off California, and in the San Benito Islands, off Baja California (see map on p. 41). The occasional specimen still turns up on the beaches of San Miguel Island in the former group. However, like all the other fur seals, they were subject to heavy hunting pressure. Guadalupe Island itself once supported at least four sealing stations known to be active between 1834 and 1881 by the dates engraved on their walls. The last known sealing was in 1894 and the seals were then believed extinct. In 1892 Charles Townsend collected four skulls from one of the rookeries on Guadalupe Island and these were the basis for the description of the new species. Merriam, who described the skulls, named the species after Townsend. For more than 30 years, the seal was known only from the skull characters, but in 1928 a collecting expedition organized by the San Diego Zoological Society returned a pair of young males to the Society's zoo, where they were exhibited.

The Guadalupe fur seal is completely protected by Mexican laws which declare Guadalupe Island to be a sanctuary for the fur seals and two other pinnipeds that occur there: the Northern elephant seal and the Californian sea lion. The fur seals seem to be increasing slowly, or at any rate slowly increasing their distribution on the island and reoccupying parts of their historical range. The most recent count (in 1977) indicated 1,073 animals on Guadalupe, which makes it by far the rarest fur seal.

New Zealand fur seal

The New Zealand fur seal, *A. forsteri*, was named after the German naturalist, George Forster, who accompanied Captain Cook on his second voyage round the world and who drew seals killed at Dusky Sound, South Island, New Zealand. Today, fur seals breed on many islands off the west coast of New Zealand from Open Bay 44°S to Fiordland on the south-western corner, including Dusky Sound. Colonies are found also on all the major islands and island groups to the south of New Zealand: Solander Island, Stewart Island and its off-lying islets, and on the Chatham Islands, Bounty Islands, Snares Island, Antipodes Island, Aukland Island, Campbell Island and Macquarie Island. Non-breeding groups occur round much of the coast of South Island and in winter, colonies appear on the south coast of North Island.

The species occurs also in Australia, where it ranges from about 117° to 136°E. Breeding colonies occur at the western end of Kangaroo Island, at South Neptune and Four Hummocks Islands in South Australia and at the Récherche Archipelago in Western Australia.

The population in New Zealand and its outlying islands numbers perhaps

Distribution of southern fur seal (2).

50,000, with another 5,000 New Zealand fur seals in Australia. There does not seem to be any definite trend, either upwards or downwards, for these populations, but as there are no obvious pressures on these seals and as they are protected in both countries, it seems likely that they are increasing slowly.

Subantarctic fur seal

The clumsily named Subantarctic fur seal, *Arctocephalus tropicalis*, received the second half of its scientific name as a result of the first specimen described being said to have come from the tropical north coast of Australia. In fact, it is a native of the subtemperate islands of the Indian Ocean, with a strong colony in the South Atlantic on Gough Island. Taking the various populations from west to east, the Subantarctic fur seals breed on Gough Island, 40°S, 10°W, where something like 200,000 seals live. Occasional stragglers are found on the neighbouring Nightingale and Inaccessible Islands and Tristan da Cunha. In the Prince Edward Islands, 47°S, 38°E, about 2,200 km (1,400 miles) south-east of Cape Town, Subantarctic fur seals are found on both

45

New Zealand fur seals at a breeding site on Open Bay Islands.

Subantarctic fur seals on Gough Island.

Marion Island and Prince Edward Island itself, to a total of about 35,000. Further thriving colonies occur to the east, on the Crozet Islands (46°S, 52°W), where about 350 seals are present on Possession Island, and on Amsterdam Island (38°S, 78°E), with a large population of about 35,000 – the seal is sometimes known as the Amsterdam Island fur seal. Another small population of a few hundreds occurs on the nearby St Paul Island. Stragglers occur on the South African coast.

Subantarctic fur seals are found on Macquarie Island, although the species most often seen there is the New Zealand fur seal. From 1981 breeding territories containing female Subantarctic fur seals and Antarctic fur seals, together with pups, and bull Subantarctic fur seals, have been noted. These mixed groups of seals have produced a few pups each year since the 1950s and it seems likely that the Subantarctic fur seal was the original indigenous species on Macquarie Island before the arrival of the sealers.

The total population of this thriving and vigorous species was estimated at 300,000 in 1984 and it is probably considerably higher now. This species, and the next, are great wanderers, and further colonizations may be expected.

Antarctic fur seal

The Antarctic fur seal, *Arctocephalus gazella*, named after the ship of the German Transit of Venus Expedition, which located the seals when they landed at Iles Kerguelen in 1874, is also sometimes known as the Kerguelen fur seal. As its name suggests, this is a seal of significantly colder waters than the other members of the genus (see map on p. 45). The headquarters of the species is at the western end of the island of South Georgia, in the South Atlantic at 54°S, 38°W. The most recent count here (in 1989) revealed a population of some 1.5 million seals and as further extensive colonization is continuing at South Georgia and elsewhere, it is probable that the current total is well in excess of this. Much smaller populations, numbering from a few hundreds to a few thousands, are found on the Antarctic South Shetlands, South Orkneys, and South Sandwich Islands and at Bovetøya. The more temperate Heard and MacDonald Islands and Iles Kerguelen support a few thousand Antarctic fur seals and there is a small population, numbering 160 in 1982, on Marion Island, where the more usual species is the Subantarctic fur seal. Although there are clear specific differences between these two animals, they are capable of interbreeding and hybrids have been observed on Marion Island. The occurrence of female Antarctic fur seals on Macquarie Island, breeding with bull Subantarctic fur seals, has been noted above.

The Antarctic fur seal is a great wanderer, and specimens have been identified on Macquarie Island and on the Juan Fernandez Islands. Because of the rather small differences between the southern fur seals, which make specific identification difficult for untrained observers, it seems likely that this species may also visit other areas, such as Tierra del Fuego, or the New Zealand islands, without being detected.

Cape fur seal

There is one more species of southern fur seal, but this is divided into two subspecies, with very different distributions (see map on p. 45). The Cape fur seal, *Arctocephalus pusillius pusillus*, breeds at 23 colonies around the coasts of

Antarctic fur seals inhabit colder waters than other members of the genus. This rookery is on Bird Island, South Georgia.

Cape fur seals at False Bay. The harem groupings can be distinguished easily.

South Africa and Namibia. Exceptionally, in this species the four largest colonies are situated on the continental mainland. However, these mainland colonies are backed by the Namib Desert, which lacks large predators that might prey on the breeding seals. The most northerly colony is found at Cape Cross, 22°S, 14°E, and scattered groups occur along the coast as far eastwards as Algoa Bay, 34°S, 26°E. Many people have taken a tour boat out to look at the fur seals on Seal Island, in False Bay just south of Cape Town. There were once many more colonies but uncontrolled sealing brought the stock to very low levels and extirpated many island colonies. The notorious Robben Island, where South African political prisoners were held, was named by the early Dutch settlers after the seals that used to occur there. Since the control of sealing in 1893, however, the seals have increased very rapidly. Despite sealing harvests in almost every year since then, there are now about 1.1 million Cape fur seals. Most of this growth has taken place at the three largest land colonies (Wolf Bay, Atlas Bay and Kleinsee), whereas 13 of the 17 island colonies have declined. A curious feature is that the harvested colonies are increasing faster (on the mainland) or decreasing more slowly (on islands) than those where sealing does not take place.

Australian fur seal

The other subspecies is the Australian fur seal, *Arctocephalus pusillus doriferus*. Here I might comment on the origin of the scientific name. The *pusillus* part, which means small, derives from the fact that this, the largest of all the fur seals, was first described from the picture of a young pup in its black natal pelage. *Doriferus* comes from two Greek words meaning hide-bearer, and refers to the fact that these seals were the object of skin hunters, as were all fur seals. The very wide separation of the two groups is the real basis for the division of

An Australian fur seal family at Seal Rocks.

the species into two subspecies. There are few anatomical differences, of which the most significant seems to be a difference in the length of the crest that unites the mastoid process with the jugular process of the skull. This is greater in Australian specimens.

Australian fur seals are found in south-eastern Australian waters, mostly off Tasmania and Victoria, but also off southern New South Wales. The ten major breeding colonies are situated in the Bass Strait between Victoria and Tasmania, though there is one colony at Seal Rocks in New South Wales, about 180 km (110 miles) north-east of Sydney. No complete counts of Australian fur seals appear to have been made, but it has been estimated that about 10,000 pups are born annually. This would be equivalent to about 40,000 seals of all ages. Unlike the same species in South Africa, the Australian fur seal does not seem to be increasing. This may be associated with inadequate feeding conditions in the nutrient-poor waters of the Bass Strait compared with the highly productive waters of the Benguela Current, where the Cape fur seals feed.

Northern fur seal

The remaining species of fur seal is the Northern fur seal, *Callorhinus ursinus*, 'the bear-like animal with the beautiful hide' (fur seals were at one time known as 'sea bears'). This is found in the cooler waters of the North Pacific. The Northern fur seal was first known to science in 1742, when Georg Wilhelm Steller described it on Bering Island in the Commander Islands (55°N, 166°E). Four years later, the first of the Pribilof Islands, St George (57°N, 170°W), was discovered with its teaming seal rookeries, and the following year, 1747, the other main Pribilof Island, St Paul, was discovered. The Pribilof Islands are the principal breeding grounds of the Northern fur seal, with a population of about one million animals. More seals are found on the Russian Commander Islands in the Western Bering Sea, and on Robben Island in the Sea of Okhotsk. A few small groups are found on the Russian Kurile Islands. These groups together amount to about a quarter of a million seals (see map on p. 52).

Northern fur seals, like their southern cousins, have been subjected to relentless exploitation since their discovery, which is described in Chapter 9. Although the American-controlled hunt on the Pribilofs was in general very well managed, the population has decreased significantly over the last four decades. There has been a very small increase in the size of the herd on the Pribilofs since 1990, but this appears to be the result of an increase in the number of male fur seals because of the cessation of the commercial harvest in 1984. Conditions in the Russian stocks seem to be similar, if not worse, and the reason for the decline in Northern fur seals is being urgently sought. Entanglement in fishing nets or shortage of food appear likely causes, and these are discussed in Chapter 10.

The Northern fur seal has an outlying breeding population far to the south of its normal breeding range. This is on San Miguel Island in the Santa Barbara Channel Islands, off the coast of California (36°N, 121°W). This is a rapidly growing population, with immigration from other stocks of fur seals contributing to the increase. About 1,500 pups were born on San Miguel in 1981 and there are certainly many more now.

A bull Northern fur seal shows his teeth.

A breeding rookery of Northern fur seals.

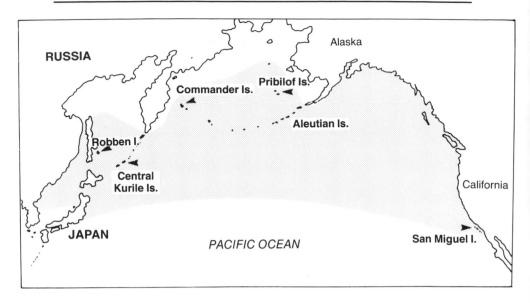

Distribution of the Northern fur seal.

FOOD AND FEEDING

Fur seals, like most seals, are rather general feeders, though there is one striking exception. A great deal of careful work has gone into determining the diet of the Northern fur seal. This has shown, not surprisingly, that diet varies both seasonally and by location. Thus, off the coasts of British Columbia in May, the seals are taking nearly half their food in the form of Pacific herring. In the Gulf of Alaska in the same month, sand lance (which was not eaten at all off British Columbia) made over half the diet. Similarly, off British Columbia, a species of squid replaced the herring as the principal item of food. In all, 53 species of fish and ten species of squid were found in Northern fur seal stomachs. It is hard to say in concise terms what constitutes the diet of such a catholic feeder, but 60 per cent small schooling fish, 23 per cent other fish and 17 per cent squid gives a good approximation.

Other fur seals have not been studied so extensively, particularly with regard to animals taken actually on their feeding grounds. While it seems that the Northern fur seal feeds mainly near the top of the water column, other fur seals feed at different levels in the sea. Some species, such as the Juan Fernandez seal, feed on the bottom, taking benthic organisms, such as octopus and rock lobsters. The New Zealand fur seal is believed to feed mainly on squid and barrcouta at the surface at night, but it also takes octopus from the sea floor during the daytime. This species also takes significant numbers of rockhopper penguins. The Subantarctic fur seal also kills penguins on Amsterdam Island. Antarctic fur seals are often seen chasing and killing macaroni penguins on South Georgia, but I do not believe that these form a significant part of the diet. It is mostly the subadult males that do this, and it

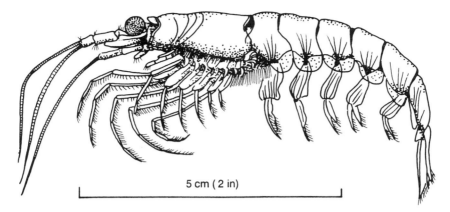

Fig. 2.2   Antarctic krill, *Euphausia superba*, the organism that forms the main food of so many Antarctic animals.

seems more of a play activity than serious feeding, as the penguins, once killed, are never seen to be devoured and are left to be disposed of by giant petrels and other scavenging birds.

The Antarctic fur seal is remarkable in that its diet consists predominantly of the small shrimp-like crustacean Antarctic krill, *Euphausia superba*. The seals take krill ranging between 35 and 65 mm (1½ and 2½ in) in length which they appear to capture mostly at night. By equipping foraging fur seals with small instrument packages which record depth against time, it has been possible to obtain a record of all the dives made during a foraging excursion by a seal. The seals chosen for this were females that were feeding their pups. It was a comparatively easy task to capture a seal while ashore with her pup and glue the recorder to her fur. When the seal subsequently departed to hunt her own food, the recorder would be switched on by contact with sea water and thereafter it would record the depths reached by a light beam controlled by pressure transducers moving across photographic film. On analysing these records, it was found that most dives took place during the hours of darkness, with the deepest dives being near the beginning and end of the period of activity and shallower dives around midnight. This corresponds with the vertical migration of the krill on which the seals feed. During the day, virtually all the krill are below 50 m (164 ft) depth, but between 21.00 and 06.00 hours a substantial proportion of the krill rises towards the surface and the seals dive as far as they need to obtain the krill. This behaviour ensures that the seals obtain their food in the most economical way, avoiding deep dives which are energetically more costly than shallow ones.

Although more than 90 per cent of the female and juvenile Antarctic fur seals' food is krill, they do take very small quantities of squid and fish (mostly the small fish that are often associated with krill swarms). There is some evidence, however, that adult male fur seals take more squid and fish, which may make up 25 per cent of their diet. One study showed that the South Georgia fur seal herd in 1983, when it was believed to comprise 1.1 million animals with a biomass of 40,000 tonnes, consumed in the course of a year 1.1 million tonnes of krill, 180,000 tonnes of squid and 297,000 tonnes of fish. These are quite staggering totals, bearing in mind that there are many other krill consumers (and consumers of squid and fish) based at South Georgia.

BREEDING BEHAVIOUR

The breeding patterns of fur seals are all rather similar. I shall describe that of the Antarctic fur seal, since this is an animal I am very familiar with and because it occurs in a strongly seasonal environment which imposes a rather stringent pattern on its breeding behaviour.

During the austral winter, the fur seals are dispersed on the feeding grounds, which at present are unknown. They may move to some definite location, where favourable current systems ensure a supply of food, or they may simply disperse throughout the ocean. A few adult males may be present on the beaches during the winter, but this is exceptional. Most of the breeding bulls arrive in late October and establish territories on the beaches. This is done by displays and by actual fighting with neighbours. The display consists of the seal sitting upright with the chest out and the head nearly vertical. A vocal threat of a surprisingly high-pitched whimper is also employed. Once a hierarchy has been established on the beach, fighting is comparatively rare, but when fights do ensue, as for example when a new bull arrives from the sea, they are violent. The bulls slash at each other with their formidable canines, and inflict wounds mostly on the wrists and head. The thick mane largely protects the neck and shoulders, but severe wounds can be inflicted in these places too. The bulls also use their bulk to repel intruders, pushing them with their chests.

Successful fighting means that a bull establishes a territory on the beach. Fur seals usually choose rocky beaches with plenty of natural features that can indicate territorial boundaries. This perhaps helps to avoid territorial disputes, neighbouring bulls recognizing their limits. Into these territories the cows arrive from the sea. The cows seem to control in which territories they give birth. There is a very strong instinct for them to return to the colony where they were born and to the place where they previously gave birth. Favoured territories by the cows are those near the water's edge, but well protected from storm tides, and these are the ones most sought for by the bulls.

The first cows arrive in the second week of November, but the main body not until the end of the month. There is very little variation from year to year in the time of arrival of the main herd. Bulls make no attempt to gather cows in their territories, but they do try (usually unsuccessfully) to prevent a cow escaping that wishes to leave. The number of cows that a bull eventually has in his territory averages between 11 and 16, but it is highly variable; some bulls managing to acquire only a single cow, while others may have 30 or more.

Cows give birth about two days after arriving from the sea. Birth is a simple and speedy affair (30 seconds to 7 minutes), but a cow often assists the process by taking hold of the emerging pup with her teeth and dragging it towards her. The umbilical cord breaks at the time of birth in about half the cases, but in the others it remains attached to the placenta, which is expelled about 4 to

A female Antarctic fur seal helps to deliver her pup by pulling it towards her.

12 minutes after the birth of the pup, until the cord is shed at 2 to 3 days after birth.

The pup is active from the time of birth, but the mother will not as a rule feed it for at least half an hour. Meanwhile, she exchanges calls with the pup. The high-pitched, whining duet between mother and pup, which is terminated only when the cow allows her pup to suck, is one of the most characteristic sounds of a fur seal breeding beach. It is a feature of the greatest importance, for it is during this stage that the cow and pup learn to recognize each other. During this bonding process, the cow repeatedly sniffs at her pup's muzzle, and this is the second and even more important part of the bonding. Cows will feed only their own pups and their smell is the deciding factor, a feature which seems to be common to all seals that have been studied. Very rarely a cow is seen feeding two pups, but this is exceptional behaviour and may result from confusion on a crowded beach at the time of two nearly simultaneous births. Genuine twinning is exceedingly rare in this species, as in all other pinnipeds.

The mother suckles her pup at about six-hourly intervals for the eight days after birth. At the end of this period, she comes into oestrus and is mated by the bull in whose territory she was. Thereafter, the cow returns to the sea to feed and synthesize more milk for her pup. She is away for three to six days and then returns to suckle her pup for three days or so. On returning to the beach, she first calls to her pup, which will normally have left the breeding beach itself to take up a position on the shoreward side of the breeding seals. The pup hears its mother calling and returns the cries, waddling down to meet its mother. When they make contact, the cow sniffs at the pup to confirm that it is her own (hungry pups will often answer any cow) before leading it to a quiet place where she can feed it.

This pattern is repeated for the whole of the summer – about 110 to 115 days. The pups grow rapidly, males gaining about 98 g (3½ oz) per day from an initial birth weight of 5.9 kg (13 lb). Females, born at about 5.4 kg (12 lb) grow more slowly, at about 84 g (3 oz) per day. The pups begin to moult their black natal fur at about 50 to 60 days old, when the hairs begin to loosen on the top of the head. They have usually completed the moult by the end of February or the beginning of March. Weaning takes place abruptly, and appears to be initiated by the pups, which leave the beaches to feed for themselves. By the end of April the beaches are deserted once more until the next breeding season.

During the active part of the breeding season, the bulls never leave their territories and lose weight at about 2 kg (4½ lb) per day. After most of the females are mated, however, the territorial system begins to break down, with bulls leaving for short periods and their places being taken by newcomers. Non-breeding adult and juvenile bulls penetrate behind the beaches and take up places on the slopes behind. They may climb to heights of several hundred feet and lie about among the tussock grass. Occasionally, a young female may produce her pup inland and the pair will soon be joined by a young male, which defends the cow as a harem. Juvenile females are rarely seen ashore, and perhaps spend most of their time at sea.

If the Antarctic fur seal lives in the most seasonal environment, it is certain that the Galapagos fur seal, right on the Equator, lives in an environment with the least seasonal variation. Nevertheless, breeding is synchronized to a large extent, the season extending from August to November, with a peak of births in the first week of October. Territories established by the bulls are much larger than those of the Antarctic fur seal, reflecting the much lower density of the females, which seek out spots with some shelter from the sun. All territories have access to the sea, so that the bulls can enter the water at midday to cool off.

As in the Antarctic fur seal (and others of the genus), the females give birth about two days after coming ashore and come into oestrus about a week later. After mating, the females embark on foraging excursions, each lasting from one to four days. A striking difference from the Antarctic species is that lactation can last an astonishing two to three years! All females mate at the post-partum oestrus but only some 15 per cent give birth the following year if they are still feeding a pup. Of females without dependent young, some 70 per cent give birth. The presence of an older sibling has a bad effect on the chances of survival of the new pup. If the older sibling is a yearling, the new pup almost always dies in the first month; if the sibling is a two-year-old, the young pup's chances of survival are about 50 per cent. This clearly reduces

This female Antarctic fur seal has chosen the denuded stool of a clump of tussock grass on which to lie while feeding her pup. Seals like to lie on the tussocks, to keep out of the mud of the rookery floor, but this eventually kills the grass and leads to erosion.

the potential fecundity of the females. A female which first pups at age five can raise only about five offspring if she survives to age 15.

Most fur seals have higher fecundities than this, the females generally becoming mature at age four. The very successful Antarctic fur seal becomes mature a year earlier, at age three, and this accounts for the very rapid increase of this species. Bulls take longer to mature, though they grow more quickly. They attain breeding status usually between the ages of seven and ten, but because of the intense polygyny of these seals, many bulls, though fully mature, never get a chance to mate at all.

The Northern fur seal has a reproductive pattern very similar to that of its southern cousins. On the Pribilof Islands, the first bulls begin to haul out on the beaches in early June. A bull that had established a territory in a previous year will often return to the same site year after year. The cows arrive by mid-June, by which time the bulls have generally sorted out their territories and most of the serious fighting is over. It is often claimed that Northern fur seal bulls actively collect females for their harems. It is true that a bull may grab a passing female with his teeth and toss her into his territory, but in fact the bulls have little control of the females. Even when the number of females in a territory is low (fewer than ten), the bulls cannot effectively prevent departures. Despite this, the bulls spend a good deal of time moving about their territories, herding their females. Harems are large in the Northern fur seal, with an average of 30 or more.

Pups are born one to two days after the cows come ashore, with a peak of pupping on St Paul Island on 7 – 8 July and oestrus follows in about a week, after which the cows commence the series of feeding/sucking bouts. Successive trips to sea become longer, lasting eight to nine days eventually, but the suckling vists to shore remain about two days in duration. By October, the pups have moulted into their silvery yearling coats and by November they are weaned.

After breeding in the summer, the seals leave the islands and migrate south. The seals that breed on Robben Island winter in the Sea of Japan; those from the Commander Islands move down the coast of Japan; the Pribilof seals migrate down the west coast of North America. On both sides of the Pacific, the final southern limit of migration is about 32°N. The smaller seals, the cows and juveniles, make the longest migrations and some of the adult bulls may stay in the cold waters around the breeding sites throughout the year (as is the case with the Antarctic fur seal).

Chapter 3
The Sea Lions

INTRODUCTION

The five species of sea lion are rather more diverse than the closely similar fur seals. Each is placed in its own genus and all have characteristic and, for the most part, separate distributions, though the Steller sea lion and the California sea lion do overlap to some extent. The best one can do to characterize them as a group is to say that sea lions are otariids that do not have abundant underfur. There are other anatomical features that characterize the group. Sea lions are larger than fur seals (apart from the very large *Arctocephalus pusillus*); they usually have only five upper cheek teeth, as opposed to the fur seals' six, and the third upper incisor is large, with a circular cross-section; finally, the tip of the sea lion baculum (the penis bone that is found in all carnivores) is broad, whereas it is narrow in fur seals.

Californian sea lion

The California sea lion, *Zalophus californianus*, is probably the most familiar of all pinnipeds because of its popularity as the trained seal of circuses. Whether California sea lions are really especially easy to train, and were thus chosen for this role, or whether it was their ready availability to trainers that caused them to be selected is not known. There is no doubt that they are very trainable, and they can go through much more complex routines than balancing balls on their noses. The US Navy trained sea lions to carry instrument packs to dive on lost ordnance to retrieve it. Sea lions could locate an object and label it by depositing an acoustic 'pinger' or even attach a retrieval harness. The extent to which these animals were used by the Navy is not yet fully revealed, but it is believed that they were involved in the retrieval of a nuclear weapon lost in the sea off the coast of Spain. The ethics of using animals for this type of work has been questioned.

California sea lion males reach on average about 2.25 m (89 in) from nose to tail and weigh nearly 400 kg (882 lb): though weight of course, varies seasonally. Females are much smaller, 1.74 m (69 in) and a mean weight of 110 kg (243 lb). The males are dark brown, though there is some variation in colour from nearly black to light brown. Females are always lighter than males, mostly a tan colour. The pups are born in a very dark-brown natal coat which they moult to the tan coloured yearling coat at about six months. A very characteristic feature of this species is the high bony crest on the head of the adult bull. This starts to develop in the animal's fifth year and it may reach 4 cm (1½ in) in height by the time it is ten. It is from this crest that the name *Zalophus* is derived. It is made up of two Greek words, *Za*, an intensifying element, and *lophos*, meaning crest.

The California sea lion is, as its name suggests, found chiefly around the coasts of California, but the species has been divided into three subspecies. *Z. californianus californianus* is the sea lion of the Pacific coast of North America. It

California sea lions. The pronounced crest on the head of the male is well seen in this photograph.

is found from Vancouver Island, British Columbia, about 50°N, to the Tres Marias Islands off Mexico, at 21°N. The breeding range is currently from the southern limit of distribution (i.e., the Tres Marias Islands) to San Miguel Island in the Santa Barbara Channel Islands. A few pups are born on islands further north, mainly the Fallaron Islands near San Francisco.

The California sea lion is a flourishing, vigorous species. A count in the late 1970s revealed that there were at least 75,000 present, and despite losses from entanglement with fishing nets, it seems unlikely to have declined from this total.

Another named form, Z. *californianus wollebaeki*, is found on the Galapagos Islands. This population is clearly geographically distinct from the California one and it is likely to have been genetically isolated for many thousand years. However, there are few physical differences detectable in the rather scanty material that is available, chief of which is that the Galapagos sea lions, like the fur seals, are slightly smaller than their continental cousins. Sea lions are found on all the Galapagos Islands, and they breed on most of them. The total population numbers about 40,000 animals and appears stable.

Less than a hundred years ago, sea lions were common in the Sea of Japan, more than 8,000 km (5,000 miles) from the nearest present-day colonies in California. No living zoologist has seen one of these animals and until recently only ten skulls were known. Since them, however, Japanese archaeologists have unearthed sea lion remains (another seven skulls and some mandible pieces) from a shell midden in Hokkaido. With so few remains to go on, it is difficult to say anything definite about these animals. The conventional view

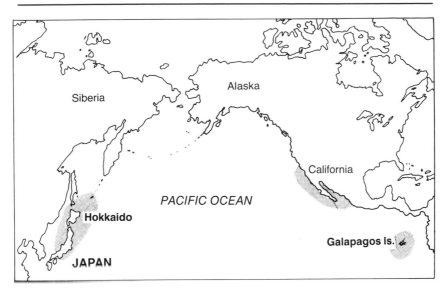

Distribution of the California sea lion.

is that the Japanese sea lion is a distinct subspecies, *Z. californianus japonicus*. However, the more recently discovered material from Hokkaido suggests that the variation from the Californian sea lion is substantial (the Japanese animals were larger, with wider skulls and six, rather than five, upper post-canine teeth) and that separation at a specific level is appropriate, making the Japanese sea lion *Z. japonicus*.

Knowledge of the distribution of this sea lion is fragmentary. In 1951 it was reported in a Japanese newspaper that 50 to 60 sea lions were living on Take-shima (37°N, 132°E), near the Korean coast. Others were once found around Kyushu and Shikoku. The Hokkaido specimens came from Okushiri-tö, off the south-western corner of Hokkaido. It is just possible that some living specimens still exist on the remote islands of the Sea of Japan or on the disputed islands between Japan and Russia, but I think it very unlikely. If the Japanese sea lion is, in fact, a full species, and it is actually extinct, it shares the doubtful distinction of being one of only two pinnipeds to have become extinct in historical times.

Australian sea lion
The Australian sea lion, *Neophoca cinerea*, shows more colour variation than is usual in otariids. Its Linnaean name, which means the 'ashy-coloured new seal', refers to the silvery grey colour of the back of some of the females. Others are fawn on the back but all are creamy or pale yellow beneath. Adult bulls are a rich chocolate-brown, but unusually for otariids, show an age-related change of pattern. After the moult of the rich dark brown natal fur, the young male resembles the female in colour for the first two years of life. Then the chest begins to develop darker spots and the muzzle becomes darker. As the seal ages, it becomes generally darker, but on the top of the head and

Australian sea lion, Kangaroo Island.

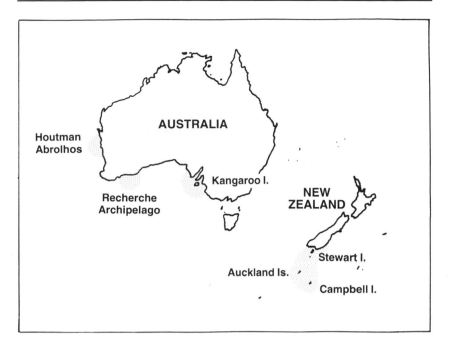

Distribution of the Australian sea lion and Hooker's sea lion.

continuing down the nape of the neck, a pale patch develops. A white-to-yellowish mane of coarse guard hairs develops around the shoulders. Australian sea lions are about the same size as the Californian species, but few measurements are available. Adult males reach 2 to 2.5 m (79 to 98 in) in length and probably weigh around 400 kg (882 lb), and females 1.7 to 1.8 m (67 to 71 in) and 80 to 105 kg (176 to 231 lb).

The Australian sea lion is restricted to the south and south-western coasts of Australia, from Houtman Abrolhos (28°S, 114°E) in Western Australia to just east of Kangaroo Island in South Australia (36°S, 138°E). Prior to commercial sealing in the nineteenth century, the range extended eastwards to the Bass Strait. Their bones are commonly found in the middens of the aboriginal Tasmanians. The Western Australia population probably numbers about 3,100 and that of South Australia 6,900. The sea lions are fully protected in Australia and as far as is known, the population is stable, though being small, it is rather vulnerable to chance hazards.

Hooker's sea lion

Hooker's sea lion, *Phocarctos hookeri*, is very similar in size to the Australian sea lion. The bulls are black or very dark brown with a mane of rough hair about their shoulders. Like the Australian sea lion, they are lighter when first moulted from the natal coat, and darken with age. Bulls have a very characteristic rounded muzzle. The females are virtually identical to the Australian species, silvery grey dorsally and creamy ventrally.

Hooker's sea lion, Sandy Bay Rookery, Auckland Islands.

Hooker's sea lion has a very restricted distribution. It inhabits mainly the New Zealand 'Subantarctic' islands of Auckland and Campbell between latitudes 51° and 53°S. A few pups are born on the Snares Islands (48°S). Stragglers, mostly young males, turn up on the New Zealand mainland to the north-east and at Macquarie Island to the south-west. Recent population estimates for this sea lion have been boosted by the discovery of a major new breeding ground. It had previously been thought that the majority of the sea lions bred on Enderby Island, in the Auckland group. However, in 1992 a survey was made which included a complete count on Dundas Island, a small exposed wave platform in the Aucklands, where more than 2,000 pups were counted. Estimates for the total population are now around 12,000. Net-entanglement kills a good many sea lions each year, but it appears that they are holding their own.

Southern sea lion

The Southern sea lion, *Otaria flavescens*, is quite variable in coloration. The males are generally very dark brown but frequently they have a much paler mane about their shoulders and neck. Some specimens are pale gold all over. *Flavescens* means becoming yellow in Latin, though this name was originally used by Shaw in 1800 to describe a very young pup of the species, rather than referring to yellowish adults. Females are dark brown to light orange or yellow and often have masks that are paler than the general coloration. In both sexes, the belly is a dark yellow. The pups are born black, with a brownish belly. There is probably more variation in this sea lion than in any other otariid. In one of the early accounts of Magellan's journey round South

Southern sea lion.

America in 1520, mention is made of 'sea wolves of many colours', which probably referred to these animals.

Adult males reach 2.5 m (98 in) in nose-to-tail length and are very massively built, reaching weights of 350 kg (772 lb). They appear to have huge heads with a characteristic broad, upturned snout that is quite typical of this species. Females are small, about 2 m (79 in) nose to tail, and weighing up to 144 kg (317 lb).

The Southern sea lion has a much wider distribution (see map on p. 66). The northernmost breeding location on the Atlantic coast is at Recife dos Torres (29°S, 50°W), off southern Brazil. The first major breeding station, however, is at Islas de Lobos, in the mouth of the River Plate. Breeding colonies occur also around Bahia Blanca, at Peninsula Valdés, and thereafter southward along the Patagonian coast wherever a sufficiently secure breeding spot can be found. Isla de los Estados and Tierra del Fuego support a number of breeding colonies, and the seals continue up the coasts of Chile and Peru to reach Isla Lobos de Tierra, at 6° 30'S. The skeleton of a dead southern sea lion was found on the Galapagos Islands in 1973, but this was clearly an exceptional vagrant.

Besides these colonies on the South American mainland, or on islands close to it, the southern sea lion is found on the Falkland Islands. Here it was once very abundant, with many breeding colonies, chiefly on West Falkland and surrounding islands. In the 1930s an accurate count of pups yielded an estimate of a total population of 370,000. The next survey was in the mid-1960s, when no more than 30,000 sea lions could be found. The most recent counts indicate that only about 3,000 survive in the Falklands. Although there

Distribution of the Southern sea lion.

has been some sealing activity in the Falklands in the last 60 years, it is not enough to account for this decline. In particular, since the count in the 1960s and the most recent survey, there has been no organized hunting of the sea lions and probably very little casual shooting. The reason for this drastic decline remains a mystery.

The size of the South American population is not well known. The huge number of small islands around the tip of the continent and up the Chilean coast, and their remoteness, makes anything like a complete census impracticable. While numbers at some colonies (e.g., those at Islas de Lobos and Punta Norte at Peninsula Valdés) are well known, this is not the case with the Tierra del Fuego or Chilean colonies. A total figure of 240,000 has been suggested, but this is uncertain. Some hunting and killing by fishermen continues, but there is no evidence for as drastic a decline in the continental population as was seen in the Falkland Islands.

Steller's sea lion

The remaining sea lion, Steller's sea lion, *Eumetopias jubatus*, is the largest of the group. Adult males can reach 3 m (118 in) in length and weigh approximately 1 tonne. Females are smaller, but still very large, at 2.4 m (94 in) in length and a weight of around 273 kg (602 lb). Both sexes are light reddish-brown, which fades to a pale yellow before the moult. The males, like all sea lions, have an ample mane, and the trivial name *jubatus*, which means

Steller's sea lions mingle with Califonian sea lions on Año Nuevo Island.

having a mane, refers to this. *Eumetopias* comes from the Greek and means having a broad forehead. These sea lions, like the California species, have a crest on the top of the head, though it is not as well developed as in the latter.

Steller's sea lion inhabits coastal areas along the rim of the North Pacific Ocean, from Hokkaido, in northern Japan, northwards as far as 66°N in the Bering Sea and thence along the coast of Alaska southwards as far as the Santa Barbara Channel Islands, off California (see map on p. 68). There are important breeding colonies in the Kurile Islands, Kamchatka; on islands in the Sea of Okhotsk; the Aleutian Islands; on the Pribilof Islands (their northernmost breeding station); on the Alaskan-British Columbian coast; and in Oregon. A substantial breeding colony at Año Nuevo Island, off California, which produced more than 1,000 pups a year in the mid-1980s, has declined precipitously in recent years.

DECLINE OF STELLER'S SEA LION

There is no doubt that Steller's sea lions have declined severely throughout most of their range. Censuses of major rookeries and haul-out areas in the Gulf of Alaska, the Aleutian Islands and in the Kuril Islands reveal declines of more than 90 per cent in some areas over the last three decades, and principally in the last ten years. A total figure for the species of around a quarter of a million in the late 1950s had fallen to about 65,000 in 1989 and there is reason to fear further decline since then.

The reasons for this decline are unknown. Sea lions had been extensively

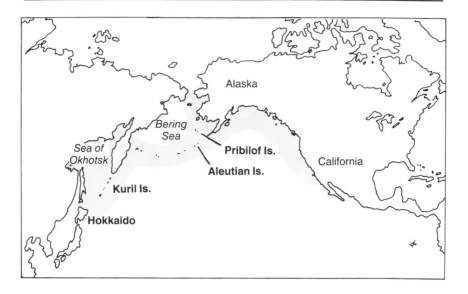

Distribution of Steller's sea lion.

hunted in the nineteenth century for their hides and for what was known as 'trimmings' (the whiskers, lips and penis bones, which were valued in the Far East medicine trade), but by the mid-1970s they were considered to be at or very near their pre-exploitation level. Since then, they have crashed to about a quarter, and in some areas to only a tenth, of this level. There are a number of factors that could cause the population to decline. Hunting is an obvious one, but there has been no commercial hunting since the 1970s and only minimal subsistence hunting by native peoples. Deliberate shooting or harassment at rookeries or haul-out place are other possibilities, and fishermen in particular are likely to shoot seals. However, the scale of this activity is much too small to account for the observed decline. Adult Steller's sea lions are at the top of their food-chain, so increased predation on adults is ruled out. Pups are eaten by a few predators, but there is no reason to suppose that this has increased since the 1970s. Although diseases do occur in the sea lions and pollutant residues can be detected in their tissues, there is no evidence that these have caused the fall in numbers.

What is left as a possible cause? Fishing activity has increased very markedly in the Gulf of Alaska and the Bering Sea in the last 30 years. Incidental catches of sea lions and other marine mammals are frequent. Sea lions can also become entangled in scraps of discarded netting and drown. And, perhaps most importantly, intensive fishing may have resulted in a shortage of food fish for the sea lions. In the central Gulf of Alaska, where the only long-term studies have been made, Steller's sea lions seem to be growing more slowly and reaching sexual maturity later than in the past, suggesting that decreased food availability may be at least part of the cause of the decline. This whole question of the effect of fisheries on pinnipeds is examined in greater detail in Chapter 9.

It is tempting for the wildlife zoologist to suppose that, unless interfered with, animal populations continue at about the same level indefinitely. This is probably true for many, though not all. Cyclical fluctuations are well documented in several populations of carnivores and their prey. Other populations are known to be very much affected by seasonal conditions. Living in the sea, the Steller's sea lions ought to be insulated from casual environmental changes, but we should not suppose that environmental changes do not take place and that these cannot affect marine mammals. It is difficult to think of any other reason to account for the collapse of the Falkland Islands' population of southern sea lions than a change in their environment that made it less suitable for them, and the same may be true for Steller's. Precisely what factor might change in the environment and cause these collapses is not known. It would most likely be one that affected the food resources of the sea lions, since mammals can tolerate even quite considerable physical changes. This is supported by the changes in growth rate noted above.

The case is still open. In the USA the National Marine Fisheries Service in 1990 designated Steller's sea lion as threatened under the Endangered Species Act and it established a Steller Sea Lion Recovery Team to advise on measures necessary to stop or reverse the population's decline. So far, the Recovery Team has used satellite tracking to locate feeding areas, made genetic and physiological studies to determine stock discreteness and food requirements, determined potential prey and the depths at which juvenile sea lions feed and established a geographic information system to manage the data acquired. There is much more to be done if the decline is to be halted and reversed. Biologists and all interested in seals will await the team's findings with interest.

FOOD OF SEA LIONS

For so familiar an animal, the feeding behaviour of the California sea lion is poorly known. What is known, however, indicates that these sea lions are (like many pinnipeds) opportunists who can feed on a large variety of food organisms. On one occasion, remains of 24 different species of fish were recovered from 24 sea lion stomachs. Another study showed that (in Monterey Bay, California) the sea lions were feeding mainly on anchovy, salmon, midshipmen, hake, rockfish, flatfish, small sharks, and several species of cephalopod. Another view is that the sea lions take squid and octopus as their principal prey. These soft-bodied molluscs are likely to be under-represented in the remains found in stomachs, as, apart from squid beaks, they tend to be fully digested. Fish, on the other hand, are often identified from their otoliths, or ear-stones, which are resistant to digestion and can be recovered from the stomach or gut or even from the droppings, or scats.

Even less information is available for the Australian sea lion. These animals are rigorously protected, so stomachs cannot be obtained from animals shot at sea. They have been seen tearing out the livers of school sharks (*Galeorhinus*) caught in nets, but while this shows the versatility of feeding methods of these sea lions, it can scarcely represent a natural feeding pattern. Other reports are of the sea lions feeding on Australian 'salmon', (*Arripis trutta*) and whiting

(*Sillaginoides*), damaging fishermen's nets while doing so. They have been seen taking crayfish (*Jasus*), tossing them into the air to break them free of their shells. An old account (from 1925) is of sea lions feeding on Little penguins while the sea lions remain ashore during the breeding season. It is unusual for most pinnipeds to feed during the breeding season, and even more unusual for them to catch prey while ashore, so this report perhaps needs further examination. Like many seals, Australian sea lions are often found to have quantities of stones in their stomachs. A full set of these gastroliths, which are usually lumps of granite up to tennis-ball size, may exceed 2 kg (4½ lb) in weight.

The feeding habits of New Zealand sea lions are likewise poorly known. However, they are known to take squids and octopus, as well as rock lobsters and a swimming crab, *Nectocarcinus*, as well as smaller swimming crustaceans, such as *Munida* (the larva of a rock lobster) and *Nauticaris* (a prawn). Small fish, penguins and other sea-birds are also taken. Gentoo penguins are said to be the main item of diet of the few New Zealand sea lions that turn up at Macquarie Island, but this may be only the result of the normal diet not being available there.

The Southern sea lion is known to feed on schooling fish, such as anchovies, *Engraulis anchovita*, squid and crustaceans. J. E. Hamilton, who made a study of these sea lions in the Falklands in the 1930s, thought that it was possible to distinguish what the sea lions had been feeding on by studying their scats at haul-out sites. Grey scats indicated a fish diet, and indeed, fish bones and scales can often be seen in these scats. Bright brick-red scats, often containing crustacean exoskeletons, indicated a diet of *Munida*, which is very abundant round the Falklands, while very liquid, bright yellow scats were the result of feeding on squid. Hamilton supposed that the action of the digestive juices of the sea lion on the squid ink produced the yellow colour. The red pigment in the *Munida*-containing scat was the characteristic crustacean pigment that makes boiled shrimps and crabs pink. Hamilton's observation can be applied to other pinnipeds that feed on these resources, such as the South American fur seals that also occur in the Falkland Islands.

Besides anchovies, southern sea lions also take hake, (*Merluccius gayi*), sardines (*Clupea bentinckii*), redfish (*Sebastiodes oculatus*), horse mackerel (*Trachurus lathami*) and a variety of other fish. In many places, these sea lions have been seen to take penguins or even fully grown female fur seals in the Falklands. Their appetite for stones is remarkable, up to 9 kg (20 lb) of pebbles and sharp-angled stones being found in a single stomach.

Like the other sea lions, Steller's sea lions take a wide variety of prey. There are regional and seasonal variations: for example, off Kodiak Island predation on capelin (*Mallotus villosus*) and salmon (*Oncorhynchus spp*) is limited to the spring and summer, reflecting the seasonal nearshore distribution of these fish associated with spawning. Fishermen make much of the predation on salmon by sea lions, which is frequently conspicuous. In one study, however, when sea lions were watched feeding off the mouth of the Roque River, Oregon, they were seen to take 87 per cent of lampreys to only 2 per cent of salmon (the remainder were unidentified). Sea lion lovers would point out that because lampreys parasitize salmon, the sea lions were actually benefiting the salmon stocks. Several studies have shown that the type of prey most frequently identified in stomach contents are flat-fishes, cephalopods and walleye pollock (*Theragra chalcogramma*). Sandlance (*Ammodytes spp*) and rockfish (*Sebastes spp*) are also frequently taken. When feeding on schooling fishes, like pollock or sandlance, the sea lions hunt in large groups of up to 50, whereas in the absence of schooling prey, they hunt singly or in small groups of two to five animals.

Besides the fish and squids that make up most of their diet, Steller's sea lions take bivalve molluscs, shrimps and crabs. They are also notorious predators on other marine mammals. They have frequently been seen feeding on the pups of other pinnipeds, such as Harbour seals, Spotted seals, Ringed seals and Bearded seals, and on sea otters. These probably form an insignificant part of the diet, but at St George Island in the Pribilofs, sea lions are estimated to kill between three and six per cent of the fur-seal pups produced there. The sea lions take the young pups when they first enter the sea at about five months old. Strangely, at St Paul Island, only 65 km (40 miles) away, this type of behaviour has not been observed.

BREEDING BEHAVIOUR

Most sea lions are present around their rookeries throughout the year, so there is not always the dramatic assembly of breeding animals at a previously deserted beach that is seen, for example, in Northern fur seals or Antarctic fur seals. California sea lion bulls begin to establish territories at about the same time that the pregnant females arrive to pup. In California this begins in early May, reaching a peak in early July. By the first week of August the territorial system has mostly broken down. Individual males hold their territories for between 12 and 41 days. The females are gregarious and seem indifferent to the territorial boundaries established by the bulls.

Females are very attentive to their pups for the first few days, often maintaining physical contact, and dragging the pups towards them if they stray. Females come into oestrus and mate about two weeks after the birth of their pups. The female actively solicits and terminates copulation. Pups are suckled at least until the next pup is born and sometimes beyond then. Pups begin to enter the sea and swim when about one to two weeks old. They moult into the adult coat at about five months and shortly afterwards begin to feed for themselves.

In the Galapagos Islands, these sea lions spread their breeding season to cover most of the cool season of mists and drizzle, the *garua*, which lasts from May–June to December–January. Births may extend over six to eight months, with the peak of pupping being earlier on Fernandina, the most westerly island, than on Española, the furthest south-east. Mating in the Galapagos generally takes place in the water, and all bull territories have access to the sea.

Australian sea lions seem to have a very indefinite breeding pattern. The dominant bulls establish territories and may remain ashore in them for up to 14 days, but more usually they enter the water frequently for periods of two or three hours. On returning, they have to re-establish their right to their territories, but usually have no difficulty in doing so. Territorial males actively herd cows and try to prevent them leaving, but no definite harem structure is

A huge breeding colony of Californian sea lions on San Miguel Island, California.

developed because of the mobility of the cows, and perhaps also the bulls.

At Dangerous Reef and South Neptune Island, most pups are born in October, but the season can extend into early January. At Kangaroo Island in one year (1975), most pups were born in June, though in the following season the main pupping was in October and pupping has been recorded throughout the year. Pregnant females come ashore about three days before giving birth. Often, cows about to give birth are seen to be suckling the pup of the previous season and on one occasion a newly born pup was ignored by its mother for nearly a day while she suckled a juvenile.

The cows are mated at about six to seven days after giving birth and stay with their pups for about 14 days before going to sea and returning at intervals to suckle the pup. At three months old, the pup has perfected its swimming by playing in rock pools and it is capable of entering the sea to feed for itself.

The Hooker's sea lion bulls select sandy beaches for their territories. These have no fixed boundaries – it is rather that each bull defends a 'personal space' around itself and as the bulls move about as a result of storms or disturbance, this space moves with them. The bulls start to arrive about the beginning of November and are followed by the cows about a month later. Birth takes place soon after the cows' arrival and births are much more synchronized than in the Australian sea lion, most pups being born between early December and early January. Mating takes place about six to seven days after birth. For two or three days after birth, the pups stay close to their mothers, but after this they become much more active, congregating in large groups, or pods, except when sucking from their dams. Lactation is assumed to last a year, or longer, since cows are not infrequently seen suckling yearling animals. Milk stealing is common in this species, and pups have been observed making the round of sleeping cows, searching for available milk.

In the Southern sea lion at Punta Norte, Peninsula Valdés, in Argentina (42°S), the breeding cycle begins with the arrival of the breeding bulls and cows in the first half of December. These animals establish themselves in a dense aggregation along the water's edge on the open pebble beach. Although the breeding bulls contend fiercely with each other, there are no clear boundaries between the males. Peak numbers of both sexes occur during the third week of January, each resident male being associated with about ten females.

Mating takes place about a week after birth after which the females go to sea to feed, returning periodically to suckle their pups. Pups enter the water for the first time when three to four weeks old, but it is not known when they begin to feed for themselves.

A peculiarity of these sea lions at Peninsula Valdés is that gangs of subadult males, which lurk on the periphery of the breeding aggregation, from time to time make raids, distracting the resident bulls and carrying off cows and pups, which they then attempt to mate forcibly. It is unlikely that these matings are successful, since the cows do not appear to be selected and hence are unlikely to be on heat. Pups are frequently killed in these forays.

A breeding group of Southern sea lions. The blood in the water is from a recent birth.

Breeding activity begins to decline by the end of January and by February the bulls are extremely thin and have lost much of the aggression that characterized them at the start of the breeding season. The breeding aggregation disintegrates and the sea lions become more spread out.

Dominant males of Steller's sea lion, which are usually at least nine years old, establish breeding territories on the rookeries in early May. There they remain for the following 40 days, or even up to 68 days, without feeding, while they defend their territories from other males and mate with the females in heat. The pups are born between the middle of May and the middle of July, mostly in the first two weeks of June. They come into oestrus about 11 to 12 days after the birth. Mating seems to be most common during the day, with less activity at night, and the same is true of births, which are twice as frequent during the day.

Most females stay with their pups until they are mated, and then go to sea to feed. Some, however, make one or two short trips to sea before they come on heat. A female Steller's shows a very definite display to the bull, crawling towards him, rubbing her neck and shoulders against him and nibbling at him. This display is said not always to mean that the female is receptive, and copulation does not always follow.

Feeding–suckling cycles are short in Steller's sea lions, averaging only 17 hours for both the at-sea and onshore phases. By four weeks old, pups are accompanying their mothers to sea and by five weeks they have become proficient swimmers. The parental bond is maintained for at least a year, with the young animal usually being weaned just before the next pup is due. Non-pregnant females will retain the bond with their young for longer, and it is not unusual to see a female suckling both a yearling and a pup. One remarkable account was of a large female observed suckling a smaller female which in turn, was suckling a juvenile. Sexual maturity in the females normally occurs between ages two and eight years.

Chapter 4
The Walrus

INTRODUCTION

The walrus is surely one of the most widely known pinnipeds, even if it is really not very familiar to most people. Of all the pinnipeds, it is the most instantly recognizable; Tenniel's illustrations in *Through the Looking Glass*, which picked unfailingly on the two key characters of this strange animal – its tusks and ample moustache – having fixed it in our memories. Even though most people think they know what a walrus looks like, I shall give a description.

DESCRIPTION

Walruses are among the largest of the pinnipeds, second only to the elephant seals. Their bodies are very stoutly built, with much less tapering to the rear than is seen in seals or sea lions. The head appears small in relation to the massive body and the eyes are small and situated high up on the head. There are no external pinnae to the ears, but the ear opening is protected by a fold of skin. The snout, with its array of about 450 very coarse whiskers, is square, with a heavy upper lip below which protrude the tusks. The flippers are small in relation to the body and walruses are not fast swimmers.

The skin of the walrus is quite characteristic. It is exceedingly thick, from 2 to 4 cm (0·8 to 1·6 in), and is thrown into a maze of creases and folds. It has been suggested that this is a development to act as an armour against the tusks of other walruses (and perhaps the teeth of Killer whales). On the neck and shoulders of adult males, which spend more time sparring with their tusks than other classes, the skin is even thicker, reaching 5 cm (2 in), and has numerous raised nodules 3 to 4 cm (1·2 to 1·6 in), in diameter and about 1 cm (0·4 in) high. These nodules appear at the time of puberty and are a secondary sexual character.

The skin is covered by rather sparse coarse hair, about 1 cm (0.4 in) length, which imparts a coarse velvety texture in the females and young males. The hair is less dense on the adult males, and absent on the raised nodules. Walruses are a cinnamon brown colour overall, but there is variation with age and sex. Young individuals tend to be darkest, their hair being the most pigmented and their skin nearly black. Both hair and skin become paler with age, the old males sometimes being so light as to appear albinistic. When walruses are immersed in the frigid water they inhabit, the blood supply to the skin is restricted and the animals are at their palest. On hauling out to bask, however, capillaries of the skin become engorged with blood and the walruses turn bright pink. Male walruses moult in June and July and the females somewhat later.

Walruses, like fur seals and sea lions, are sexually dimorphic, the males being about 20 per cent longer, and 50 per cent heavier than the females.

Male Pacific walruses.

There is also some regional variation in body size. Pacific walruses are the largest. Males can reach 4.2 m (165 in), though an average length would be about 3.2 m (126 in) and weight 1,215 kg (2,679 lb). Females average 2.6 m (102 in) and 812 kg (1,790 lb). Atlantic walruses are about 3 per cent shorter and 10 per cent lighter than those from the Pacific.

The skull and tusks of the walrus deserve special mention. The skull is much modified because of the presence of the huge tusks. These are the upper canine teeth. They erupt when the young walrus is about six to eight months old, but they do not become visible externally for another year, since until then the 2.5 cm (1 in) long tusks are hidden under the upper lip. The tusks grow continually in length by the addition of dentine (ivory) and cement at the root. A thin enamel cap is present at eruption, but this is soon worn away and disappears within four to six years. The inner core of dentine is made up of globular, or marbled, dentine. This very characteristic ivory exists only in trace amounts in the teeth of other mammals, and its presence can be used to identify walrus ivory.

The tusks of males are larger and heavier than those of females, and a single tusk may reach 1 m (39 in) in length and a weight of 5.4 kg (12 lb), though averages for Pacific walruses are 55 cm (22 in) for adult males and 40 cm (16 in) for adult females. At all ages, the tusks of females are rounder in cross-section and more slender and curved than those of males. The tusks of old walruses become shorter as abrasion and breakages remove material from the tips faster than it is replaced at the roots. The remainder of the dentition consists of four flat-surfaced teeth on each side of both the upper and lower jaw. These are single-rooted and represent in the upper jaw the third incisor and three cheek teeth. These are premolars, since they are preceeded by milk-teeth in the almost vestigial deciduous dentition. The teeth in the lower jaw are the canines and three premolars. A glance at the lower surface of the skull shows all these teeth lying between the tusks. This is because in embryonic development the upper canines migrate laterally out of the tooth row to take up their position at the corners of the upper jaw, which of course has become much modified in consequence. The back of the skull has also become much modified, for here there have to be attachments for the very powerful muscles that support the weight of the tusks at the opposite end of the skull, and allow the animal to use them in fighting. There are no supraorbital processes in the skull of the walrus, a feature that it shares with the phocids. All otariids have well-developed supraorbital processes.

These features of the walrus skull are reflected in its behaviour. Indeed, it may be truer to say that they are the result of its behaviour. Walruses are social animals which live in groups. The primary purpose of the tusks is to establish the animal's position in the social hierarchy of which it is a part. An animal without tusks is a juvenile, and at the bottom of the social ladder. The animal with the biggest tusks is usually at the top and unchallenged in this position. Walruses adopt postures to display their tusks and, by doing so, can cause animals with smaller tusks to give way. When walruses of equal tusk size encounter one another, they may spar with their tusks, stabbing at each other and occasionally inflicting serious wounds. Most encounters are soon ended by one animal turning away and accepting the dominance of its opponent.

The tusks are not used in feeding, despite early beliefs to the contrary (see

Atlantic walrus.

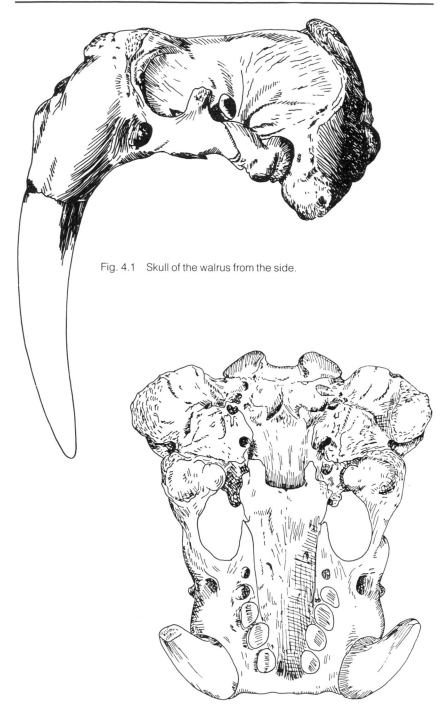

Fig. 4.1   Skull of the walrus from the side.

Fig. 4.2   Skull of the walrus from below.

page 81). They are, however, sometimes used as a fifth limb, when these very bulky animals are emerging from the water on to an ice floe. (It was probably an account of this behaviour that caused the zoologist, Brisson, in 1762 to name the walrus *Odobenus*, which is derived from Greek words for 'tooth-walker'.) Big tusks require a massive skull to accommodate them, and the walrus has turned this to advantage. In winter, walruses are often found in areas of heavy pack from which other pinnipeds are excluded by their inability to keep breathing-holes open in the ice. However, a walrus is able to make new breathing-holes in new ice up to 20 cm (8 in) thick simply by smashing through it with its head.

DISTRIBUTION AND STATUS

Walruses are typically inhabitants of the pack-ice area over the shallow waters of the Arctic continental shelf (see map on p. 80). They have a circumpolar distribution but two subspecies are recognized. *Odobenus rosmarus rosmarus* is the Atlantic walrus. It gets its specific name, *rosmarus*, from an Old Norse word *rossmaar*, which meant walrus. Another Norse word, *hvalross*, gave us walrus directly, supplanting the previously used 'morse', itself derived from the Lappish *morsa*, a name said to come from the noise made by the animal. The Atlantic walrus is found in the eastern Canadian Arctic, mainly in the northern part of Foxe Basin and in northern Hudson Bay. There are smaller groups in Ungava Bay, on Baffin Island and Ellesmere Island. Walruses are found in both west and east Greenland, but they are absent from the southern tip. Once abundant at Svalbard, they are now much reduced there, but recovering. In the Russian Arctic, walruses are found in the Barents Sea, around Novaya Zemlaya and in the Kara Sea.

The Pacific walrus, *O. rosmarus divergens*, got its subspecific epithet from the belief that the tusks were more curved than in Atlantic animals. This is not in fact the case, but since the type specimen from which Illiger described the subspecies in 1815 no longer exists, we cannot see how curved were its tusks. The Pacific walrus is found in the Bering and Chukchi Seas and around Wrangle Island. It reaches Bristol Bay, on the Alaskan side of the Bering Sea, and the Gulf of Anadyr, on the Siberian side, with some extending down the eastern side of the Kamchatka Peninsula as far as 57°N. In the Chukchi Sea, it ranges from Point Barrow in the east to Kolyma Bay in the west. A third subspecies, *O. rosmarus laptevi*, has been described from a few specimens taken in the Laptev Sea, but its validity is doubtful. Laptev walruses seem in skull character more similar to the Pacific subspecies.

Walruses once ranged further than this – around Iceland, for example – but they have been depleted by hunting. Young animals are often seen well outside the usual range. One came ashore at Aberdeen, Scotland, in 1954 and in 1986 two were seen in Shetland and one in Orkney.

Walruses have been severely depleted by hunting for their tusks, skins (which at one time were extensively used to make leather buffing wheels) and oil. The Atlantic walrus population numbers about 30,000. The Pacific subspecies is in much better shape, with a population of about 260,000. There are probably fewer than 10,000 walruses in the Laptev Sea. Commercial hunting of walruses has ceased, but there is a substantial subsistence take by aboriginal peoples in the walrus's range. Currently, about 6 to 7 per cent of

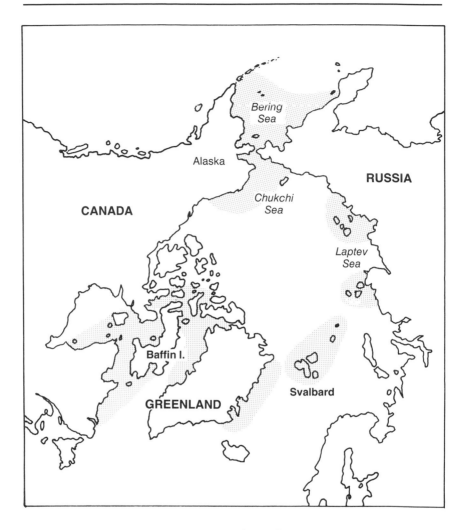

Distribution of the walrus.

the stock is taken each year by Inuit in eastern Canada and Greenland and it is not clear that this level of exploitation can be maintained. From the Bering – Chukchi population, only 2 to 4 per cent are taken annually, and the population seems to be supporting this. The United States and Russian governments are co-operating in walrus research and there are good prospects for the continued survival of this species if aboriginal subsistence take can be adequately controlled.

FOOD AND FEEDING

Walruses are predominantly benthic feeders, that is to say, they find their food on the sea floor. Typically, they feed at depths between 10 and 50 m (33 and

164 ft), though occasionally they descend to as much as 80 m (262 ft). There is one exceptional account of a walrus feeding at 115 m (377 ft). The food the walruses find on these shallow parts of the continental shelf is composed almost entirely of filter-feeding bivalves – clams and cockles – though a large variety of other bottom-dwelling organisms may be taken, including shrimps, crabs, whelks, polychaete worms, priapulids, octopus, sea cucumbers and tunicates. Rarely, fish are taken and some walruses occasionally eat seals.

The most common food organisms, the soft-shell clam (*Mya truncata*) and the cockle (*Serripes groenlandicus*), as well as many other molluscs eaten by walruses, normally live buried in the bottom sediments, the cockle within a few centimetres, but the clam often 10 to 20 cm (4 to 8 in) below the surface. For many years it was assumed that the walruses rooted out these shellfish with their tusks. However, a careful examination of the wear patterns on the tusks, which are abraded on the front and sides, and on the whiskers, indicates that walruses glide slowly along over the bottom with the snout and tusks in contact with the sediments, locating their prey by touch. The upper lip is highly callused and it seems likely that, if any digging is necessary, it is done by rooting with the snout, pig-fashion. Feeding walruses leave a series of furrows and shallow pits on the sea floor where they have disturbed the sediments. The pits may be excavated by squirting water out of the mouth. Location of prey must be by touch, since even in shallow waters visibility is poor over the muddy sediments where the walruses feed, and further reduced by the turbidity stirred up by the feeding of the walruses themselves. Furthermore, the position of the eyes near the top of the head is not well adapted to seeing what is happening near the mouth. Walruses in captivity are often seen exploring the bottom of their pools, paddling slowly with their hind flippers and maintaining contact with the bottom with their whiskers. While doing so, their eyes are usually closed.

Walruses are highly selective feeders. The content of stomachs does not correspond to what is known of the variety of fauna on the sea floor where the animals have been feeding. Furthermore, the stomachs contain almost nothing of the shells of the molluscs. The stomach of a male walrus was recorded as containing 23 kg (51 lb) of clam siphons and 16 kg (35 lb) of the feet of cockles. These fleshy parts had been separated from the shells. The means by which walruses do this is not fully understood, but it is probably by suction. Walruses reared in captivity have been shown to be able to produce a negative pressure of 1,013 millibars, amply sufficient to remove a siphon from a clam. Just how the suction is applied has not been explained. Presumably the shellfish are taken into the mouth, the soft parts sucked out and the shells rejected. Empty mussel shells have been seen around walrus breathing-holes. It is not likely that the molluscs are crushed with the cheek teeth, since the flattened surfaces of these do not show the scratches that would result. What causes the very smooth abrasion of these teeth is not known. Judith King suggested it might be sand and gravel swallowed with the food, but these substances are not commonly found in walrus stomachs.

An aberration in feeding patterns, observed most frequently in male walruses, is eating seals. Remains of young Bearded, Ringed and Spotted seals have been found in walrus stomachs. In the Pacific walrus this was very rare in the two decades prior to the 1970s (only three out of more than 4,000 stomachs examined), but it increased in frequency in the 1970s and 1980s, when eight out of 645 stomachs contained seal remains. This increase in seal-eating paralleled an increase in the abundance of walruses and a decrease in their fatness, and so it might have been the result of a shortage of more traditional food. Walruses have been seen to kill seals with their tusks. Lev Popov, a Russian seal biologist, and some companions were watching a Harp seal pup on an ice floe when a walrus rose in the water alongside it, stabbed it with its tusks, but then, seeing the men, withdrew and swam away. Bud Fay, the American doyen of walrus-workers, has seen a walrus grasp a seal with its fore flippers, tear it open with its tusks and then devour it. Lacking teeth designed for biting off pieces of flesh, Fay hypothesized that walruses use their extraordinary oral suction to tear our chunks of viscera. It seems they mostly consume strips of skin and attached blubber, usually from young tender animals.

Walruses that habitually feed on seals are said to be easily recognizable by their blubber-stained tusks and skin. Native peoples avoid eating the flesh of these animals and the liver is customarily discarded. Seal-eating walruses accumulate large quantities of vitamin A in their livers and consuming these gives rise to symptoms of hypervitaminosis. The same thing is true of polar bears, which feed largely on seals. The vitamin A is acquired from the blubber of the seals, where it is present in large quantities, and is then concentrated in the liver of the predator. Another reason the Eskimos have for avoiding these walruses is that they may be infected with larvae of the nematode *Trichinella spiralis*, and if eaten without adequate cooking, they can give rise to the debilating symptoms of trichinosis, where the larvae penetrate the intestinal walls and encyst in the muscles of the consumer.

Even more remarkable than killing and eating seals, is taking birds. During a joint Soviet – American research cruise in 1984, a walrus was collected near St Lawrence Island in the Bering Sea. Its stomach contained the remains of three prey items: 3 kg (6·6 lb) of tissue from a Ringed seal (including its intact stomach), 95 g (3·4 oz) of pieces of a Black guillemot, and a single siphon from a soft-shelled clam. There are some other anecdotal records of walruses eating birds, but so far no one has suggested how they are captured.

BREEDING AND SOCIAL BEHAVIOUR

Walruses are highly social animals with complex behavioural patterns that are still being elucidated. We know most about the Pacific walrus, because of the long history of research by Bud Fay and his American and Russian colleagues. The breeding cycle starts in the late winter, in January, while the walruses are in the central and southern parts of the Bering Sea. Females and their calves congregate in small groups of 10 to 15 animals in traditional breeding areas. These groups travel and feed together, but may coalesce with other similar groups when they haul out on ice floes between feeding bouts.

Each group of females is attended by one or several males which mostly remain in the water and there display to the females. The display takes the form of producing clacks and whistles at the surface and, when submerged, set sequences of knocks and haunting, bell-like tones. These bell-like sounds seem to be produced by resonance in one of a pair of inflatable pharyngeal sacs in the throat of the male walrus. They are quite unlike the usual barks and

A herd of basking walruses.

growls that walruses use at other times of the year, and they are a courtship song, analogous to the mating songs of many birds or, even more aptly, the humpback whale.

As the groups of females move about, so the males follow, displaying incessantly. Subadult or subordinate males (walrus males do not reach social maturity until about 15 years) remain peripheral to the groups and do not usually display. Mating, which has not been directly observed, is believed to take place in the water. The mating system has been described as a 'mobile lek', where the displays of the male attract oestrous females to leave the resting group and enter the water to copulate beneath the surface. Perhaps the system is not as reliant on female choice as all that, for the males fight with each other to establish a dominance hierarchy, so that only one is effectively available for the females in the group to choose to mate with. Whatever the system of choice, the outcome is that a dominant male will mate with all the females that come into heat while he is in attendance, and thus a polygynous breeding system exists. Bud Fay found that in the area he studied, the ratio of males to females in March and April varied from 1:5 to 1:17. However, the ratio of *displaying* males to potential mates was from 1:5 to 1:67, with an average of 1:23, so the degree of polygyny is high.

Most matings take place in February, but can occur from January to March. The pups are born 15 months later, in May of the following year, though there are records of unusually late or early births. This very long gestation period is unique in pinnipeds. Because it lasts more than a year, it cannot be followed by the usual post-partum oestrus (or else the births would get out of synchrony with the seasons), so female walruses breed only once every two years, and it appears that as they grow older, the interval between births becomes longer. This means that the walrus has a very low reproductive rate, the lowest of all the pinnipeds and one of the lowest among all mammals, comparable with that of the elephant, or sperm whale, for example.

The walrus calf at birth is about 1.1 m (43 in) long and weighs about 60 to 65 kg (143 lb). Observed births have taken place on an ice floe, but the calf can swim within a few minutes of birth, which may take place in the water. Bud Fay was told by some Eskimos that they had captured a walrus with a new-born calf at least 30 km (19 miles) from the nearest floe.

The calf feeds only on milk for at least the first six months. Its mother is very solicitous, carrying it on her back and defending it fiercely from potential predators. It is very unusual for a calf to become separated from its mother. Cows will herd their young into the water when alarmed, ensuring that they escape before they leave the floe themselves. Calves whose mothers have been shot usually remain with them and are easily captured by the hunters. Occasionally, an orphaned calf is 'rescued' by another walrus, which grasps it with its fore flippers and swims off with it.

By the end of its first year, the calf has tripled in weight and grown tusks about 2.5 cm (1 in) long (but still concealed by the upper lip). For another year it remains with the mother, perfecting its ability to feed for itself, though still receiving some milk. At two years old, it separates from its mother, who then normally produces another calf. The calves continue to travel in the same group as the mothers, but over the next couple of years the young males break away, joining bull herds.

MIGRATORY CYCLES

Overlaid on the reproductive cycle is a migration cycle. During the winter, the female walruses are in the Bering Sea. Following the mating season, around April, they begin a slow northward migration to the Chukchi Sea. It is during this migration that the gravid females produce their young. By July, the herds have reached the Chukchi Sea, where they spend the summer, turning southward in October, to reach the Bering Sea again in January. Most of the bulls gather in separate feeding areas in the Bering Sea during the spring, while the cows and young are migrating northwards. They remain separate during the summer, but meet up again with the females in the vicinity of the Bering Strait in the autumn and follow them to the wintering–breeding areas in the Bering Sea. The immature males detach themselves from the breeding males at this time and form their own herds.

This pattern of movement and separation of the sexes serves to spread the impact of the walruses on their food supplies and minimizes potential impacts between the males which become highly aggressive during the breeding season.

PREDATION

Because of its huge size, the walrus is secure from all but the largest or most skilled predators. Killer whales and polar bears are the only natural predators. Polar bears feed mainly on Ringed seals and Bearded seals, but they are often found to have been feeding on walrus. Often, this will be walrus carrion that the bears have discovered, following an Eskimo kill, but bears have been seen to stalk and attack walruses. Usually, it seems the bears do no more than scare basking walruses into the water, though sometimes in the confusion of scrambling to the sea, the adult walruses may crush a calf which the bear can then seize. Big male walruses, with their formidable tusks, can successfully outface a bear. Their very thick skins render them more or less impregnable to the bear's claws and their tusks can kill.

Killer whales attack walruses in the water. A Russian observer watched a pod of 15 Killer whales surround a herd of 60 or 70 walruses. Two whales entered the herd and cut out a group of ten or a dozen walruses, which were then torn to pieces by the whales. Probably, it is young walruses that are most at risk from Killers. The great size and thick skin of the adults would make them difficult prey for killers. However, adult males have been found with internal injuries consistent with having been rammed by a Killer whale.

Walrus herds can be panicked by the presence of Killer whales and there are accounts of large numbers of walruses perishing when they were crushed piling up on the beach, but whether these were the result of harassment by Killer whales is not certain: aircraft movements have been observed to affect walruses in this way.

Since the development of coastal cultures in the Arctic, probably about 15,000 years ago, Man has been a significant predator on walruses. Walruses provided essential resources for Eskimos: hide for ropes, tusks for harpoon tips, and so forth (see Chapter 9). In the eighteenth and nineteenth centuries, walruses were taken commercially for their ivory, hides and oil but now they are hunted only by aboriginal peoples. Little of the carcass is used for subsistence nowadays and often the only part taken is the head, for the sake of the tusks. When carved, these are sold to tourists to provide a cash input into the aboriginal economies.

The combined harvest of walruses by aboriginal peoples in Alaska and Russia for the ten years to 1989 averaged about 6,750. However, this figure does not include those animals that are shot and escape mortally wounded without being retrieved. This may amount to about 40 per cent of the animals killed.

Chapter 5
True Seals – the Northern Seals

INTRODUCTION

The first true seals – phocids – that I shall consider are a rather diverse group. The ten species of northern phocids are divided between four genera, all with one species except for *Phoca*, with six which themselves are divided into several subspecies, some of doubtful validity. They include all the true seals found in the Northern Hemisphere, except for the monk seals and the Northern elephant seal, which are related to the Antarctic seals (and, of course, the Southern elephant seal), and are collectively described as the southern phocids.

In more technical terms, the northern phocids make up the Subfamily Phocinae, with three tribes: the Erignathini, including the Bearded seal; the Cystophorini, the Hooded seal; and the Phocini, the Grey seal, the Harbour seal, the Spotted seal, the Ringed seal, the Caspian seal, the Baikal seal, the Harp seal and the Ribbon seal.

All these seals share a number of common skull characters, but the only obvious external feature that separates them from the remaining phocids is that the northern phocids all have well-developed claws on both fore and hind flippers. At the extreme microscopic level, the southern phocids have 34 chromosomes, while the northern seals have 32, except for the Bearded seal and the Hooded seal, which have 34. I might in passing note here that all otariids have 36 chromosomes and the walrus has 32.

The Bearded Seal

The Bearded seal, *Erignathus barbatus*, gets its generic name from two Greek words (*eri* and *gnathos*) that refer to its heavy jaw. The other part of its Linnean name means bearded and refers to its most characteristic feature, the conspicuous and very abundant whiskers. These whiskers arise from the fleshy mystacial pads on either side of the snout, and represent a moustache rather than a beard. Each whisker is smooth along its length, and not beaded, as is the case with other true seals (except for monk seals, which also have smooth whiskers). When dry, these whiskers curl very elegantly, giving the Bearded seal a raffish look.

Bearded seals are large seals, reaching about 2.25 to 2.7 m (89 to 106 in) in nose-to-tail length and from 275 to 340 kg (606 to 750 lb) in weight. The sexes are about the same size. Adults are greyish-brown in colour, darker on the back, rarely with a few faint spots on the back or dark spots on the flanks. Occasionally the face and neck are reddish-brown. Pups are born with a greyish-brown natal fur with scattered patches of white on the back and head.

The Bearded seal is so named from its luxuriant whiskers.

They are 87 to 120 cm (34 to 47 in) long and weigh 25 to 43 kg (55 to 95 lb), but it is not certain that these dimensions are for newly born pups. Bearded seals are unique in the Phocinae in having two pairs of nipples, a feature they share with the monk seals. They are characterized by having rather square-ended front flippers, which has given rise to the name 'square-flipper' sometimes used in Newfoundland and by Norwegian seal hunters.

The Bearded seal has a circumpolar distribution throughout the American, European and Asiatic Arctic (see map on p. 88). (Two rather doubtful subspecies are described: *E. barbatus barbatus*, from the Laptev Sea to Hudson Bay and as far south as the Gulf of St Lawrence, and *E. barbatus nauticus*, from the western Canadian Arctic to the central Siberian coast.) It is found in the Sea of Okhotsk, and occasionally as far south as Hokkaido. The population size, like that of all ice seals, is difficult to estimate, but it has been put at 600,000 to a million. Probably about 450,000 of these are found in the Pacific sector (i.e., Laptev Sea, Chukchi Sea, Bering Sea, Okhotsk Sea and around Japan). There is some hunting, mostly by aboriginal hunters, but there seems to be no risk of over-exploitation.

Bearded seals spend the winter mostly in heavy offshore ice. From mid-March to late April, females give birth to their young on pack ice. The lactation period lasts from 12 to 18 days and the pups can and do enter the water soon after birth, a habit which may help to protect them from polar bear predation. Bearded seal males produce a distinctive underwater song. (Some people believe that both males and females sing.) This may be part of a

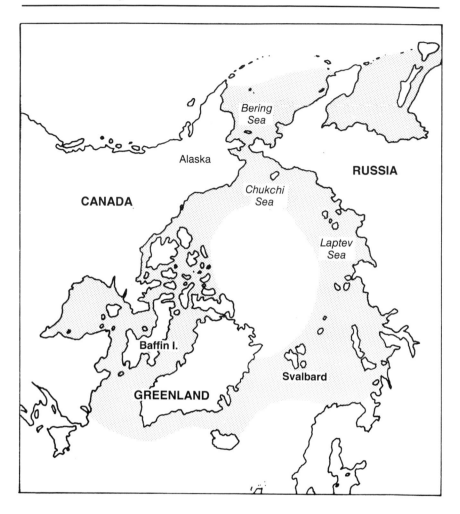

Distribution of the Bearded seal.

territory-defence system beneath the pack ice. The males are probably polygynous, mating with as many females as they have access to, but the social structure of these seals is not well known. Outside the breeding season, Bearded seals are solitary, though occasionally several animals will haul out around the perimeter of a large floe, each well spaced from its neighbour and each facing in a different direction.

Bearded seals are mostly benthic feeders, finding their food on or near the bottom of shallow seas. Invertebrates, such as molluscs, both gastropods and bivalves; crustaceans, including crabs and shrimps; and various 'worms', including priapulids and echiuroids as well as the more usual polychaetes, make up the majority of the diet, but some fish, such as sculpin, flounder, Arctic cod and octopus, are also taken. Bearded seals possibly overlap to some extent with walrus in their feeding habits and may also use suction to extract molluscs from their shells. Like the walrus, the Bearded seal usually has extremely worn cheek teeth. The palate is more arched and higher than in other phocids and the mandibles are very deep, resulting in a very large buccal cavity, presumably a modification for suction feeding.

The Hooded seal

The Hooded or Crested seal, *Cystophora cristata*, is another large seal. The generic name means 'bladder-bearer' in Greek, from the peculiar inflatable appendage on the nose of the adult male. The trivial name, *cristata*, means crested in Latin and also refers to this. Males are noticeably larger than females in this seal, reaching a weight of over 400 kg (882 lb) and 2.6 m (102 in) in length. Females are around 300 kg (660 lb) and 2 m (79 in) in length. Both sexes are silvery grey with black spots and mottling, more pronounced on the back and flanks. The hood of the adult male is formed from an enlargement of the nasal cavity. In the passive state, the hood starts from just behind the level of the eyes and extends to its tip, hanging down over the front of the mouth. When the seal is excited, the nostrils are closed and the hood inflated to form a vast sac about twice the size of a football. The hood is in two parts, one at the front and one at the back, and air can be passed from one chamber to the other. Seals sometimes inflate their hoods when lying quietly on the ice and gently move air from one part to the other. In general, however, the hood is inflated only during agonistic behaviour with other males. Besides the hood, males can extrude an extraordinary membranous balloon from one nostril, usually the left. This is the very distensible internasal septum, which divides one nostril from its neighbour. The balloon appears when the seal closes one nostril and blows air into the other, forcing the

A Hooded seal triad. While the female is undoubtedly the mother of the pup, the male in attendance may not be its father. It will, however, father the female's next pup.

septum to extrude as the balloon. When the balloon is inflated, the seal can make a loud 'pinging' noise by shaking it violently from side to side. All this is part of the aggressive display used by the bulls to establish dominance and hence access to the females during the breeding season. Because display does not always settle the matter, and fighting is often resorted to, the bulls usually bear wounds resulting from sexual fighting during the breeding season.

Hooded seals are found in the north-west Atlantic from around Svalbard, past Greenland to the Canadian Arctic and Gulf of St Lawrence. They congregate at a few discrete breeding sites: the West Ice (around Jan Mayen), Davis Strait at about 64°N, the Front (off Newfoundland) and in the Gulf of St Lawrence. Moulting takes place in two locations: Denmark Strait (between Greenland and Iceland) for the seals from the North American breeding grounds, and off north-east Greenland for the Jan Mayen breeders. Apart from the breeding and moulting season (mid-June to mid-July), the seals disperse widely. Because Hooded seals have been extensively exploited for the skins of the weaned pups, quite good data are available on pup production, and hence total population size. The north-west Atlantic stock is estimated to number abut 325,000 and the Jan Mayen stock about 200,000, giving a total of 500,000 to 600,000. As far as is known, the population is stable.

Distribution of the Hooded seal. The four breeding areas are indicated in black.

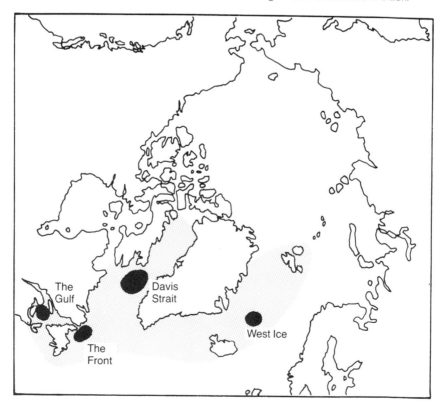

A 'blue-back', the pup of a Hooded seal, aged about three days.

Hooded seals gather in loose aggregations on old, heavy ice floes to breed. The pups are born from mid-March to early April. At birth they weigh about 20 kg (44 lb) and measure 1.05 m (41 in) in length. Male pups are larger than females, and this difference persists throughout life. The pups shed a pale grey natal coat while still in the uterus and are born with a very handsome coat, blue-grey on the back and silvery grey beneath. This was once the most valued pelt in the northern sealing industry and gives the Hooded seal pup its common name, 'blue-black'. Hooded seal pups are born in a very advanced stage, even with some blubber laid down beneath the skin. The mothers are extremely defensive of their young and vigorously threaten, and even attack, intruding males. Lactation is astonishingly short, from three to five days, and it is followed by oestrus. The mother – pup pairs are attended by one or more bulls, which display their hoods or fight to drive off other bulls, as they compete for proximity to the female and the opportunity to mate.

Hooded seal adults are pelagic, deep-diving predators that feed mainly on demersal fish, including Greenland halibut, redfish, polar cod, and the squid *Gonatus fabricii*. The young seals take smaller prey, such as capelin and amphipod shrimps.

The Grey seal

The Grey seal, *Halichoerus grypus*, is the first of the Phocini and the only member of its genus. It got its trivial name, *grypus*, meaning 'hook-nosed', from the Danish name, *krumsnudede sael*, used by Fabricius in 1791 in his memoir on the Seals of Greenland, which means the same thing: it refers to the Roman-nose profile of the adult bull. *Halichoerus* means 'sea-pig' in Greek but it does not seem especially appropriate to this seal.

The Grey seal is the third and last large seal in the Phocinae. In the eastern Atlantic, males are 1.95 to 2.3 m (77 to 91 in) long and weigh 170 to 310 kg (375 to 683 lb); females are considerably smaller, 1.65 to 1.95 m (65 to 77 in) and 105 to 186 kg (231 to 410 lbs). In the western Atlantic, the Grey seals are larger, bulls reaching over 400 kg (882 lb) and cows 256 kg (564 lb). Besides the differences in size between males and females, there are differences in shape too. The shoulders of the adult bulls are very massive and the skin in this region and over the chest is thrown into heavily scarred folds and wrinkles. The female, on the other hand, preserves the usual sleek, seal-shaped profile. The snout of the adult male is elongated with a convex outline above the wide and heavy muzzle, giving the Roman-nose appearance. The Canadians call this seal 'horse-head', but I see little equine about this profile. The top of the female's snout is flat and the muzzle is more slender.

Although the term 'grey' is accurate for most seals, there is a lot of individual variation. Some bulls are almost entirely black, while some cows are creamy-white with only a few scattered black markings. Apart from a generally darker back and lighter belly, there are two tones of colour pattern: a lighter and a darker. In males, the darker tone is predominant, forming a continuous background with lighter patches and reticulations. In the female, this is reversed, darker markings occurring on a paler background. Pups are born in a silky white natal fur which is moulted by the end of the lactation period to reveal a weaner coat that matches the adult pattern.

The Grey seal has three distinct populations: one centered on the western North Atlantic, one on the eastern North Atlantic, and a relict population in the Baltic Sea. They are separated both geographically and physiologically by

Distribution of the Grey seal.

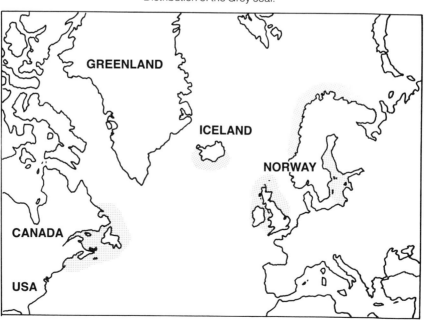

There is considerable difference in size between the sexes in the Grey Seal. Here a cow responds aggressively to the attentions of a bull.

differences in the breeding season. Probably, there was a continuous population in the last interglacial period, from Labrador via Greenland and Iceland to north Norway. About 100,000 years ago, in the last glacial period, the southward extension of the ice separated the western stock from Grey seals on the coast of France and the Iberian Peninsula. With the retreat of the ice, the eastern group spread northwards into its present range, but the isolation of the Baltic Sea, as the Ancylus Lake about 9,000 years ago, separated the Baltic population from the other eastern seals.

The western Atlantic group is found around the coasts of Newfoundland and Nova Scotia and the Gulf of St Lawrence, within the limits of Cape Chidley in the north of Labrador and Nantucket Island, Massachusetts, in the south. Breeding colonies are found on the Magdalen Islands, Amet Island in Northumberland Strait, Sable Island (a large and rapidly expanding colony), Point Michaud on Cape Breton Island and on the fast-ice of Northumberland Strait and George Bay. Outside the breeding season, large concentrations of Grey seals are seen at Miquelon Island, south of Newfoundland, and in estuaries, such as the Miramichi.

In the eastern group, Grey seals are found rather sparsely in Iceland, particularly on the east coast, in the Faroe Islands and on the coast of Norway from Møre northwards to North Cape. A very few breed on the Murman coast near the mouth of the White Sea. The great majority breed around the coasts of the British Isles. The largest groups are in the Hebrides, North Rona, Orkney and the Farne Islands, with smaller groups in Cornwall and the Scilly Isles, Wales, the Isle of Man, the Shetlands and East Anglia. A very few breed in Brittany.

The Baltic population is now much reduced. The remaining seals are found from Öland and the Gulf of Danzig in the south to the Gulf of Bothnia in the north, mainly on the eastern side.

The two main stocks are increasing rapidly. The western Atlantic stock numbers between 80,000 and 110,000. The eastern Atlantic stock is between 120,000 and 125,000, of which some 99,500 are found in the British Isles and they are increasing at about 7 per cent annually. The Baltic population is estimated at between 2,000 and 3,000 seals and it is either stable or declining.

The breeding pattern of Grey seals is perhaps the most diverse of any pinniped. The stocks breed at different times of the year, with a spread of the main breeding season from September to March. In the British Isles alone, breeding spreads from September to December, with pups recorded in every month of the year.

Although the peak of breeding occurs in different months in different parts of the range, the relative stages of the breeding cycle seem to be fairly constant. The seals begin to assemble around the breeding grounds a short while before the first cows haul out at their chosen pupping sites. These are usually on isolated skerries or uninhabited islands. The seals show a preference for smooth sandy or shingle beaches, sometimes of considerable extent, as on the Monach Islands in the Hebrides, or Sable Island in Canada. In many suitable sites, the seals will heave themselves several hundred metres inland to give birth on the grassy swards. In less suitable environments, the seals may use caves for breeding, but this is usually characteristic of low-density colonies. With spring-breeding seals in Canada and in the Baltic, the chosen breeding area is often on sea ice. Males come ashore (or on to the ice) as the first females pup, and they take up positions among them. The bulls fight among themselves for access to the females, but they do not defend discrete territories. Where the terrain is favourable (e.g., restricted by narrow gullies), a bull may exclude others from ten or so females, while at sites with open access, the effective sex ration may be one bull to two cows.

The pup weighs about 14 kg (31 lb) at birth and is fed at 5 to 6 hourly intervals for 16 to 21 days. At isolated breeding assemblies, the cows remain with the pups for the whole of the lactation period and they will defend their pups from other cows and bulls. At sites liable to disturbance, the cows come ashore to feed their pups and then retreat again to the safety of the water. Any form of disturbance at breeding sites results in the disruption of the maternal bond, with females losing pups, or feeding others at random, almost always with increased mortality rates for the pups, except for the few fortunate ones who get extra milk.

Mating takes place towards the end of the lactation period. Each female may be mated on land, or in the water, several times, by one or more males. Soon after mating, the cows leave and return to sea. Some bulls remain ashore for the whole duration of the breeding season, up to eight weeks, and neither males nor females feed at this time. Males may lose weight at 2.2 kg (4.9 lb) per day, females, with a pup to feed, at 3.8 kg (8.4 lb) per day.

The autumn-breeding Grey seals in the north-east Atlantic stock are something of a puzzle. No other pinniped in a seasonal environment produces its young at this time of the year, when, as newly independent feeders, they have to contend with winter storms. It is possible that the north-eastern stock has changed its breeding season comparatively recently, as a response to

Although the white coat of the pups betrays an ice-breeding ancestry, most Grey seals now breed on land. Here, on Muckle Greenholm in Orkney, cows may wander nearly three-quarters of a kilometre (a quarter of a mile) inland to produce their pups.

prehistoric human predation on this rather vulnerable terrestrially breeding seal.

Grey seals feed on a wide variety of fish, mostly benthic or demersal species, taken at depths down to 70 m (230 ft) or more. Sandeels (*Ammodytes spp*) are important in their diet in many localities. Cod and other gadids, flatfish, herring and skates are also important locally. However, it is clear that Grey seals will eat whatever is available, including octopus and lobsters. They are often identified as feeding largely on salmon, and this is probably true for individuals near salmon rivers, and more particularly, those near salmon nets; but salmon does not seem to be an important food for the species as a whole. The average daily food requirement is estimated to 5 kg (11 lb), though the seals do not feed every day and, as noted earlier, fast during the breeding season.

THE GENUS *PHOCA*

The remaining seven species of phocines are all in the genus *Phoca*. The most familiar and widely distributed of these is the Harbour seal, *Phoca vitulina*. *Phoca* is a Latinization of the word for seal in Greek and it is said to be derived from a Sanskrit root which means to swell up, and refers to the plumpness of seals. The trivial name, *vitulina*, means calf in Latin. Five (or six) subspecies have been named – three in the Atlantic part of the range, and two (or three) in the Pacific. I will deal with these when describing the distribution.

The Harbour Seal

The colour and pattern of Harbour seals are very variable. Basically, the seals are darker above and lighter below, with a mottle of dark spots on the silvery or creamy-grey belly and flanks. On the back, the dark spots coalesce to produce a dark reticulation. In some specimens from Hokkaido, the dark markings on the back may show a pattern of rings. There may be a dark vertebral stripe running down the back. Males are generally darker than females. This description refers to freshly moulted specimens. As the coat wears, it fades until near the next moult it may be a uniform brownish tinge. It has been noted both in the British Isles and in British Columbia that seals from sandy estuaries tend to have duller and more uniform coat patterns than those from rocky habitats. Pups are born in the adult-pattern coat, or very occasionally in a white natal coat, but this is usually shed before birth, in the uterus.

Harbour seals are medium-sized seals. In Europe, males are from 1.3 to 1.61 m (51 to 63 in) long and weigh 55 to 130 kg (121 to 287 lb); females are smaller, 1.2 to 1.55 m (47 to 61 in) and 45 to 106 kg (99 to 234 lb). The Harbour seals from the western part of their Pacific range are larger, males about 2 m (79 in) and 185 kg (408 lb), females 1.7 m (67 in) and reach 142 kg (313 lb). Pups (in Europe) weigh 10 to 16 kg (22 to 35 lb) at birth for males and 8 to 14 kg (18 to 31 lb) for females.

The Harbour seal has a circumpolar distribution, but in more temperate latitudes. In the North Atlantic, Harbour seals are found from Murmansk along the Norwegian coast, around the Danish coast and into the southern

A Harbour seal mother and her pup from the east coast of Scotland.

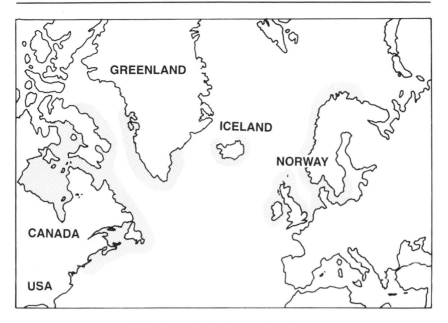

Distribution of the Harbour seal: 1. Atlantic.

part of the Baltic, where they are found sparsely. They occur in the Wadden Sea along the German and Dutch coasts, and around the British Isles, though not in the south of England and Wales. There are also Harbour seals in southern Iceland and southern Svalbard. These seals which are collectively described as *Phoca vitulina vitulina*.

On the other side of the Atlantic, Harbour seals are found from Maine north along the coasts of Newfoundland and Labrador to Ellesmere Island in the Canadian Arctic and west into Hudson Bay. They are found on the Greenland coast from Upernavik, in the west, to Angmagssalik, on the eastern coast. All these seals are referred to as *Phoca vitulina concolor*. Although this subspecies has a characteristic range, there seems to be no way animals from the two populations can be distinguished and to name two separate subspecies seems otiose. Even more purposeless was the designation of a population of seals living in a pair of freshwater lakes in the Ungava Peninsula (Hudson Bay) as *P.v. mellonae*. These are the same animals as their neighbours in Hudson Bay and should share their name.

Harbour seals are found along the western seaboard of North America from Alaska to Cedros Island in Baja California, Mexico. Westwards, the seals are found through the Aleutian chain to the Pribilof Islands. These seals are called *Phoca vitulina richardsi*, though sometimes the more southern seals are described as *P.v. geronimensis*, another example of the unnecessary scattering of subspecific epithets on this seal.

On the other side of the Pacific, Harbour seals are found in the northern parts of Hokkaido, northwards along the Kurile Islands and eastern Kamchatka as far as the Commander Islands and in the western Aleutian

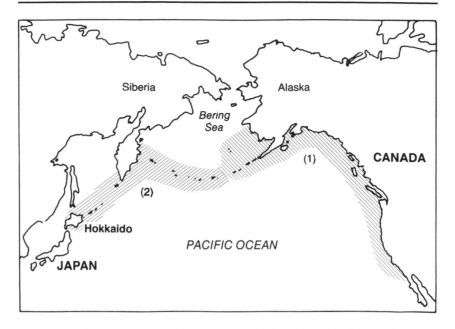

Distribution of the Harbour seal: 2. Pacific. The point at which *P. vitulina richardsi* (1) gives way to *P. v. stejnegeri* (2) in the Aleutian chain is not certain.

Islands. This form is the most clearly differentiated from other Harbour seals by its larger size and somewhat different coat pattern (the presence of ring markings). It is named *Phoca vitulina stejnegeri*, after Dr L. Stejneger who collected the original specimens in 1883 at the Commander Islands.

Harbour seal numbers have fluctuated greatly in the eastern North Atlantic as a result of sterility caused by pollutants and viral infections. Probably between 40,000 and 50,000 Harbour seals are to be found in this part of the range and now that recovery from the viral infection of 1988 (see Chapter 11) seems under way, it is likely that most populations will become stable or will increase. In the Baltic and Wadden Sea, however, chronic pollution problems may check recovery of the seals.

The western Atlantic stock numbers between 40,000 and 100,000 and as far as is known it is stable. The stock size of *P.v. stejnegeri* has been estimated at about 4,000; in Hokkaido it is threatened by fishermen who trap and shoot seals. The remaining Pacific Harbour seals number about 380,000 and apart from some localized catastrophic declines, this population appears stable.

Harbour seals give birth on sandbanks or rocks, usually in the intertidal zone. Occasionally, pups are born on ice in the more northern parts of the range. Births take place in any one location over a period of a month or six weeks. The peak of pupping varies from April to August in different parts of the range, generally in late spring. Pups can swim within a few hours of birth (some births may even take place in the water) and usually swim off with their mothers when the tide rises for the first time after birth. The cows remain in very close contact with their pups, often carrying them on their backs, or

Harbour seals often breed on sandy beaches or tidal sandbanks. These are on San Miguel Island, California.

This Harbour seal from Hokkaido shows ring markings on its coat.

forcing them under the surface if danger threatens. Lactation lasts three to four weeks and as weaning approaches, cows may leave their pups for longer periods. Mating occurs soon after weaning (not after the moult in late summer, as has previously been suggested), usually in the water. Bull Harbour seals fight for access to the females but because of their very aquatic nature, it is difficult to determine the mating system: probably the bulls are serially polygynous, mating with cows as they become available and repelling other bulls as far as they can. It has been suggested that *P. v. stejnegeri* is more terrestial in its breeding, with bulls and cows establishing themselves ashore, rather like Grey seals, but there are few observations on this subspecies.

Harbour seals feed on a wide variety of fish and invertebrates, taking species which are locally abundant and easy to catch. In Scotland, gadoid fish, particularly whiting and saithe, herrings and sand-eels, are important. In estuaries and off sandy coasts, flatfish, such as flounders, predominate. In British Columbia, Harbour seals gather at the mouths of salmon rivers to feed on the fish as they congregate before ascending the river. Molluscs, such as whelks and octopus, are also eaten. Newly weaned pups in some parts of the range feed primarily on shrimps.

The Spotted Seal

Closely allied to the Harbour seal (and sometimes regarded as another subspecies of it) is the Spotted seal, *Phoca largha*, a seal of the pack ice of the North Pacific and the adjacent parts of the Arctic Ocean. The trivial name is the local name given to this seal by the native Tungus of Siberia. The Spotted seal is a small seal. Males, which are slightly larger than the females, reach 1.7 m (67 in) in length and a weight of 80 to 110 kg (176 to 243 lb), though an exceptionally large seal might reach 120 kg (265 lb); the females are 1.5 m (59 in) long and weigh about 80 kg (175 lb). In appearance, the Spotted seal is very similar to the Harbour seal. The coat has a background of silvery grey, which weathers to a brownish-yellow, peppered with black spots which may coalesce on the back to produce a dark mantle. The pups are born in a greyish-white natal coat which is moulted to reveal the adult pelage.

Spotted seals are found in the Bering and Chukchi Seas from Chaun Bay in the west to Herschell Island in the east. They occur also in the Sea of Okhotsk, extending as far south as Sakhalin and northern Hokkaido in the winter. There is a separate population in the Po Hai Sea and the Yellow Sea (see map on p. 102). The Bering Sea population has been estimated at 100,000, but this may be too high; the Sea of Okhotsk population is said to be 130,000. There are no estimates for the Chinese population. Spotted seals are exploited by local seal hunters in Siberia and Alaska. Recent Russian quotas have been 13,000 seals, but the actual kill is uncertain. How hunting and other killing is affecting the population is not known.

Pups are born on the ice floes in late March or April, mainly during the first two weeks of April. The pregnant cows seek the shelter of ice hummocks and crevices where these can be found. Lactation lasts three to four weeks. During this period, the mother and pup remain on the floe and are attended by a male which usually floats in the sea near the floe. The cow comes into heat at the end of lactation and is mated by the attendant bull.

A Spotted seal triad. The male is just visible in the water by the floe.

Spotted seals usually remain over the continental shelf. They are not deep divers, feeding in relatively shallow waters on fish, such as capelin, pollock, herring, smelts, sand-eels, saffron cod and sculpin. During summer and autumn, the seals move to the coasts and concentrate near rivers where salmon are assembling before spawning. Besides fish, Spotted seals eat a variety of invertebrates, such as crabs, shrimps and octopus.

The Ringed Seal

The Ringed seal, *Phoca (Pusa) hispida,* is grouped with the Caspian seal and the Baikal seal in the subgenus *Pusa. Pusa* is said to be derived from the general term used by the Greenland Inuit for seals; *hispida* comes from the Latin for rough or bristly, and refers to the harsh coat of the adult. Ringed seals are small seals, common throughout the Arctic. Males reach 1.5 m (59 in) in length and a weight of 65 to 95 kg (143 to 209 lb), exceptionally 107 kg (236 lb); females are slightly smaller, 1.38 m (54 in) and 45 to 80 kg (99 to 176 lb). Some very small Ringed seals have been described, but these are probably the result of an interrupted suckling period. The coat has a light grey background spotted with black, the spots often being surrounded with lighter ring markings, from which this seal gets its vernacular name. The dark markings often run together on the back and there may be a dark vertebral stripe. The belly may be free of spots and a clear silvery grey. Pups are born in a silky white natal coat, though the pups of Ringed seals from Ladoga are born in grey coats.

Ringed seals are distributed throughout the Arctic, as well as in the Baltic

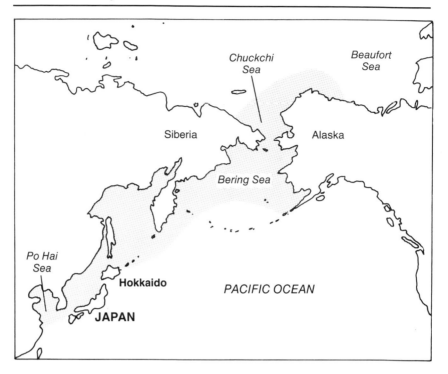

Distribution of the Spotted seal.

area (see map on p. 104). The seals which are found around north Norway, Greenland, the Canadian Arctic, Alaska, the Bering Sea and north of the Russian coast are *Phoca hispida hispida*. In the Sea of Okhotsk and around Sakhalin and Hokkaido, they are usually called *P. h. ochotensis*, but there is little evidence that these are a separate subspecies or even effectively isolated from the former. In the northern part of the Baltic Sea and in the Gulfs of Bothnia and Finland, there is another population, named as *P. h. botnica*. These seals have been isolated since at least Ancylus Lake times and perhaps deserve their subspecific status. They are said to be slightly bigger. In Lake Saimaa, in Finland, and in Lake Ladoga, in Russia, both near the eastern end of the Gulf of Finland, there are two further named populations, *P. h. saimensis* and *P. h. ladogensis*. They are in freshwater lakes, but it is not clear if there are real subspecific differences between these and *P. h. botnica*. The circumarctic population of Ringed seals is huge – perhaps 2.5 million. The Okhotsk seals number about 800,000 to a million. In the Baltic Sea and the two gulfs, there are probably no more than 5,000 to 8,000 Ringed seals. This population has suffered severely from reproductive failure as a result of pollutants in the sea water. The Ladoga seals number about 10,500 to 12,500, with a tendency to increase. In Lake Saimaa, the seals are not doing as well: habitat disturbance and general persecution has reduced what was once a flourishing population to no more than 160 to 180 seals.

A Ringed seal.

The Ringed seal is an ice-breeding seal. Characteristically, the pregnant female makes a snow lair in the fast ice. In the spring, she selects a place on the lee side of a pressure ridge, where the drifting floes have rafted up over each other, and she scrapes away the snow with her well-developed claws in the snowdrift that has formed in the lee of the ridge. Having excavated a lair, she keeps open an access hole through the ice to the water beneath, also with her claws. Here the pup is born in early April, with some protection from the weather.

Lactation in this relatively protected environment is longer than in other ice-breeding seals. The Ringed seal suckles its pup for up to two and a half months, but the length of the lactation may be affected by the break-up of the fast ice. Pups on stable ice wean at a greater weight than those from less stable areas. Little is known about mating, but this is presumed to take place in the water beneath the ice. Lairs are usually widely separated, so it seems unlikely that males could defend more than one female at a time. However, males call underwater, produce a strong and very characteristic scent and often carry wounds that look like the results of sexual fighting, so there may be some sexual competition. Because males become sexually mature at seven years old, two years later than females, this could imply a limited form of polygyny.

Not all Ringed seals make breeding lairs. The seals from the Sea of Okhotsk and around the Baltic give birth on the surface of drifting ice. At least in the case of the Okhotsk seals, the lactation period is short – about three weeks.

Ringed seals feed on a wide variety of organisms. In much of their range, the winter diet consists largely of fish, including polar cod and Arctic cod; in the summer they feed extensively on planktonic crustacea, such as euphausiids and the amphipod shrimp *Parathemisto*.

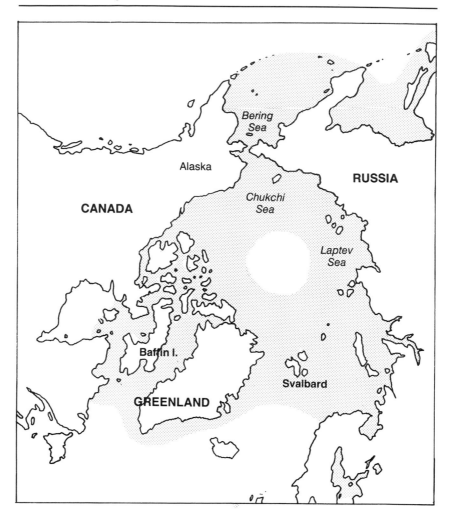

Distribution of the Ringed seal.

The Caspian Seal

In the Caspian sea, between northern Iran and the south-western part of the Commonwealth of Independent States, lives a near relative of the Ringed seal, the Caspian seal, *Phoca (Pusa) caspica*. (The trivial name refers to its origin.) These are small seals measuring 1.3 to 1.4 m (51 to 55 in) and weighing 50 to 86 kg (110 to 189 lb). Very large specimens may reach 1.8 m (71 in) and 86 kg (190 lb). The background coloration is silvery grey, with dark spots on the back and sides. Males are said to be darker than females. Pups are born in a silvery grey natal coat.

These seals are found only in the Caspian Sea. They are dispersed throughout the sea during most of the year, but they concentrate in the north-

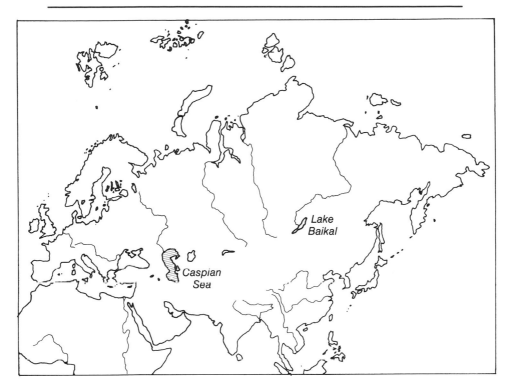

Distribution of the Caspian and Baikal seals.

eastern corner in December. By this time, ice has formed and the floes become rafted against each other. The pregnant cows select sheltered places among the jumble of floes and produce their pups from late January to the beginning of February. Lactation is variously said to last two weeks or a month.

Caspian seals feed on a wide range of small fishes, including shad (*Alosa spp*), cyprinids and gobies, and crustaceans. The seals enter river estuaries to eat carp, roach and pike-perch.

The population size is estimated to be about half a million and there is some harvesting of pups, with a current quota of 50,000. Although the population is thought to be stable, degradation of the habitat and overfishing of the fish stocks are seen as threats, and the Caspian seal is regarded as vulnerable.

The Baikal Seal

Another freshwater relative of the Ringed seal is the Baikal seal, *Phoco (Pusa) sibirica*. Lake Baikal is a huge freshwater lake in Siberia (whence the trivial name), near the border with Mongolia. Baikal seals are probably the smallest of all the pinnipeds. They grow to about 1.2 to 1.4 m (47 to 55 in) long and weigh 63 to 70 kg (139 to 154 lb). The coat is generally a uniform steely-grey colour, though there may be a scattering of dark spots on the upper surface. As the coat weathers, it becomes brownish.

Baikal seals bask in the sun on the shores of the deepest lake in the world.

Pups are born in white silky natal fur in late February to early April on the ice that covers the lake. Like the Ringed seal, the Baikal seal female makes a lair in a snowdrift in which to produce her pup. Lactation lasts for eight to ten weeks and it is followed by mating. The seals are reputed to be polygynous.

The seals are said to be found mainly in the surface waters of the deeper parts of this very deep lake. Their food consists of more than 19 species of fish, largely deep-water forms. These include two species of *Comephorus (Golomynka* in Russian) and sculpins *(Cottocomephorus)*.

Baikal seals number about 60,000 TO 70,000 and there is a substantial harvest, mainly of pups, of about 5,000 to 6,000 seals.

The Harp Seal

The Harp seal, *Phoca (Pagophilus) groenlandica,* is a medium-sized seal. It was at one time placed in its own genus, *Pagophilus* (from Greek for 'snow-loving'), but this has now been reduced to subgeneric status. The trivial name, of course, refers to Greenland, from where these seals were first described. Both sexes of Harp seals are about 1.7 m (67 in) long and weigh about 130 kg (287 lb). These are one of only a few seal species with a distinct colour pattern. Adult male harp seals are light silvery grey over most of their bodies, but there is a black mask to the face and a black patch over the shoulders which extends down and backwards over the flanks. This has been described as

A Harp seal white-coat pup.

harp-shaped (hence the name Harp seal), but it bears no resemblance to a harp. It has also been compared to a horseshoe, but this is not apt either. In the female, the dark markings are paler and tend to be more broken up. Juveniles are grey with black spots and mottlings. The adult markings develop gradually through successive annual moults, though some females never attain the full pattern. Pups are born in a dense white natal coat.

When dispersed, Harp seals are found from the Laptev Sea, around Greenland to Baffin Bay, in Foxe Basin and northern Hudson Bay and down the Labrador coast as far as the Gulf of St Lawrence. As with most seals, wanderers are quite often found outside this range, but these are exceptions. During the spring, however, all the Harp seals congregate in four places to breed. Harp seals living in the nort-west Atlantic off eastern Canada (the largest population of about 2 to 2.4 million) divide into two groups, one off the coast of Newfoundland, the 'Front', and one off the Magdalen Islands in the Gulf of St Lawrence, the 'Gulf'. The Harp seals off northern Russia, about 0.5 to 1 million, congregate on pack ice in the mouth of the White Sea. A third group breeds on the 'West Ice', between Ja Mayen and Svalbard. This population numbers about 100,000 to 400,000 seals. Harp seal numbers everywhere have been much affected by hunting and it is difficult to be

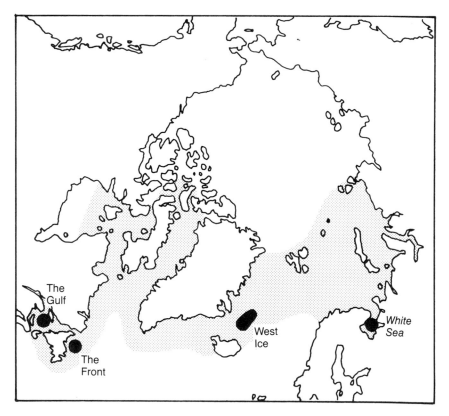

Distribution of the Harp seal. The four breeding areas are indicated in black.

An adult female Harp seal, showing the characteristic pattern.

Male Ribbon seal.

positive about trends, though it is likely that the north-west Atlantic and West Ice seals are increasing. The White Sea stock may be decreasing.

Although the timing of events differs slightly from site to site, in general Harp seals move southwards before the freezing pack ice. After winter feeding, the females assemble on the ice in the traditional whelping areas. (Although the young of most seals are called 'pups', Harp seal young are usually called 'whelps' and grey seal young may be called 'calves'.) The White Sea seals whelp from mid-February to early March; those in the Gulf from late February to mid-March; the Front seals about five days later; and the West Ice seals from mid-March to April. The pups are born on the surface of the floes, without any special protection, and they are fed by their mothers for 9 to 12 days. Males usually remain in the water alongside the floes with the females and mating occurs in the sea at the end of lactation. After weaning their pups and mating with the bulls, the cows, accompanied by the bulls, assemble on ice to the north of the whelping patches to moult. After moulting, the seals follow the melting ice northwards to their summer feeding grounds. The pups, having completed their moult, follow the adults. By September, the seals are beginning to move south again to renew the cycle.

The feeding of Harp seals has been extensively studied because of the perceived interaction with fisheries. Most of the data come from the north-west Atlantic population. The diet varies with the age of the seals, time of year and location, and more than 100 food species have been identified, but the most important food items are capelin (*Mallotus villosus*), polar cod (*Arctogadus glacialis*), herring (*Clupea harengus*), Arctic cod (*Boreogadus saida*), and amphipod and euphausiid shrimps.

The Ribbon Seal

The last member of the Phocini is the Ribbon seal, *Phoca (Histriophoca) fasciata*. This was once classified in the genus *Histriophoca*, which comes from a Greek word for a stage-player, plus *phoca*. The name, now downgraded to subgenus, refers to the striking pattern of this seal; so, too, does the trivial name, which means banded in Latin.

Ribbon seals are a little smaller than Harp seals, reaching about 1.6 m (63 in) in length and a weight of 95 kg (209 lb) in both sexes. In appearance, they are the most striking of all seals. The adult male is a dark chocolate-brown with broad white, or yellowish-white, bands around the neck, the hindquarters and the insertion of each fore flipper. As in the Harp seal, the females are paler and the markings less distinct. Pups are born in a white natal coat and after moulting this, they become blue-grey on their backs and silvery beneath.

Ribbon seals occupy the Pacific Arctic as Harp seals have occupied the Atlantic Arctic. They are found mainly in the Bering Sea and Sea of Okhotsk, but extend in the summer some way into the Chukchi Sea. The population numbers about 60,000 in the Bering Sea and 133,000 in the Sea of Okhotsk.

Pups are born on relatively heavy ice floes from early April to early May, with most births in the first two weeks of April. Pups are suckled for three to four weeks and increase their birth weight of 10.5 kg (23 lb) to 27 to 30 kg (60 to 66 lb) in this times. Males attend oestrous females and are probably serially polygynous.

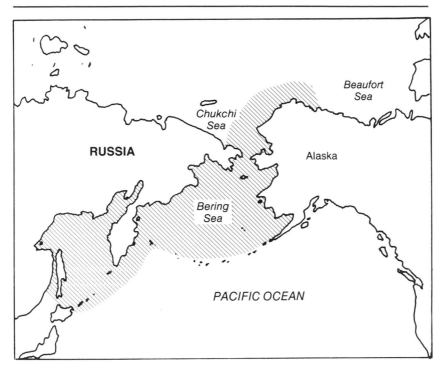

Distribution of the Ribbon seal.

Ribbon seals feed primarily on pelagic fish, like pollack, (*Theragra chalcogramma*), eelpout (*Zoarces viviparus*) and Arctic cod (*Boreogadus saida*), as well as cephalopods and crustaceans, such as crabs and shrimps and other bottom-dwelling invertebrates.

Chapter 6
Monk Seals and Elephant Seals

INTRODUCTION

The final group of seals comprises the most primitive, the hugest and the most remote. These are the monk seals, the elephant seals and the Antarctic seals of the subfamily Monachinae, which takes its name from the monk seals, *Monachus* (from the Greek for a monk). Why these seals were so named is not clear; it has been suggested that the rolls of fat around the neck of the Mediterranean monk seal suggested the cowl of a monk, but this seems far-fetched to me. Although the skeletal characteristics that unite the Monachinae are quite clear to the anatomist, it is not easy to find useful external features that can identify the group in the field: almost the only one is that the claws on the hind flippers are always reduced. Another less useful feature is that the birth coat of a pup is never white, varying from black in the monk and elephant seals to smoky-brown or grey in the Antarctic seals. But three of the four Antarctic seals give birth on floating pack ice, and their pups are rarely seen. In this chapter I shall describe the monk seals and elephant seals, leaving the Antarctic seals for Chapter 7.

MONK SEALS

Monk seals (the Tribe Monachini) are unusual among phocids in that they are all found in relatively warm waters. They have two pairs of nipples and the young are born in black natal fur. They are the most primitive of living seals, and one of the three recent species – the Hawaiian monk seal – can almost be regarded as a 'living fossil'. Monk seals are among the most endangered of all marine mammals. One species has become extinct during this century (the only pinniped to suffer this fate, and indeed, with Steller's sea cow, one of only two marine mammals to have been exterminated in the last few centuries). The two surviving species are reduced to remnant populations which require very active conservation management if they are to continue to be part of the extant pinniped fauna.

The Hawaiian monk seal

The Hawaiian monk seal, *Monachus schauinslandi*, received its name because the first skull known to science was brought back from Laysan Island by Dr H. Schauinsland. This is a moderate-sized seal, the females reaching 2.3 m (91 in) and about 250 kg (551 lb), the males slightly smaller at 2.1 m (83 in) and 170 kg (375 lb). The coat is grey above, but turns brownish with weathering. Beneath, it fades into buff or pale grey. Like all monk seals, new-born pups are clad in a black natal fur. Although probably once generally

Hawaiian monk seals resting on the beach on Lisianski Island.

distributed throughout the Hawaiian archipelago, it is now restricted to the more remote, mostly uninhabited, western islands from Kure Atoll to French Frigate Shoals (see map on p. 115). There are five main breeding islands: French Frigate Shoals, Laysan Island, Lisianski Island, Pearl and Hermes Reef, and Kure Atoll. Of these, French Frigate Shoals is the most important location, about half the total population – 1,500 to 1,600 animals – and the same number of births occurring there. A few births occur on other islands and, exceptionally, two births have occurred in the main Hawaiian Islands.

Pups are born on sandy beaches, above the reach of the tides, over an extended period from late December to mid-August, but mostly between the middle of March and the end of May. Females are gregarious but aggressive towards males. The pup weighs about 16 kg (35 lb) at birth, doubling this weight at 17 days and quadrupling it at six weeks, by which time weaning usually takes place.

There are no archaeological or Polynesian records of seals in the main Hawaiian Islands, but they probably occurred there before the arrival of the first canoes. By the mid- to late 1800s, their numbers had been significantly depleted by commercial sealing and casual killing by plumage hunters and beachcombers.

The US government has taken strong measures to protect this seal. The north-western Hawaiian Islands were designated a reservation to protect sea-birds by Theodore Roosevelt in 1909. Today, as the Hawaiian Islands National Wildlife Refuge, this is managed by the Fish and Wildlife Service, with the seals as one of its priorities. The first counts were made in the 1950s.

Over the next 20 years, numbers declined by about a half, perhaps because of human interference from military and Coast Guard personnel (and their dogs!) stationed on some of the critical breeding islands. The monk seal was listed as endangered under the Endangered Species Act in 1976 and the Marine Mammal Commission collaborated with the Fish and Wildlife Service to develop a research programme and prepare a recovery plan.

The teams involved have taken steps to increase the survival of pups during their first months after weaning by supplementary feeding; they have documented and endeavoured to minimize interactions with commercial fisheries; they have freed seals entangled in fishing nets and cleared beaches of similar debris; and they have worked with the Coast Guard and the Navy to reduce disturbance to monk seals on the beaches.

This has done much to reduce the decline – the present monk seal population is about the same size as it was in the early 1980s – but the species' status is still very precarious. A worrying decrease occurred in the late 1980s and early 1990s, mainly at French Frigate Shoals and Laysan Island. At French Frigate Shoals, this was perhaps the result of food limitation in this area which might be connected with commercial fishing activities, but the cause at Laysan Island is not apparent. Perhaps the underlying general cause is a change in ocean circulation patterns which has made this not very productive area less capable of sustaining the seals.

Factors limiting the recovery of the seals are varied. They include interactions with commercial fisheries, declines in available prey, entanglement in debris, human disturbance, disease, shark predation and, at some places, attacks on adult females and pups by aggressive males.

This 'mobbing' behaviour, as it is known, is puzzling. At Laysan and Lisianski Islands, the sex ratio is strongly skewed towards males (for an

A Hawaiian monk seal pup entangled in a gill net.

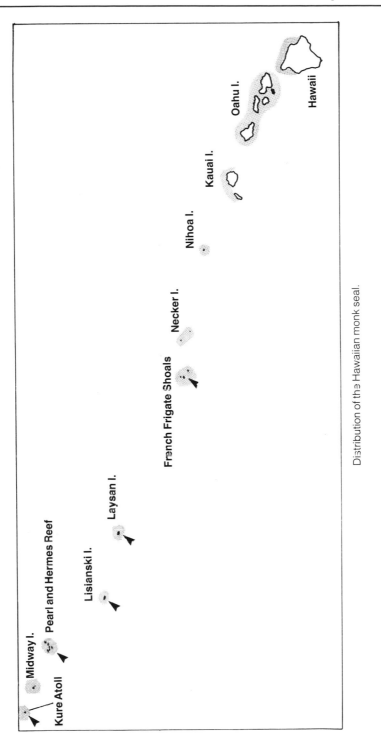

Distribution of the Hawaiian monk seal.

Kure Atoll

Midway I.

Pearl and Hermes Reef

Lisianski I.

Laysan I.

French Frigate Shoals

Necker I.

Nihoa I.

Kauai I.

Oahu I.

Hawaii

unknown reason) and groups of males mob females or pups and attempt to mate. Four females were known to have been killed by this in 1992. The Recovery Team has planned to address this by physically removing some of the males and treating others with a testosterone-suppressing drug to reduce their aggressiveness. The programme began in 1992, but it is too soon to say whether it has been effective.

Vigorous efforts are being made to help the Hawaiian monk seal, but they are hampered by lack of funds. Another major problem is the deterioration of the airstrip on Tern Island, which is vital to the programme. Biologists have been using this strip, but the sea-wall protecting it has deteriorated and massive erosion appears imminent. If the runway is lost, the biological station will have to be evacuated, with dire consequences for the Wildlife Refuge. The scientific importance of the Hawaiian monk seal, as the most primitive seal alive today, is undoubted, but there are other issues. Here is a species, breeding wholly in the territory of the richest state in the world, which has passed some of the most comprehensive protection legislation for the environment and for marine mammals in particular. If the Hawaiian monk seal loses its tenuous foothold and slips into extinction for the want of a few thousand dollars, what can the American public, and indeed, the rest of the world, think?

The Caribbean monk seal

William Dampier, an English buccaneer, in a description of the 'Alacrane Islands' (now Arricife Alacrane), off the Yucatan Peninsula of Mexico, wrote:

> *An. 1675* Here are many Seals: they come up to sun themselves only on two or three of the islands, I don't know whether exactly of the same kind with those of colder Climates, as I have noted in my former Book, they always live where there is plenty of Fish.

> Though here was great store of such good Food and we like to want, yet we did neither salt any, nor spend of it fresh to save our Stock, I found them all but one Man averse to it, but I did heartily wish them of another mind, because I dreaded wanting before the end of the Voyage; a hazard which we needed not to run, there being such plenty of Fowls and Seals (especially of the latter) that the Spaniards do often come hither to make Oyl of their Fat

Perhaps food on English pirate ships was better than often reported, or perhaps Caribbean monk seals were specially unpalatable. Most probably, English sailors, then as now, tended to be a bit picky about local foods.

Caribbean monk seals, *M. tropicalis* (the trivial name is a reference to its habitat) were once widely distributed in that area, from the northern coast of Yucatan northward to the southern point of Florida, the Bahamas and Jamaica and southward along the Central American coast to about Latitude 12°. The seals were found on remote sandy beaches or, more usually, small islets where they were secure from hunting by the indigenous peoples. However, that changed as Western ships began to arrive. Columbus himself started the depredations in 1495, when he killed eight 'sea wolves' that he

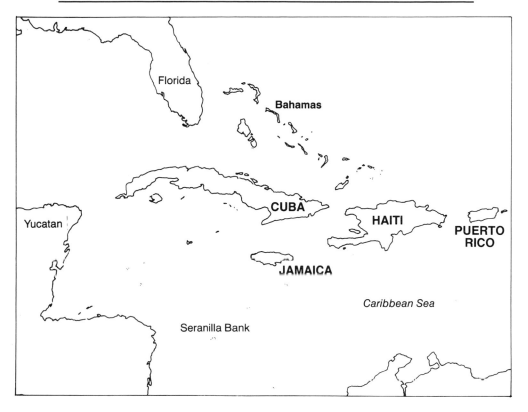

The region where the Caribbean monk seal was once found.

found asleep on a rocky island south of Haiti. At least one commercial sealing expedition operated from Jamaica, but it was probably casual killing for oil, and perhaps meat, that reduced the seals to a mere remnant. The last remaining colony was at Seranilla Bank, about midway between Nicaragua and Jamaica, but there have been no confirmed sightings since 1952. In 1973 an aerial survey was made of all the sandy islands and atolls in the area, but no seals were seen. What was observed was evidence of occupation by fishermen, and since monk seals would be unlikely to share a small islet with fishermen, one must conclude that the seals have gone. However, hope springs eternal, and there are claims of sighting a seal-like animal in Puerto-Rican waters as recently as 1984. I believe the Caribbean monk seal is extinct, but as Karl Kenyon (the person who conducted the aerial survey in 1973) pointed out: 'You can't prove anything is extinct – you can only say that no one has seen one'.

There are some Caribbean monk seal skulls in museum collections, but there are few reliable descriptions of the living animal. They were probably about 2 to 2.4 m (78 to 80 in) in length, brownish or greyish-brown, and produced black pups like the other monk seals. Pups were born about the beginning of December.

The Mediterranean monk seal

The Mediterranean monk seal is *Monachus monachus*. Recorded weights seem to indicate that this seal is slightly larger than the other monk seals, the females reaching 2.7 m (106 in) and 300 kg (661 lb) and the smaller males 2.5 m (98 in) and 260 kg (573 lb), but weights almost certainly fluctuate widely depending on the condition of the seals. Some very large dimensions (e.g., 3.8 m/150 in in length, and a male weighing 400 kg (882 lb)) have been recorded, but these are perhaps doubtful. The coat varies between light fawn and a dark chocolate-brown, paler beneath and often with a large irregularly shaped pale creamy patch on the belly. Pups are born in a black natal fur, again often with a white patch beneath. The shape of these patches can be used to identify individuals.

The Mediterranean monk seal was at one time an abundant species. Aristotle was familiar with it and noted several features (such as the seal's notched tongue and its unusual kidney) that showed he must have examined several specimens. Its former range included the coasts of the Black Sea, throughout the Mediterranean and westwards to Madeira and the Canary Islands, as well as the African coast as far south as Cap Blanc. There have been reports from Senegal and the Gambia. Today, there are probably none left in the Black Sea, perhaps 200 to 250 around Greece, 20 to 50 off the Turkish coast, about 45 in the Adriatic, 30 or so off Algeria and perhaps 20 on the Mediterranean Moroccan coast. Isolated individuals are reported from Cyprus, Sardinia, and Tunisia. There may be as many as 20 in Libya, or the species may be extinct there: we don't know. Outside the Mediterranean there are 8 to 10 at the Desertas Islands by Madeira, but the seals seem to be extinct in the Canaries. The largest colony is in Morocco, where about 130 seals live on the coast near the southern boundary with Mauretania. At Cap Blanc, a small peninsula divided by the disputed boundary between Western Sahara and Mauretania, there is a haul-out of male monk seals, numbering perhaps a dozen or so. Until recently, there were believed to be about 70 to 80 seals near

Distribution of the Mediterranean monk seal.

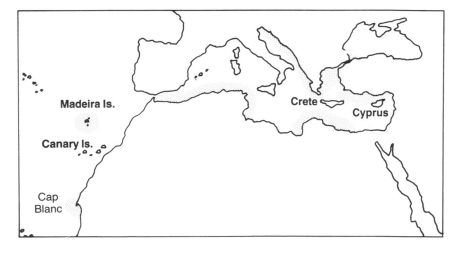

A Mediterranean monk seal in a cave on Kefalonia.

the tip of Cap Blanc. Recent reports of as many as 130 monk seals at Cap Blanc were based on erroneous calculations of scaled-up counts from cliff tops.

Because of the occurrence of isolated individuals at other locations, it is not really possible to give a total population figure, but I feel it is unlikely that there are more than 600 Mediterranean monk seals left in the world and there may be as few as 250.

Because of its rarity and reclusive nature, not much is known about the biology of the Mediterranean monk seal and what is known may be modified by human pressures. For example, monk seals now commonly give birth to their pups in caves, though historical descriptions show that they used open beaches until the eighteenth century. They now typically live in groups of five to six individuals, but this may be only because there simply are not enough seals to form larger groups. Births occur from April to December, with a peak in September–October. The pup is fed for about six weeks, though one report claims lactation lasts as long as 16 to 17 weeks. This seems abnormal to me. As in the Hawaiian monk seal, the Mediterranean species seems to be a generalist feeder, taking both fish and cephalopods, with the occasional crustacean.

Like the Hawaiian monk seal, the Mediterranean monk seal has attracted the attention of people anxious to prevent yet another valued species becoming extinct. There are more problems in the case of the latter, however. There is no single national authority to bring in protective legislation and few of the countries that host the seals have much money to spare for conservation. Nevertheless, a number of national and regional groups have got together and are doing what they can to secure the future of the seals. But the task is a hard one. Although the monk seal is a nominally protected species, in most, if not all, of the countries where it occurs, this does not mean very much in the remote localities favoured by the seals. From Aristotle's time, and no doubt before, fishermen have been the enemies of the seals and it is likely that fishermen still shoot or dynamite them. It is hoped that educational programmes will change these attitudes: there clearly are not enough seals to affect fishermen's catches significantly and local people can be persuaded to take a pride and interest in their seals once they see how highly regarded they are by some people. But there is another problem that affects all wildlife in the Mediterranean: this is the increasing number of tourists visiting this area each year, more and more of whom search out the secluded spots that can be critical habitat for the seals and other wildlife. This problem appears insoluble. The seals on the Moroccan–Mauretanian border were benefiting from the reverse situation. The warring factions, and particularly the Polisario guerrillas, had deterred visitors and discouraged fishermen in this area. Since a truce was declared between Morocco and the Polisario, this stretch of coast has been opened up to commercial fishing and there have probably been substantial accidental mortalities of seals entangled in nets, as well as a probable reduction on the available food supply.

Reserves for monk seals have been created in the Northern Sporades in Greece, the Desertas Islands in Madeira, Portugal, as well as the reserve at Cap Blanc, Mauretania, and a protected area around Monte Cristo, Italy (though it is not certain that there are resident seals here). Some successful rehabilitation schemes have been operated. From one of these in the Northern Sporades, a washed-up pup, named Theodorus, was released and has become very friendly to humans. The local fishermen all know and like him and he functions as a star performer for public relations and educational purposes.

Unfortunately, there is a lack of unanimity in the various conservation groups. In particular, one group wishes to take monk seals from the wild and set up a captive breeding programme, with the aim of building up a substantial stock to be released in suitable locations. This aim, which has proved successful for some other endangered species, is strongly opposed by other groups, who consider that existing wild populations are not large enough to provide the breeding stock and that catching them will cause much disturbance. However, the scheme has received financial support from the European Community and looks likely to go ahead. My own view, which I admit is a minority one, is that prospects for the Mediterranean monk seal in the wild are so exceedingly gloomy that it would be a prudent move to take at least some animals into a restricted, but nevertheless extensive, marine environment where, with supplementary feeding, a stock could be built up in safety. I really do not believe that adequate safeguards can be put in place to prevent the continued decline of these fascinating seals in the wild.

A 'living fossil'

I mentioned at the beginning of this chapter that the Hawaiian monk seal is the most primitive of all living seals, and that it can be regarded as a 'living fossil'. This is the view of two of the most respected seal palaeontologists –

Charles Repenning and Clayton Ray, both from the US. Their views are based on some rather obscure anatomical features, which are not easy to understand, but I feel I should do something to try to explain how this conclusion was reached.

Firstly, it was influenced by the structure of the ear region of the skull. As explained in Chapter 1, seals had to make adaptations to their ears when they entered the sea. In most seals, the dorsal part of the bone (the petrosal) which houses the cochlea is enlarged, increasing its sensitivity to water-borne sound by increasing the mass of the bone opposite its attachment to the rest of the skull. However, in the Hawaiian monk seal, the dorsal part of this bone is actually smaller than the ventral part, and the degree of development of this specialization is less than in any living phocid seal and even less than in any fossil, including the 14.5-million-year-old *Monotherium wymani*, the oldest known fossil monachine seal. Furthermore, there is no exaggeration of the basal whorl of the cochlea, as shown in most phocid seals and interpreted as reflecting increased sensitivity to the direction of sound in water. Further back in the skeleton, the Hawaiian seal shows a separate perforation in its pelvic bone for the obturator nerve. This is regularly found in fur seals, but it is known in no other living or fossil phocid seal.

Another primitive feature is that the fibula (the smaller bone in the shank of the leg) is not fused at the knee end with the tibia, a condition that is common in fissiped carnivores, but unknown in other seals, except for a few fossil otariids and occasionally in the walrus.

Finally, the posterior vena cava (the vein that brings blood from the posterior part of the body to the heart) of the Hawaiian monk seal is much simpler than in other phocids. Of course, there is no fossil record of this vein.

These may appear to be small anatomical points, of rather little significance to those whose interests are in the living animal and how it takes its place in the ecology of its region, but they are the sort of point that palaeontologists use to reach their conclusions about the evolution of our modern fauna. And if we think of the Hawaiian monk seal as a living fossil, perhaps we will value it a little more highly and strive a little bit more to keep it and its one surviving close relative present in our world.

THE ELEPHANT SEALS

There are two species of elephant seals, the Southern and Northern elephant seal. They can be regarded as making up the Tribe Miroungini. The generic name, *Mirounga*, was given by the anatomist James Gray in 1827, and it is derived from an Australian aboriginal word, *miouroung*, said to mean 'elephant seal'. Joel Asaph Allen, a North American seal scientist in the nineteenth century, complained of the barbarous nature of this name, but we are stuck with it, as the name *Macrorhinus* (big nose in Greek), earlier given by Cuvier to this seal, had already been used for a genus of beetles.

The Southern elephant seal

The Southern elephant seal is *M. leonina*. The second part of the name means lion-like, and it is said to refer probably to the animal's size and roaring. I believe, however, that it may have arisen from confusion caused by Anson's description, in 1740, of the sea lion of the Falkland Islands, which is very lion-like, with its abundant mane and stubby snout. Captain Cook, 35 years later, noticed the error. Writing of elephant seals at South Georgia, he said:

> There were some of those which the writer of Lord Anson's voyage described under that name [lions]; at least they appeared to us to be of the same sort; and are, in my opinion, very improperly called lions, for I could not see any grounds for comparison.

Whatever the origin of the name, the Southern elephant seal is certainly an extremely large seal. Breeding males can reach a nose-to-tail length of 4.9 m (193 in) and a weight of 3,200 kg (7,055 lb), perhaps even at times 4,000 kg (8,818 lb)). Females are substantially smaller, at 2.6 to 2.8 m (102 to 110 in) and 400 to 900 kg (882 to 1,984 lb).

In appearance these seals are unmistakable, and they could be confused only with their northern cousins. They are dark grey, sometimes with a darker vertebral stripe, lighter beneath but fading to shades of brown as they approach the moult. There is considerable variation from almost yellow to almost black, the darker animals seeming most often to be males. The pups are born in a black woolly lanugo which is moulted at about three weeks to reveal a steely-grey coat which lasts till the following year, when they moult into the adult pelage. By three years of age, the males are conspicuously larger than the females and are beginning to develop the characteristic proboscis. Older males also develop scars about the head and neck, the result of fighting, at first with other young males, but later as the result of serious fights when contending for dominance in breeding assemblies (see Chapter 8). Mature

The proboscis of a bull Southern elephant seal, from which the species may have received its name.

A bull Southern elephant seal inflates its proboscis and roars a challenge.

A female Southern elephant seal and her new-born pup on South Georgia.

females often have a pattern of white scars on the back of the neck, where they have been gripped by the teeth of the bull during copulation.

Southern elephant seals breed mostly on the islands on either side of the Antarctic Convergence. The breeding areas fall into three groups, which perhaps represent three subspecies. The first of these comprises South Georgia, the South Shetland Islands, the Antarctic Peninsula, Gough Island, the Falkland Islands and Patagonia north to the Valdés Peninsula in Argentina at 42°S. The second group of islands, in the Indian Ocean, consists of the Kerguelen Archipelago, Heard Island, the Prince Edward Islands and Crozet Island. The final group is Macquarie Island and Campbell Island, off New Zealand. Scattered births occur elsewhere – on the coasts of South

Breeding distribution of Southern elephant seals. Non-breeding animals may stray far to the north and south of the indicated areas.

Africa, Australia and New Zealand, for example – and adult animals may wander far, bulls often being seen near the coasts of continental Antarctica, but they rarely enter pack ice. An extraordinary record was of an adult female which swam into the Gulf of Oman (24°N) in January 1989. The poor creature was promptly shot (it was considered 'a potential threat to children') and its skeleton now adorns the Oman Natural History Museum.

The total population of Southern elephant seals numbers about 650,000. It appears to be stable in South Georgia, where rather fewer than half the total are concentrated, but the Indian Ocean and Macquarie Island stocks appear to be declining, for no very apparent reason.

The Northern elephant seal

The Northern elephant seal, *M. angustirostris*, was recognized as a separate species in 1866. Its trivial name means narrow-snouted and this is the obvious character separating it in appearance from the southern species. The noses of both males and females are more pointed and the trunk of the adult male is longer and more pendulous. The males are smaller, reaching only about 4.2 m (165 in) and 2,300 kg (5,071 lb), while the females, at 3.1 m (122 in) and 900 kg (1,984 lb), are much the same size as the southern species, so there is less sexual dimorphism in the northern one. In colour they are very similar, though the chest of the mature males of the northern species develops a distinct pinkish hue that is not seen in the southern seal. A detail that is not apparent on casual examination is that the cheek teeth of the Northern elephant seal sometimes have small cusps and double roots. In the Southern form, the teeth are simple, with single roots.

Northern elephant seals breed on islands off the west coast of North

A bull Northern elephant seal.

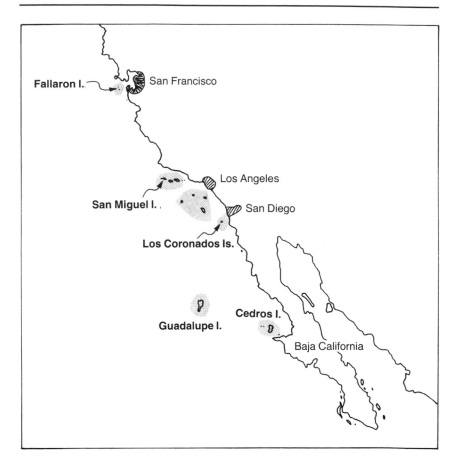

Breeding distribution of Northern elephant seals. Animals disperse widely outside the breeding season.

America, from the Fallaron Islands at 38°N, through Año Nuevo Island (near Santa Cruz), the Santa Barbara Channel Islands, Los Coronados (near San Diego), and the Cedros Islands (off Baja California) at 28°S. The oceanic island of Guadalupe was the haven from which this species, following its near-extinction by nineteenth-century sealers, repopulated most of its original range, and the seals still breed there. From perhaps as few as 20 animals remaining in 1890, the population has built up to a present 125,000.

Food and feeding of elephant seals

Elephant seals are deep-water feeders, taking squid, octopus and bathypelagic fish. Their diet was known from examination of stomach contents and the remains in faeces, but where and how they caught their prey remained a mystery. Elephant seals were practically never seen at sea, even in the near vicinity of their breeding or moulting grounds. The reason for this was made clear when it became possible to make the seals record their diving behaviour

Northern elephant seal bulls are slightly smaller than the southern species, but have longer trunks and more impressive dermal shields on their chests.

and, ultimately, their position while still at sea. This research was started by a group working with Burney Le Boeuf of the University of California, Santa Cruz. Burney's team captured two elephant seal cows at Año Nuevo in February 1983. To one was attached a small instrument package that measured depth against time and recorded the results on photographic film. This time–depth recorder (TDR) weighed 500 g (18 oz) and would work for about 14 days on its batteries. Then it would have to be recovered and its film processed and read. To the other seal was attached a depth-histogram recorder. This was designed to record the depths of dives in four pre-set intervals, ranging from 6.8 to 667 m (22 to 2,188 ft).

When the females returned to the rookery and the instrument packages were recovered, the results were astonishing. From the time the cow went to sea to the time the recording film ran out 211 days later, the seal had dived repeatedly. Dives averaged 61 a day, each lasting about 20 minutes followed by only 3 minutes on the surface. Only 13 of the surface intervals exceeded 4 minutes. The mean depth of the dives was 333 m (1,093 ft), with a maximum of 630 m (2,067 ft). Only 6 per cent of dives were to less than 200 m (656 ft). The very small amount of time spent at the surface (11 per cent) showed why elephant seals were so rarely seen at sea.

By 1990 things had moved on. The TDRs were now electronically instrumented, were lighter and would record for longer. It was possible to deal with larger seals. Bob DeLong and Brent Stewart immobilized eight bull elephant seals at the end of the breeding season at San Miguel Island in the

Channel Islands. These were fitted with the improved TDRs and VHF transmitters so the seals could be located when they returned to moult in summer. The instrument packages were glued to the hair on the backs of the seals with epoxy glue, avoiding the problem of straps which often cut into seals.

When six of the seals returned in July, they were immobilized again (using an anaesthetic called ketamine), the instruments recovered, and the seals' stomachs washed out to recover prey remains.

The TDRs had recorded depths every 30 to 60 seconds and over 36,000 dives were made during the five months the seals were at sea. Most often, these were to depths of 350 to 450 m (1,148 to 1,476 ft), though maximum depths of 1,333 m (4,373 ft) and 1,529 m (5,016 ft) were recorded. These were the greatest depths ever known for any seal, or any air-breathing vertebrate, for that matter. These seals spent 86 per cent of their time submerged, rarely spending more than 5 minutes at the surface between dives; 99 per cent of all surface intervals were shorter than 10 minutes. Dives averaged 21 to 24 minutes; the longest was 77 minutes. (Even these astonishing records have since been surpassed. Recent work with TDRs on Southern elephant seals at Macquarie Island recorded a female that dived for 120 minutes!)

There is no evidence that the seals ever sleep during the time they are at sea. Perhaps, as has been suggested for dolphins, they sleep with one side of the brain at a time, alternating the sleeping hemispheres, so that foraging can continue. Or perhaps they sleep during the descent, as they sink slowly through the water, to rouse again as they ascend, though this seems less likely to me, as they would miss opportunites for encountering prey.

The prey recovered from the stomachs of the seals would have represented no more than the last eight days' feeding (this is the time it takes for squid beaks to pass through the gut of captive elephant seals), but even so, it confirmed the view that cephalopods make up the greater part of the diet. The prey was similar to that taken by the females: primarily squid that migrate towards the surface at night and descend again at dawn. The daily pattern of the seals' diving – deeper during daylight, and less deep during darkness – corresponds to pursuit of these prey, though occasionally creatures, such as octopus, would be taken from the sea floor.

These results, fascinating though they were, do not give direct information on where the seals were feeding. To do this it would be necessary to have some kind of positioning system fitted to the seals. This was partly solved by equipping the instrument packages (which by now were miniaturized electronic recorders) with light and temperature sensors. From day-length recorded by the light sensors could be calculated (roughly) latitude, while sea water temperatures could be looked up on existing charts to verify the position. For Northern elephant seals, which are constrained in the direction of their migration by the continental coast, this worked well and Bob DeLong and Brent Stewart were able to produce some useful plots of migrations.

A fully accurate system became possible when the Argos satellite-positioning system was developed. This was originally designed for military purposes, but it was later extended to allow positioning at sea. The system depends on measuring the Doppler shift in frequency of a radio transmission from a particular location on the surface of a satellite and from this,

A bull Southern elephant equipped with a data logger and satellite transmitter.

computing the position of the source of the transmission. Scientists at the Sea Mammal Research Unit in Cambridge constructed a specially designed, low-power data logger interfaced to a transmitter unit and connected to sensors detecting submergence, depth and velocity. Four elephant seal cows at South Georgia were anaesthetized and had the instrument packages glued to their necks, just behind the head. In this way, the antenna of the transmitter would emerge when the seal surfaced. The package on one of the seals soon failed when it was seized by a male attempting copulation, a hazard the designers had not sufficiently allowed for. However, the other three packages provided striking records.

When the seal surfaced following a dive, the transmitter started to transmit, providing the Argos satellite system with an accurate position. At the same time, the data on dive depth and velocity which had been gathered in the logger were squirted out to the satellite. This could then be interrogated by one of the scientists in Cambridge and a plot of the seal's track, or records of its dives, would appear on a computer screen.

Initially, all three seals swam in a directed manner towards the south-west. One of the seals was fitted with an extended-life transmitter battery and this provided the clearest record. The first phase of its journey was a transit to the feeding grounds, though the variability of dive depths and durations

A computer representation of the track of a female Southern elephant seal as she swims along the west side of the Antarctic Peninsula to reach a feeding ground near a sea-floor canyon. The seal's track is shown in white. Each vertical line represents a dive, the length of the spike being proportional to the depth of the dive. The sea floor is contoured in blue at 500 m (1,640 ft) intervals. The seal swam in the upper 1,000 m (3,280 ft) during its traverse of the ocean and then dived to the bottom when over the continental shelf off the Antarctic Peninsula.

suggested that there was some opportunistic feeding. The second phase showed longer average dive velocities, and dives often to the sea floor. In phase three, the seal dived repeatedly to the sea floor in targeted feeding. These dives were shorter than those in phase one and this may be associated with the capture and digestion of food. Assimilation of food is known to increase the basal metabolic rate and, by using oxygen stores, this may have reduced the time the seal could spend submerged.

Before this work, it was known that the elephant seals dispersed from South Georgia outside the breeding and moulting periods, but nothing was known of where they fed. Not all South Georgia seals go to the same place. Further studies have shown seals setting off in other directions, so this is not a definite species migration, as takes place with Northern fur seals, for example. The development of this data logger has allowed for the first time visualization of the track of a marine mammal as it moves freely through the most remote parts of the ocean and it will open up a new window on the behaviour of marine mammals.

Breeding in elephant seals

The two species of elephant seals follow a very similar breeding pattern, except that the Northern elephant seal has its breeding calendar about four months later than the southern species. While the breeding season in the south starts in the southern spring in September, it is not till January that the Northern elephant seal begins to gather together on the breeding beaches. One might have expected an even later season if these seals too were to breed in the spring, but it is likely that the warmth of a California spring would be too stressful for the vigorous activities of the breeding bulls.

Elephant seals prefer open sandy beaches on which to breed. Cows begin to haul out in mid-September in South Georgia (about two to three weeks earlier at Peninsula Valdés – an interval that means that the photoperiod at the time of arrival is the same at both locations). The beaches used are traditional, cows returning to the same site (probably where they were born) year after year. They are gregarious, gathering in groups, but they do not permit bodily contact, snarling and snapping at an intruder who approaches too close. Even before the arrival of the first cows, a few bulls will be present at favoured sites. Once the cows start arriving, many more bulls haul out from the sea.

The bulls compete very aggressively for sites among the cows. The larger, more experienced bulls can do this by threat alone. A bull lying prone is offering no threat. When it raises its head, it indicates a measure of dominance. A small bull, seeing an established bull do this, may back off at once. The next stage is for the bull to roar. The roar, resonating through the inflated proboscis, is a threat that not only carries a considerable distance, it also identifies the roarer. Bulls may roar either at an identified intruder, or for no reason that is obvious to an observer, except perhaps to advertise their presence.

However, if roaring does not deter an intruder, the dominant bull will rear up so as to raise the anterior two-thirds of its body clear of the ground. This is a highly conspicuous posture in the generally horizontal world of the elephant seal and it indicates a high level of arousal. A bull prepared to engage in combat will respond in a similar manner and the actual contest may begin.

Southern elephant seals line the beach at Holmestrand on South Georgia.

Few interactions between males reach the stage of exchanging blows, but when they do, the contests are enormously impressive. The two huge animals swipe at each other with open jaws, their massive necks meeting with dull thwacks. When a bite connects, severe puncture wounds can result and the shoulders and neck of the contestants are soon streaming with blood. The bulls seem indifferent to these injuries, but eventually one will retire, leaving the victor (almost always the established bull) to his position among the cows. Bulls may lose an eye, or break a jaw in a fight, but such injuries are very rare, most contests ending with the bites and minor tears on neck and shoulders. It is these areas that have developed the thickened skin – the dermal shield – during the years of sparring as a young male before entering the lists seriously as a potential breeding male. In 20 years of observation of breeding in the Northern elephant seal at Año Nuevo Island, Burney Le Boeuf recorded only five deaths from fighting. In eight seasons at South Georgia with the southern species, I saw no deaths and only two broken jaws.

As the season advances, the groups of cows grow and coalesce so that on the largest beaches a crowd of several thousand animals may be present. The largest single crowd of this kind that I have seen numbered 4,000 females, with about 400 bulls scattered among and around them.

The females give birth about six to eight days after coming ashore. The pup weighs about 46 kg (105 lb), or roughly a fifteenth of its mother's weight. Male

Northern elephant seal bulls rear up to fight on Año Nuevo Island, California.

pups are significantly heavier at birth than females. The newly born pups cry to their mothers in a high-pitched wail in the process of establishing the maternal bond, whereby the mother will recognize her pup among the many hundreds in the vicinity. However, elephant seal pups do not usually stray far from their mothers, which themselves usually stay in the same place on the beach

The elephant seal cow comes into oestrus about 20 days after giving birth and remains receptive for about four days. During this time she will be mated several times. Normally, it will be the nearest bull whose attention is attracted (whether by scent or some other cue, we do not know). The bull lumbers over and with no preliminaries, lays a flipper over the side of the cow and mates with her, often gripping her neck in his teeth. The cow will resist violently if she is not fully in heat, but whether she resists or makes her hindquarters available, she whimpers loudly. This has the effect of alerting other males to what is going on. If the copulating bull is the dominant animal, it makes no difference – even while copulating he can raise his head and threaten a subordinate male. However, if it is one of the subordinate males that has mounted the female, this alerts the beach master, who will charge up to drive off the other male.

The structure of an elephant seal breeding aggregation is thus rather different from that of fur seals. Instead of groups (harems) of cows, each

A Northern elephant seal breeding beach on Año Nuevo Island. The extreme crowding is characteristic of elephant seals.

Mating in Southern elephant seals. The bull grips the cow with a flipper and may bite her neck.

exclusively controlled by a single bull, with peripheral males who rarely get access to the females, the elephant seal cows form an amorphous mass, or harem crowd. Within this is a dominant bull, alpha male or beach master, who has access to all the cows and who can drive off, usually by threat alone, all other males. But he is not the only bull among the cows. Other bulls may be present in the harem crowd and these may have successful copulations when the attention of the alpha male is directed elsewhere. Besides these, other bulls may lie on the beach or at the water's edge, or patrol up and down in the shallows. These bulls may also have the chance to copulate with cows that are leaving the crowd on shore, having weaned their pups, but these animals have probably already been successfully mated by the alpha bull or by one of the other bulls in the harem crowd. The distinctions between the various classes of bulls are not always clear. Very large crowds may have several alpha males, since one could not possibly patrol the whole beach, and subordinate bulls may displace an alpha bull by fighting.

Weaning of the pup and departure of the cow follows soon after oestrus. Lactation lasts about an average of 23 days in the Southern elephant seal, by which time the cow has lost a great deal of her blubber reserves. She goes to sea for an intensive feeding period before returning to land once more in the southern autumn, in February, to moult.

With the departure of the majority of the females in November, the organization on the beach begins to break up. An alpha bull, which may have been ashore defending his position for up to 90 days wthout feeding, will be lean to the point of emaciation. These bulls depart, leaving the beaches to younger animals. An alpha bull, because of the great strain of the breeding season, is unlikely to have more than a few seasons of dominance, though during a successful season he may pass his genes on to 80 or more females.

The bulls leave the beaches later than the cows and return to moult later, usually in March and April. During the moult they lie about in heaps, the testosterone-mediated aggressiveness that kept them separated during the breeding season now a thing of the past.

Chapter 7
The Antarctic Seals

INTRODUCTION

The Antarctic seals comprise a group of four very distinct species, each in its own genus and having a characteristic life-style. They are sometimes grouped into the Tribe Lobodontini, a name which implies that they have 'lobed teeth'. While this is very true of two of the group, it is not specially apparent in the case of the others. The reduced claws on the hind flippers have been noted already in the previous chapter and Antarctic seals, like most phocids but unlike monk seals, have only a single pair of nipples. Their pups are born in a greyish or brownish natal fur, not the black coats of the monk and elephant seals.

The Antarctic seals colonized the Antarctic seas during the late Miocene or early Pliocene, about fifteen million years ago, at a time when the Antarctic enjoyed a more temperate climate. As the continents drifted, Antarctica moved towards the pole, and during the subsequent cooling and eventual glaciation, these seals became adapted to low temperatures and to the different food resources that developed in the Southern Ocean. The subsequent evolutionary radiation gave rise to the four distinct and very successful Antarctic seals of today: the Weddell seal, the Crabeater seal, the Leopard seal and the Ross seal. Together with the Southern elephant seal and the Antarctic fur seal in the northern part of their range, they divide up the available ecological niches between them, providing a good example of ecological radiation, and accompanying anatomical changes, based on the utilization of different prey species. Where two or more species occur together, they employ different food resources (for example, Crabeaters and Ross seals); where they feed on the same food, they are geographically separated (for example, elephant seals and Ross seals, or Crabeater seals and fur seals).

The Antarctic seals are found, as the name suggests, in the Antarctic, but there are differences in their distribution within the region related to the presence and structure of ice.

The Weddell Seal

The Weddell seal, *Leptonychotes weddellii*, was named after the nineteenth-century Scottish sealer and explorer, James Weddell, who brought back the first specimens. Its generic name, *Leptonychotes* (Greek for slender-clawed), refers to the reduced claws on the hind flippers, characteristic of all the Antarctic seals. Weddell seals are large, bulky seals, with a characteristic barrel-shaped outline. The head of the Weddell seal seems small for its body and its snout is short and wide. The fore flippers are also small; in a fat animal it is difficult for both flippers to touch the ground at the same time. The colour of the adults is very dark brown, lighter ventrally, and mottled with large darker and lighter patches, those on the belly being silvery white. Adult males

The chubby Weddell seal is a familiar sight round Antarctic coasts.

usually bear scars, most of them around the hind flippers and genital region, probably the result of intrasexual fighting. The pups are born in a silvery grey, grey-brown or sometimes golden lanugo.

Adults reach 3.3 m (130 in), but more usually 2.6 m (102 in), with the females generally larger than the males. Weights reach around 400 to 500 kg (882 to 1,102 lb) in the spring, when the seals are fat. New-born pups are 1.2 m (47 in) long and weigh about 25 kg (55 lb)

In close-up, it can be seen that the corners of the mouth turn up, giving the Weddell seal a somewhat benign appearance. When dry, the whiskers are strongly curled. When the seal opens its mouth, as it sometimes does on land to make a hooting sound or a dull glottal 'clopping' noise in its throat, it can be seen that the incisors are strongly procumbent. These, and the canines, are greatly worn down in older animals, as the Weddell seal uses its teeth to keep open ice holes during the winter. The cheek teeth have a prominent central cusp, with sometimes a smaller one behind.

Weddell seals are found most abundantly in the fast-ice region around the shores of the Antarctic continent and on a number of island groups surrounding it, and on the South Shetland Islands and the South Orkney Islands (see map on p. 139). Occasional wanderers are found as far north as Uruguay, New Zealand and South Australia, but the most northerly breeding population is a very small group of about 100 seals that live in South Georgia. Although during the summer Weddell seals are often found hauled out on shingle or rocky beaches, they much prefer lying on snow or ice, and they will seek out a snow patch on a beach, or an ice floe, on which to bask. They always produce their young on ice (or snow). In the more southerly parts of their range, they must keep breathing-holes open in the fast ice, which they do by sawing with their teeth, producing the wear that characterizes the teeth of older Weddells. Weddells are found usually singly or in small groups, but occasionally occur in close aggregations of up to 100 individuals. The total population is estimated to be about 732,000.

The Crabeater seal

The Crabeater seal is *Lobodon carcinophagus*. The specific name means crab eater in Greek. Crabeater seals do not feed on crabs, which occur only sparsely on the very fringes of the Antarctic, but on another crustacean, Antarctic krill. The name seems to have arisen by confusion with the Norwegian for crayfish, *kreps*, which might perhaps have been applied to the shrimp-like animals on which the seal feeds.

Crabeater seals are relatively slim, lithe seals with a clearly streamlined form that contrasts with the dumpy Weddells. The snout is elongated and slightly tip-tilted and the line of the mouth is level, with no up-turn at the corners. Although there is nothing remarkable about the teeth at the front of the jaws, the cheek teeth are extraordinarily elaborate, the most complex of all the mammals. Each is provided with four or five recurved, lobe-like cusps, that interlock to form a sieve. Their role will be discussed later, when feeding methods are described. The fore flippers are moderately long, about one-fifth of the body length.

Crabeater seals on a floe.

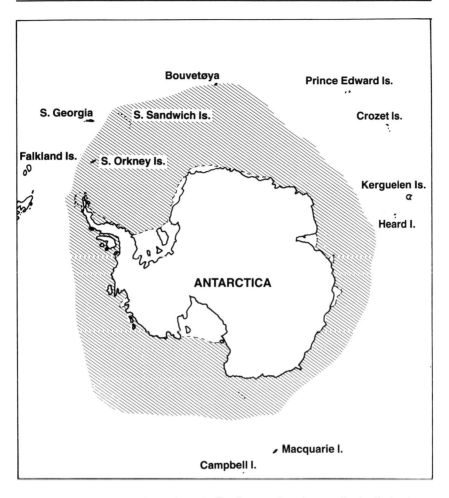

The area occupied by the Antarctic seals. The Ross seal, and generally, the Crabeater seal, are confined to the area shown, but Weddell seals also breed on South Georgia, while Leopard seals are regularly found on Subantarctic islands, particularly in the winter.

The backgound colour is mainly silvery grey when newly moulted, or golden to creamy white when the coat has faded. Older animals become progressively paler, even when freshly moulted, and may appear almost white. In younger animals, there are net-like, chocolate-brown markings and flecks on shoulders, sides and flanks, shading into the predominantly dark hind and fore flippers and head. The pattern is strongest on flanks behind the fore flippers and around the hind end of the body. Pups are light greyish-brown with dark hind flippers and indistinct spots on the body.

Crabeaters grow to 2.6 m (102 in) in length, weighing up to 225 kg (496 lb). The largest females may slightly exceed the largest males in size. New-born pups are 1.2 m (47 in) long and weigh 20 kg (44 lb).

Crabeater seals are virtually confined to the Antarctic pack ice where they breed in the spring. During the summer, they retreat to the areas of residual pack ice (about 4 million km²/1.5 million sq miles) that remain after the bulk of the ice has melted. However, they are occasionally seen hauled out on glacier ice or, much less commonly, on shore. Despite this strong affinity with ice, Crabeater seals have been seen in places as far from the Antarctic as New Zealand, Tasmania, the tip of South Africa and the River Plate. Crabeaters are the most abundant seals in the world. Because of their habitat, it is difficult to produce estimates of abundance, but the population probably numbers between 15 and 40 million, more than equal to all the other seals in the world put together.

The Leopard seal

The name of the Leopard seal, *Hydrurga leptonyx*, translates from the Greek more or less as 'the slender-clawed worker in the water'. *Leptonyx* is from the same roots as the name of the Weddell seal, *Leptonychotes*. The colloquial name, Leopard seal, was originally applied to the Weddell seal, but seems more apt for this species, because of its conspicuous predatory habits. Leopard seals are large seals with a very characteristic profile. The head seems disproportionately large, with a long, reptile-like snout, giving it a huge gape. There is a marked constriction at the neck (unique in phocid seals) and the body then widens to a high, arched thorax which tails off steeply to the flanks.

In close-up, it is often possible to view the very large, sharply pointed incisors and canines, since these seals threaten on being approached by opening their mouths widely to reveal the huge gape. The cheek teeth are massive, each with three recurved cusps. Although less complex than those of the Crabeater, they are still very much more complicated than those of any other carnivore.

In colour, Leopard seals are black or very dark grey on the back and silver or creamy, on the belly. The back is liberally spotted and flecked with pale patches, and this is reversed on the belly, where dark patches occur. There is a relatively sharp demarcation along the sides. Pups are patterned similarly to adults, unlike most other seals, but the fur is softer and thicker than in the adults.

Female Leopard seals reach 3.6 m (142 in) in length (the males are slightly smaller), and weigh about 370 kg (816 lb), or exceptionally, 500 kg (1,102 lb). The new-born young are 1.5 m (59 in) long and weigh about 35 kg (77 lb), though few have been measured.

Leopard seals have a wider distribution than the two previous species. They range from the shores of the Antarctic continent to the Subantarctic islands, such as South Georgia and Macquarie Island. The main population parallels the Crabeater seal distribution, staying with the circumpolar pack ice. It is on the floating pack that most Leopard seals breed, but pups are born on snow-covered beaches at places such as South Georgia. During the austral winter, Leopard seals are frequently seen in Patagonia, the Falkland Islands, New Zealand, Tasmania and southern Australia – and infrequently in South Africa. The Leopard seal is usually a very solitary animal, but exceptionally two or three may be seen together on a floe. The greatest number I have ever

The silhouette of the Leopard seal, with its large head separated by a pronounced neck from its rib-cage, is unmistakable.

seen together is 11 on a floe about 10 m (33 ft) across. The seals were lying quietly together, though none was in contact with its neighbour. A neighbouring piece of ice had eight Leopards on it. The reason for this unusual concentration was not discovered. Leopard seals have a world population estimated at 222,000 individuals.

The Ross seal

The Ross seal, *Ommatophoca rossii*, was named by J.F. Gray after Sir James Clark Ross, who led the *Erebus* and *Terror* expedition to the Antarctic in 1839–43. Ross took with him Robert McCormick, who made extensive zoological collections, including the skin and two skeletons of this new seal which was described by Gray, Keeper of Zoology at the British Museum. *Ommatophoca* is Greek for 'eye-seal'. Gray had noticed the enormous orbits of this animal, which are perhaps more apparant in the dried skull than in the living animal. Ross seals are the smallest of the Antarctic seals. They are plump, dumpy and rather shapeless animals. The head is short and wide and can be withdrawn into rolls of fat about the neck. When disturbed, this seal raises its head vertically, with chest enlarged and back arched. The mouth is small, with small sharp teeth at the front of the jaws and very small cheek teeth, each with a prominent central cusp and, except for the last post-canine, one or two lateral cusps. The eyes are large and protruding and the ear openings very small. The fore flippers have reduced claws and the terminal joints are elongated. The hind flippers have very long cartilaginous extensions; they reach 22 per cent of the body length, the greatest for any phocid. Ross seals are surprisingly vocal in air, inflating the windpipe and, with mouth wide open, making unique trilling, cooing and chugging sounds.

The Ross seal is the least frequently observed of all the Antarctic seals. The patterning of faint stripes behind the head is quite characteristic.

A party of observers approaches a Ross seal on a floe. Heavy pack is the usual habitat of this seal.

Ross seals are dark grey to chestnut dorsally, with little spotting and a sharp line of demarcation from the silvery white underside. A light and dark pattern about the eyes gives the head a mask-like appearance. There are often broad dark stripes from chin to chest, and on the sides of the head. The sides are spotted or obliquely striped. Fore and hind flippers are dark. Pups are dark brown – not white, as described sometimes – above, paler beneath. They show the striped pattern on the throat characteristic of the adult.

Female Ross seals reach 2.17 m (85 in) in length (measured along the curve of the back) and weigh 177 kg (390 lb); males 2.07 m (81 in) and 169 kg (373 lb). New-born pups are 0.96 to 1.20 m (38 to 47 in) and weigh about 16.5 kg (36 lb), but few have been measured.

Ross seals have a very restricted habitat and, as a result, were at one time reckoned to be extremely rare. It is certainly true that they were (and are) rarely seen. This is because they are most frequently found in areas of very heavy pack ice. For obvious reasons, ships and observers have avoided such ice and consequently, the Ross seals. It was not until powerful ice-breakers and helicopters became the usual means of transport in the Antarctic that the true abundance of Ross seals was realized. They seem to prefer certain areas, such as the King Haakon VII Sea (the area around the longitude of the Greenwich Meridian). Usually solitary, up to five Ross seals have been seen sharing the same ice floe. The population is very difficult to calculate, because of the clumped distribution, but estimates have ranged from 220,000 to 650,000 individuals.

BREEDING BEHAVIOUR

Weddell seals produce their pups from September to November in low-density colonies, along pressure cracks or tide cracks in the fast ice, or in the more northerly parts of the range, along the shore ice. They seem to prefer naturally occurring open water for breeding, but as noted above, they can keep breathing-holes open by gnawing the ice. Several females may share a single breathing-hole or length of crack, but they remain well spaced out. The breeding males spend most of their time in the water and react aggressively to other males. The bulls vocalize, display or fight in order to establish and maintain exclusive access to the females. Copulation has not been observed on land and only once (via a television monitor) in the water. However, some preliminary courtship behaviour sometimes takes place on land.

The other three Antarctic seals all breed on pack ice. The breeding of the Crabeater seal is highly synchronized, with a peak in mid-October. The basic social unit is the mother–pup pair, joined by a breeding male to form a triad which remains together until the pup is weaned at about four weeks. Male Crabeaters are very aggressive and defend an area on the floe for about 50 m (164 ft) around the female and her pup. The triads are widely spaced – 1 to 2 km (½ to 1¼ miles) apart – and the females are also very aggressive to other seals, including the accompanying male, which is fiercely rejected until near the end of the lactation period. Copulation has not been observed in Crabeaters, but it is believed to take place on the ice.

Leopard seal births peak in November–December, but young pups have been seen from September to January. Females and pups occur on floes and

The pup of the Leopard seal is born in the same pattern coat as its mother.

other Leopards (presumably males) have been seen cruising in the water near them, but interactions with the females has not been observed.

Even less is known about the Ross seals. Most births seem to take place in the first half of November. The lactation period is deduced to be four to six weeks.

FOOD AND FEEDING

Of the Antarctic seals, Weddell seals are perhaps the most typically seal-like in their diet and feeding patterns. They feed mostly on bottom and mid-water fish, though cephalopods (octopus as well as squids) and other bottom invertebrates, including crustaceans, lamellibranchs and even holothurians (sea cucumbers) are taken. In many parts of their range, Weddell seals can obtain their food at moderate depths, but those seals that live on shelf ice may have a long way to swim to the bottom, where they find most of their food. Dives of 300 to 400 m (984 to 1,312 ft) are common, but these do not usually last longer than 15 minutes or so. During these dives, prey of a considerable size may be taken. One Weddell seal was seen to catch a large nototheniid fish, *Dissostichus mawsoni*, about 1.5 m (59 in) long and estimated to weigh 31 kg (68 lb), bring it to the surface and consume it entirely in three hours! I shall return to the subject of diving and Weddell seals later in this chapter.

In contrast to the generalist Weddell seal, the Crabeater is a super-specialist. Ninety-four per cent of its diet consists of a single species, Antarctic krill. This shrimp-like crustacean (it is a euphausiid, not a decapod like the true shrimps) is the key organism in the marine food-web in the Antarctic. About 60 mm (2.4 in) in length when full grown and weighing about a gram, krill are astonishingly abundant. It has been suggested (although on rather scanty evidence) that krill make up about 50 per cent of the biomass of the

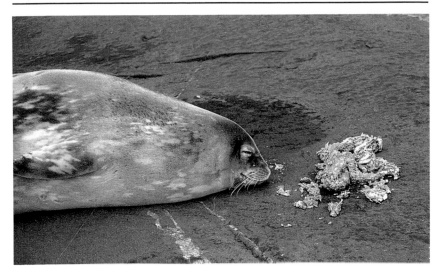

A Weddell seal, on Astrolabe Island, lies near a heap of fish remains which it has just disgorged.

zooplankton in the Southern Ocean. Krill form the link between the phytoplankton that capture energy from the sun and build up carbon into complex assimilable compounds, and almost all the major consumers in the Antarctic: the baleen whales, seals, many of the penguins and other sea-birds, squid and fish. Although the baleen whales are best known as krill consumers, it is the Crabeater seal that as a single species consumes the greatest amount of krill. The population of 15 million Crabeaters takes about 62 million tonnes of krill a year. Krill represents a huge resource, and the evolution of a species to exploit it is not surprising.

A baleen whale gets its food by taking in huge gulps of sea water, several tonnes at a time, vastly distending its pleated throat as it does so. Then, closing its mouth, it expels the water through the sieve formed by the fringed baleen plates, and finally swallows the krill trapped on the filter-bed of baleen. Crabeater seals do not feed in this way; to do so, a Crabeater seal would need a much larger mouth in relation to the size of its body, as whales do.

There are no observations on Crabeater seals feeding in the wild, but several on how they feed in captivity, where they have been observed to suck in their food. I believe that when a Crabeater seal locates a swarm of krill, it directs its snout towards an individual (perhaps using information derived from stimuli detected by its vibrissae to do so) and when close enough, opens its mouth and sucks in the krill by depressing the floor of its mouth in the same way that a pike snaps up a minnow. Once the krill is inside the seal's mouth, the jaws close and the tongue is raised, expelling the excess water through the grid formed by the interlocking teeth and out through the sides of the mouth. The process is repeated until sufficient krill have been captured to make a mouthful, which is then swallowed.

Krill swarms are common in open water, but disperse very readily – fishermen would say they show 'net evasion'. How Crabeaters prevent the

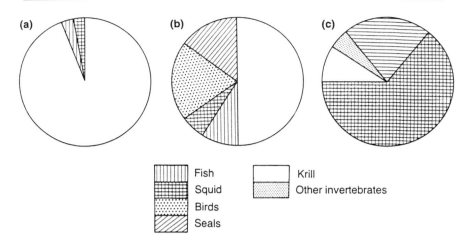

Fish
Squid
Birds
Seals

Krill
Other invertebrates

Fig. 7.1   Food composition of (a) Crabeater seal, (b) Leopard seal and (c) Ross seal.

swarm dispersing is not known, but in the open sea Crabeaters are often seen in groups. It may be that they feed co-operatively, rounding up the krill in a tight swarm as some baleen whales have been observed to do. In the winter, when the sea surface is largely covered by pack ice, the krill graze the phytoplankton that coat the under-surface of the floes. Here the seals may be able to pick them off one by one without risk of the krill dispersing.

The average meal size of a Crabeater is about 8 kg (18 lb), which represents some 8,000 krill, so the seal obviously has to make many captures to satisfy its needs. Quite clearly, Crabeater seals can do this very easily, since their abundance indicates that they are highly successful feeders.

Leopard seals also feed on krill, which make up the largest proportion of their diet. However, Leopard seals are much better known for their feeding on penguins or fish. Penguin rookeries in the Antarctic attract human observers and they have frequently reported Leopard seals waiting in the sea near the spot where the penguins enter or leave the water. Penguins are aware of this, too, and linger on the ice edge or the rocks until a number have assembled together, when they enter the water together, hoping to find some safety in numbers. Penguins return from feeding excursions in groups for the same reason, but they are more vulnerable to the waiting Leopards, probably because their full crops make them less agile. Once grabbed in a hungry Leopard's jaws, a penguin has little chance. The seal shakes the bird from side to side, often ripping its skin from its body, before tearing off chunks which can be swallowed. No seal is equipped with shearing teeth and even the fearsome dentition of a Leopard seal can do no more than hold on to the prey until a piece can be wrenched from the rest of the body. Sometimes, small penguins are swallowed whole, taking advantage of the Leopard seal's huge gape, but larger ones, like emperors, are dismembered before being eaten.

Feeding on penguins is a seasonal practice when the penguins are concentrated for breeding at their rookeries. It is not adopted by all Leopard

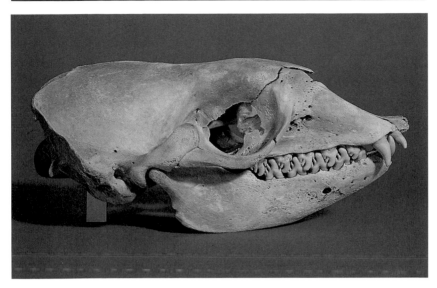

The dentition of the Crabeater seal is highly modified to form a sieve for straining krill out of the water.

The gape of the Leopard seal reveals its potential as a predator.

A Leopard seal seizes a penguin underwater.

seals and may be particularly characteristic of males. In one study of Leopards catching penguins, all those whose sex could be identified were males.

I have often watched Leopard seals catching fish in the kelp beds that fringe the coasts of South Georgia. As at penguin rookeries, the seals are well spaced out. Fishing territories are obviously valuable properties to be defended. These fish-eating seals were not all males, the sexes seeming to be present in equal numbers.

Crabeater seals form another important component of Leopard seal diet. Many years ago, it was noticed that almost all adult Crabeater seals (83 per cent) bore white, parallel paired scars. These were attributed to attacks by killer whales. Indeed, this is the origin of some of them, but the great majority are the result of encounters with Leopard seals, as careful measurement of the spacing between the scars and between Leopard seal canines showed. Leopard seals are significant predators of young Crabeaters when they first enter the water. Crabeater seals older than a year are seldom attacked and fresh wounds on adults are rare. Most animals with fresh wounds are about 6 to 12 months old. Weaned pups do not begin to show fresh wounds until late February. Presumably younger pups do not survive an encounter with a

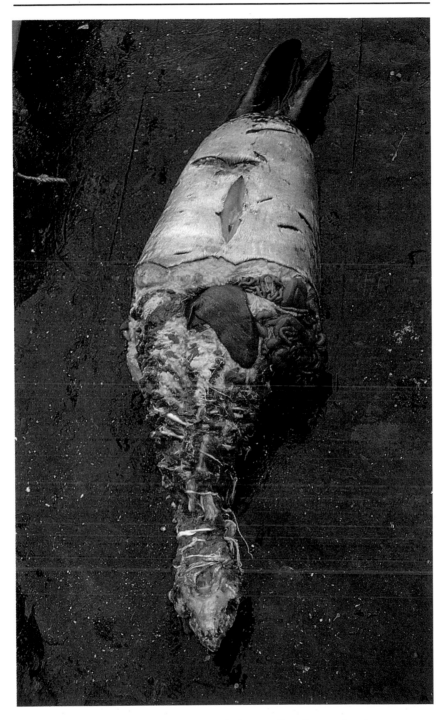

The carcase of a young Crabeater seal, partly devoured by a Leopard seal.

This old Crabeater seal bears the scars of an encounter in its youth with a Leopard seal.

Leopard seal, but the chances of escape improve as the pup grows bigger and can swim faster. By one year of age, the probability of being eaten approaches zero and in November the Leopards switch to a fresh crop of pups.

THE WEDDELL SEAL AND DIVING

Weddell seals have contributed more to the study of diving in pinnipeds than any other seal, and one worker, the American physiologist Gerry Kooyman, has made an outstanding contribution to this work. Kooyman chose to work on Weddell seals at the American research station, McMurdo, on Ross Island in the Antarctic. Here, Weddell seals keep holes open in the ice, through which they dive for their food. If a hole is isolated from others, the seal must return to the same hole from which it dived in order to breathe, and this gives researchers an opportunity to collect blood samples, or to recover recording apparatus the seal has taken down with it. Weddells are astonishingly placid seals. For the most part, they show no fear of humans and will even endure the handling involved in taking a blood sample or fitting instrument packs without complaint (though one has to be careful – they can give a pretty nasty nip if they feel like it). This made them ideal subjects for Kooyman's researches.

It was with Weddell seals that Kooyman developed the prototype of the time–depth recorder that yielded the data described in the last chapter for elephant seals. Kooyman's first TDRs were very simple instruments, consisting of a Bourdon tube (the sensitive element from a pressure gauge) connected to a lever which scratched a trace on a charcoal-dusted glass disc fixed to the front of a clockwork kitchen timer! From such simple (but very effective) instruments have developed the electronic marvels of today that record not only depth against time, but can capture details of heart rate and stomach temperature, take blood samples at predetermined times, or log swimming speed and position.

Before discussing the Weddell seal any further, I will give a general account of diving. Food exists at various levels in the oceans and is sometimes concentrated on or near the sea floor. In order to exploit these food resources, seals need to be proficient divers. All mammals can dive (that is, hold their breaths and swim below the surface), but this is for most of them a very limited faculty, involving only comparatively brief dives of five minutes or less, and relatively shallow depths of a few metres. Seals and whales, however, have adapted their anatomy and physiology to extend the period they can spend underwater and the depths to which they can descend.

As a first necessity for diving, a seal must be able to prevent water entering its body when it is underwater. The nostrils of a seal are slit-like and normally closed when at rest. To open its nostrils to take a breath, a seal has to use a pair of muscles which pull the sides of the nostrils apart. When the muscles relax, the nostrils close automatically. Furthermore, once the animal submerges, the pressure of the water on the sides of the slit closes the nostrils even more firmly. The external ear openings can also be closed muscularly and held closed by external pressure.

Obviously, if a seal is to capture food underwater, it needs to open its mouth. To prevent water flooding into the back of the throat and down into the lungs, seals close off the back of the mouth by raising the tongue and lowering the soft palate. The two arytenoid cartilages of the larynx press against the epiglottis to prevent food entering the trachaea when the seal swallows.

Breath-hold capacity in human divers is increased by breathing deeply – hyperventilating – just before diving, and then entering the water with lungs filled to their fullest extent. Seals do not do this. Seals dive with their lungs nearly empty, having exhaled before descent. Full lungs would increase a seal's buoyancy and thus make it more energetically expensive to swim down through the water. Instead of taking down their oxygen store in the lungs, seals take it down in other ways.

Besides being stored as gas in the lungs, oxygen can be stored in physical solution in the blood and tissue fluids. Much more importantly, it can be chemically combined with special oxygen-binding pigments in the body. The best known of these is the red pigment of the blood, haemoglobin.

Seals carry their major oxygen store in their blood. They have much greater blood volumes than terrestrial mammals. A Weddell seal, for example, has about 150 ml of blood per kg body weight, twice the corresponding value in humans. And the seal's blood contains much more haemoglobin, about 1.6 times as much. The combined result of this is that the seal's oxygen store in its blood is three or three and a half times the relative amount in humans. Not only do seals have very much more haemoglobin in their blood, they also have higher concentrations of another oxygen-binding pigment, myoglobin. Myoglobin is what makes meat red, and the darker the meat, the greater the concentration of myoglobin. Chicken-breast meat, for example, contains almost no myoglobin, while it is abundantly present in a beef steak. Weddell seal muscles are almost black, so great is the concentration of myoglobin, as are the muscles of elephant seals. These seals are deep divers, and need an abundant oxygen store. Crabeater seals and Antarctic fur seals, which forage for krill near the surface, do not dive for so long, and their muscles are little darker than beef.

In a Weddell seal weighing 450 kg (992 lb) there are about 67 litres (118 UK pints/142 US) of blood of which 23 litres (40/49 pints) are arterial, or oxygenated, blood. The metabolizing tissues of the seal could extract 19.1 litres (34/40 pints) of oxygen from this. Another 11 litres (19/23 pints) of oxygen are stored in the myoglobin of the muscles, giving a total store of 30 litres (53/63 pints). The average oxygen consumption rate of tissue is 250 ml per kg per hour, or 1.9 litres (3/4 pints) per minute, for our 450-kg Weddell seal. Hence, the 30 litres of oxygen should be consumed in about 16 minutes. But we know from direct observations and data collected with time–depth recorders that Weddell seals can stay submerged for much longer – up to 73 minutes. How is this done?

When a seal dives, changes occur in its blood system so that the animal functions as a heart–brain–lung system, the circulating blood being restricted to these organs. The brain is very sensitive to oxygen deprivation and its supply of blood must be ensured. On the other hand, most other organs, the gut, muscles, etc., can continue to function for a time without oxygen. What happens when the seal dives is that the heart rate slows, a condition known as bradycardia. At the same time, a muscular cuff, the caval sphincter, contracts around the main vein bringing blood back from the trunk and abdominal organs, the posterior vena cava. This prevents any more blood returning from the liver, the gut, the muscles of the back, etc. If no more blood can be returned, no fresh blood can travel to these organs. However, blood can still be pumped to the brain, returning via the external jugular vein and a vein that runs alongside the spinal cord, the extradural vein. This vein is found only in seals, and blood passing down it eventually pools in a large hepatic sinus, just posterior to the caval sphincter. Some of the blood in the extradural vein, however, drains via the intercostal veins and the azygos vein into the anterior vena cava and thence into the heart, whence it can be recirculated.

In this way, the blood flow to the brain is unimpeded, though that to the viscera, muscles, skin, etc., is reduced by about 90 per cent. Once their oxygen stores are exhausted, the organs outside the heart–brain–lung system must continue to derive energy anaerobically by glycolysis: a process in which glycogen (the energy source) is converted to lactic acid, producing energy without the use of oxygen. Glycolysis is a normal process in energetic movement in all mammals. It is the accumulation of lactic acid in the muscles that gives rise to fatigue in marathon runners, for when a muscle contracts vigorously and repeatedly, the blood may not be able to supply sufficient oxygen. During rest and recovery, oxygen is used to process the accumulated lactic acid to carbon dioxide, which is carried away in the blood and exhaled through the lungs. What differs in the seal is that it can tolerate high concentrations of lactic acid without the ill-effects that would occur in a less well-adapted mammal. Using blood samples obtained from free-diving Weddell seals, Gerry Kooyman was able to show that there was no significant increase in blood lactic acid until the dive time exceeded 25 minutes. After this, lactic acid accumulated, reaching a value of about 230 mg per cent for dives of about 60 minutes duration.

This indicates that the shorter dives made by Weddell seals (and probably other seals as well) are aerobic, using oxygen in the normal way to generate energy, but using it very much more economically than in most mammals. Of 4,600 dives measured by Kooyman, only 3 per cent were in excess of 25 minutes, the aerobic dive limit. Only in the longer dives does the full diving response of bradycardia and anaerobic metabolism come into play. These longer dives require a protracted recovery time. In the Weddell seal, a dive lasting 45 minutes requires a surface recovery time of 105 minutes, during which the heart speeds up, oxygen stores are replenished and accumulated lactic acid is oxidized to carbon dioxide. Just how elephant seals which, as we saw in the previous chapter, dive continuously for days with only brief periods at the surface, manage to top up their oxygen supplies is not clear. Most of their dives are aerobic, but the longer ones probably are not, yet they are not followed by extended periods at the surface.

The Weddell seals on the Ross ice shelf show two patterns of dives. Feeding dives are brief, from 5 to 25 minutes, but they are deep, since the seals are finding the majority of their food on the sea floor some 400 to 600 m (1,312 to 1,969 ft) from the surface. Exploratory dives last much longer, up to 73 minutes, but they are shallow, just under the surface of the ice. In areas away from fast ice, Weddell seals probably make very few, if any, of these exploratory dives which require anaerobic metabolism, since even in dense pack ice, access to the surface will never be very far away.

It is not sufficient simply to be able to hold your breath to be a successful deep diver. A Weddell seal descending to 400 m (1,312 ft), or an elephant seal at more than a kilometre below the surface, are subjected to extraordinary pressures – over 100 kg per cm² in the latter case. As human divers can discover to their cost, the effects of exposure to pressure while diving can be very serious.

Pressure has little effect on most of the tissues that make up a seal's body. These are effectively liquids and are virtually incompressible. Problems arise where there are air spaces within the tissues – that is to say, in the respiratory system and the middle ear. Even a shallow dive can demonstrate to a human diver the effects of pressure on the middle ear and the nose-blowing and swallowing of an emerging diver is an effort to equalize pressure in the ears, via the Eustacian tube that connects the air in the middle ear with the throat. Seals, diving deeply, might risk collapse of the walls of the middle ear at depth. They avoid this by means of a plexus of blood vessels which are filled with blood as the external pressure forces blood into them. As the pressure increases, the plexus expands to fill the entire air space of the middle ear, equalizing the pressure within and outside and obviating risk of collapse. Human divers will also be aware of the discomfort that can arise from their sinuses during a dive. Seals do not suffer from this at all, since there are no cranial sinuses in pinnipeds.

The lungs, of course, contain by far the largest air space in the body. As we have seen, a seal expels air from its lungs before it dives. As it submerges, the external pressure of the water forces its abdominal viscera to bulge against the very oblique diaphragm to take the space previously occupied by the air in the lungs. Some air remains in the bronchioles, the tiny cartilage-supported tubes that distribute air to the absorptive part of the lungs, and in the trachea (windpipe) and the paired bronchi, but this is only a very small fraction of what was previously present. In some seals – the Leopard seal, for instance – even the trachaea collapses completely, and in all seals it is compressed. The little compressed air that remains is probably important to the seal for producing underwater vocalizations as this air is passed over the vocal cords.

A problem for human divers is the condition known as the 'bends'. Gases are more soluble in liquids as pressure increases. A diver breathing air under pressure gradually accumulates nitrogen in his blood (the oxygen in the air is, of course, metabolized). Bends occur when the dissolved nitrogen in the blood and other body fluids comes out of solution to form bubbles as the diver rises to the surface and external pressure is reduced. The condition is often compared to the rush of bubbles released when a bottle of soda-water is unstoppered.

Seals are not liable to develop the bends since they never actually breathe air under pressure, for they exhale before submerging. It would theoretically be possible for them to accumulate nitrogen by repetitive diving if non-tidal air remained in their lungs, but the bulging abdominal viscera, as we have seen, drive the air out of the absorptive part of the lungs into the non-absorptive airways. In this way, the opportunity for nitrogen to be absorbed is greatly reduced and this, coupled with the very small amount of nitrogen taken down on a dive, protects the seal from developing the bends.

Otariids and walruses do not show such great developments for diving as do phocids. They have lower haemoglobin values in their blood and their relative blood volumes are less. Otariids exhale before they dive, but they probably retain more air in their lungs than do phocids. Certainly, it is common to see sea lions and fur seals blowing bubbles underwater. All pinnipeds can dive, but some, particularly the Weddell seal and the elephant seals, have developed this faculty to an extraordinary extent in order to exploit the ocean deeps. Other bottom feeders, the walrus for example, remain in shallow areas and, while spending quite a lot of time submerged, they do not dive deeply or for long periods. The pinnipeds thus show a parallel with the whales. All whales dive, but sperm whales and bottlenose whales have specialized in deep feeding. Their muscles, like those of Weddell seals and elephant seals, are almost black with myoglobin, while the muscles of the shallow-feeding fin whale or common dolphin are of a similar colour to those of Crabeater seals or Antarctic fur seals.

Chapter 8
Reproduction, Death and Social Structure

INTRODUCTION

The essence of mammalian organization is the birth of living offspring and the link between these and their mother in the process of suckling and rearing the young. The basic mammalian plan evolved on land and the adoption of an aquatic life by the pinnipeds has imposed constraints on this plan. The whales and sea-cows are also aquatic, of course, but because they spend all their life in the water, their reproductive strategies seem less modified than those of seals (though, of course, one could argue that since they give birth in the water, they are even more highly modified). Pinnipeds must return to the land (or to ice) to bear and suckle their young. As we have seen, the aquatic modifications of seals have made them less agile on land and hence more vulnerable to terrestrial predators. In order to minimize this risk, pinnipeds have evolved a number of strategies which affect their reproduction, lactation and, particularly, social organization.

ANATOMY AND PHYSIOLOGY OF REPRODUCTION

The female reproductive system of pinnipeds is not very different from that of terrestrial carnivores, except that the entrance to the vagina and the urinary meatus are withdrawn into the body, so that an extra segment – the urogenital sinus – is added to the tract. The paired, bean-shaped ovaries are each contained within a loose membranous sac, the ovarian bursa, formed from a double fold of peritoneum. The Fallopian tubes pursue a sinuous course around each ovary and terminate at the distal ends of the two-horned, or bicornuate, uterus. The uterus is secured in the body cavity by a pair of round ligaments that run from near the attachment of the diaphragm to the distal end of each uterine horn. A pair of broad ligaments are widely attached over the length of the horns and secure the uterus to the dorsal wall of the abdominal cavity. Externally, the two horns of the uterus combine to form a common uterus, but the lumen of each horn continues separately almost (or quite) to the cervix, so that the common uterus is non-functional.

The uterine cervix protrudes a short distance into the thick-walled vagina, the inner surface of which is ridged with complex folded ridges which allow for distension at birth. The walls of the vagina are massively reinforced with white fibrous tissue, making it a very tough organ indeed. As noted before, the vagina does not open directly to the exterior, but into another almost equal-sized part of the tract, the vestibule or urogenital sinus. It is separated from this by the remains of the hymenial fold, just below which is the urinary meatus on a small papilla, showing that it has been developed as an inward

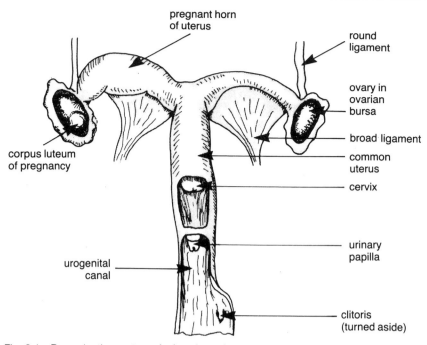

Fig. 8.1   Reproductive system of a female seal.

growth of the vulva. The clitoris is situated on the dorsal wall of the urogenital sinus, almost at its opening to the exterior. The clitoris sometimes contains a tiny bone, the os clitoridis, though in small or young seals this is represented by a cartilage only.

The external opening of the reproductive tract and the anus open into a common furrow which can be held closed by a sphincter muscle running round it.

There are no discrete accessory glands associated with the female reproductive system, though at the approach of oestrus the walls of the vagina and the urogenital sinus mucify and the secretions of many dermal mucous glands lubricate the canal.

The mammary glands are formed from two sheets of glandular tissue lying over much of the ventral and lateral surface of the trunk. They vary greatly in size. In a Weddell seal, each inactive gland measures about 30 by 16 cm (12 by 6¼ in) and has a volume of about 0.6 litres (1 UK/1¼ US pints), increasing to 2.8 litres (5/6 pints) in the lactating seal. There are two nipples in the phocids (except for the Bearded seal and the monk seals, which have four), situated at the level of the umbilicus. Supernumerary nipples, either paired or single, are not uncommon. Fur seals and sea lions have four nipples routinely. Each nipple lies flat against the body surface, except when stimulated by the sucking of a pup. The milk produced by pinnipeds is very rich in fats and I will discuss its role later.

The male system is similarly simple, the chief difference from that of

Pinnipeds, unlike cetaceans, must return to a solid substrate to breed. This Grey seal has moved inland on a remote Orkney island to produce her pup.

terrestrial carnivores being the retention of the testes within the body contour in the phocids and the walrus. In these animals, the testes lie embedded in the groin, between the abdominal musculature and the muscles and blubber of the skin. The testes of fur seals and sea lions are contained in a conventional scrotum of hairless, deeply pigmented skin. The scrotum is a device to ensure that the testes are kept at a temperature lower than that of the body core, since spermatogenesis is inhibited at body temperature. Phocids, with their internal testes, have a problem in this respect which is solved by embedding each testis in a heat exchanger. This is a venous plexus that communicates with veins carrying relatively cool blood coming from the hind flippers. In the Harp seal, the testes, which lie beneath some 8 cm (3 in) of skin and blubber, are 1 to 4°C cooler than the body core, about the same difference as in Man.

The epididymides, in which mature sperm are stored, border the testes. The vasa deferentia travel upwards to loop over the ureters before entering the prostate gland. The prostate is the only accessory gland of the male tract. It is a bulky, cone-shaped gland that encircles the base of the bladder and the urethra. It has the role of producing a secretion which dilutes, activates and nourishes the sperm on ejaculation.

The penis is contained within a pouch in the ventral abdominal wall. The opening is about midway between the umbilicus and the anus. (The anus, incidentally, opens into a vestibule with a slit-like opening, resembling that of the female and leading to frequent misidentifications of sex by untrained observers.) In all pinnipeds the most ventral of the three blocks of tissue that make up the body of the penis, the corpus cavernosum penis, is ossified in its distal part to make the os penis, or baculum. In phocids, the baculum is little more than a rod of bone, flattened or very slightly grooved on its ventral surface where the urethra runs, and sometimes enlarged a little at its proximal end, where it is attached to the fibrous portion of the corpus cavernosum. In otariids, the baculum has a much more definite architecture, which varies from genus to genus, but incorporates a slender shaft of dense bone with a

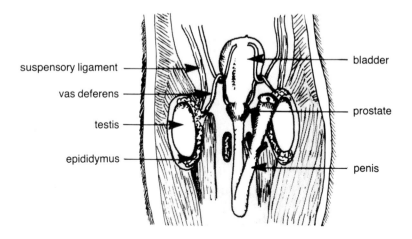

Fig. 8.2   Reproductive system of a male seal. The testes here are inguinal, or contained within the groin. In a fur seal or sea lion, they would be in an external scrotum.

Ice-breeding seals have almost limitless habitats available in the polar winters. This is a Leopard seal with a few days' old pup.

rugose expansion at its proximal end and a well-developed head at the other end. The baculum of the walrus is the largest baculum of any mammal. It is a big bone, even allowing for the size of a walrus, and very dense, like the bacula of otariids. The proximal end is enlarged to give a club-like appearance.

The function of the baculum is not very clear. It would stiffen the penis before insertion, but other mammals seem to manage this perfectly well by engorging the corpora spongiosa and cavernosum with blood. Erection of the penis in this way is required in pinnipeds in order to extrude the organ from its abdominal pouch. A baculum is found in all carnivores (except the hyenas), insectivores, bats and primates (except Man).

The surface of the glans penis is helmet-like in phocids, but flattened or even concave in otariids. There is usually a projecting papilla just above where the baculum terminates.

THE REPRODUCTIVE CYCLE

The male cycle is relatively simple. Sometime before the onset of the breeding season, and probably cued by changes in day-length, the mature male begins to secrete hormones which initiate the development of spermatocytes in the testis to mature sperm which is stored in the epididymus. At the same time, the prostate enlarges and its secretory cells become active. Changes take place also in the behaviour of the males. They become increasingly aggressive towards each other and associate with females.

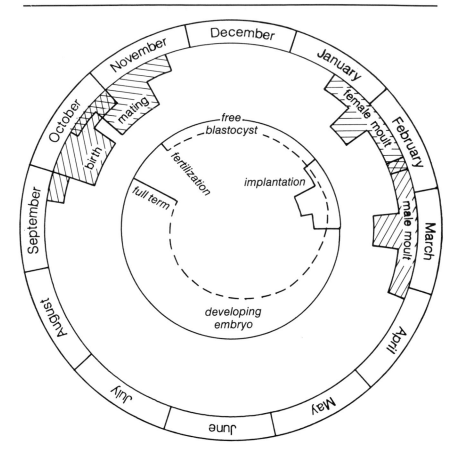

Fig. 8.3   The reproductive cycle of a typical phocid, the Grey seal.

Although in some cases the females are said to solicit the males to copulate, in general the initiative comes from the males, responding to (probably) olfactory and certainly behavioural cues provided by the females. Towards the end of the breeding season, the potency of the breeding bulls declines; the testis and prostate regress and their behaviour becomes less aggressive. In many species, fur seals, for example, the males never become sociable to the extent of permitting bodily contact, but in others, such as the elephant seals, they may gather together in heaps at the time of the moult. Curiously, at the moult there may be some signs of renewed activity in the testis, but this seems to be unaccompanied by behavioural changes.

The female cycle is more complicated. I shall start with a pinniped which has recently born a pup and is coming into heat, or oestrus. The horn of the uterus in which her newly born pup developed has shrunk to a fraction of its size a month earlier, though the scar where the placenta was established is still very conspicuous. Because the uterus contracted greatly immediately after the pup was born, there has been very little loss of blood from the raw surface where the placenta was attached and healing of the surface epithelium is already well advanced. The ovary on the opposite side contains a large fluid-filled follicle containing an egg. Hormonal changes about this time alter the female's receptivity to the male and copulation ensues.

Females are normally quite aggressive to males except at this time of oestrus. Even then, it seems in some seals, such as elephant seals, the male has to persuade the female in a somewhat drastic manner, thumping his fore quarters down on her shoulders and biting her neck. Phocid seals seem to show little in the way of pelvic thrusts. After the penis is inserted, the couple lie quietly almost without moving. What induces ejaculation is not known, but the very muscular vagina almost certainly plays a part. Otariids show more activity, with vigorous pelvic thrusting by the male. Most copulations last between 2.5 and 6 minutes.

Ovulation, at least in fur seals, appears to occur spontaneously. The follicle ruptures and the egg is shed into the lumen of the ovarian bursa and then taken up in the fringed funnel at the end of the Fallopian tube. It is conveyed down the tube by the action of the cilia that line it and is probably fertilized by the sperm at the utero–tubal junction.

The fertilized ovum descends into the lumen of the horn of the uterus. Here it begins to divide to form a hollow ball of cells, called a blastocyst. What would happen next in most mammals would be for the blastocyst to begin to establish contact with the wall of the uterus – the endometrium – and develop a placenta which then nourishes the further growth of the embryo. In pinnipeds, however, there is a departure from this process. There follows a period of inactivity or suspended development during which the blastocyst lies free in the lumen of the uterus.

Meanwhile, the follicle from which the egg was shed has developed into a glandular structure, the corpus luteum, or yellow body, which secretes hormones that govern pregnancy, including progesterone. The corpus luteum in the opposite ovary, which controlled the pregnancy that resulted in the birth of the recent pup, has meanwhile ceased to have a hormonal function. Its secretory cells have regressed and been replaced by white fibrous tissue. From its previous yellow colour, it becomes white and is known as a corpus albicans, or white body. The corpora albicantia gradually shrink but may persist for a number of years, perhaps even for life in some species, and an examination of the ovaries of a seal for the presence of corpora can reveal information about its reproductive history.

After the delay, which typically lasts about three months, some change occurs which causes the development of the blastocyst to resume. This has been shown in Harbour seals and California sea lions held in captivity to be mediated by changes in day-length. However, the condition of the females may have an important secondary role in timing after the correct day-length conditions have been recognized. It has been shown in Grey seals that resumed development of the blastocyst is associated with an increase in body condition of the female. The blastocyst swells and develops an intimate attachment to the uterine wall. This is generally referred to as 'implantation', but seal blastocysts do not truly implant, they remain superficial to the lining of the uterus at all times. However, the phrase 'delayed implantation' to describe this phenomenon is too well established in the seal biologist's vocabulary to be easily abandoned, though 'embryonic dispause' is obtaining some currency.

As the embryo develops, some of its membranes become intimately associated with the maternal tissues, so that foetal and maternal capillaries are in very close contact. Nutrients and oxygen are taken up by the developing embryo, and later the foetus, and waste products and carbon dioxide are carried away in the maternal circulation. In seal placentas, the foetal and maternal blood vessels are in much closer contact than in most other mammals. This might be an adaptation for easier gas exchange if the mother dives with a reduced heart rate. This thin barrier also allows the passage of hormones, for it is found that newly born seals have enlarged gonads. The gonadotrophic hormones responsible for this probably arise in the placenta.

The placenta is of the zonary type: it forms a cylindrical band around the foetus, intimately applied to the wall of the uterus. Around its margins in the later stages of pregnancy are lakes of degraded maternal blood. The function of these marginal haematomata is not known, but they are shown to contain porphyrins – haemoglobin from which the iron has been removed – and thus they may be a source of iron for the foetus.

As gestation progresses, the corpus luteum on the side with the foetus suppresses the growth of follicles in that ovary. However, in the opposite ovary, follicles are developing from egg cells that were laid down when the maternal seal was herself a foetus. One of these follicles begins to grow faster than the others, so that by the time birth takes place, an egg is already preparing itself for release when the seal comes into oestrus.

Birth is a simple and speedy process in seals. Although the new-born pup is large in relation to the mother, the absence of protruding limbs or a long neck makes delivery easy. Presentations may be crown or breech, the baby seal in its birth membranes presenting a neat torpedo-shaped package either way. From the first visible onset of labour until delivery may be as little as 15 minutes. The placenta may be delivered either simultaneously, still attached to the pup, or follow after a few minutes.

To some extent, the timing of birth seems to be under the control of the mother. If pregnant seals are prevented from hauling out – by disturbance at the rookery for example – when the disturbance is removed, there is a sudden surge of births, suggesting that the females can postpone giving birth until they are safely ashore. This would, of course, be a very useful trait for survival.

Thus the whole gestation period of the pinniped is almost a year, from mating, usually one to three weeks after one birth, to the subsequent birth. But when the period of delayed implantation is subtracted, it is seen that the active gestation is about nine months – a normal period for a large mammal. Why do seals have a delayed implantation? It may be that this is a device to allow births and matings to take place at the same time of assembly on land, a period of some danger to the seals, while still preserving a gestation time appropriate to the size of the animals. By postponing immediate development, the female is allowed time to recover from the strain of lactation which, as we shall see, imposes a greater energy demand than gestation.

Ovulations and subsequent pregnancies alternate from one ovary and its corresponding uterine horn to the other side and as an almost invariable rule, only single births occur. Twins have been recorded from many species of pinnipeds, perhaps because the event is so unusual biologists always pay special attention to it. A female suckling two pups has not necessarily had twins, of course, but the discovery of twin foetuses at least suggests the possibility of a twin birth. In the Ringed seal, triplet foetuses have been recorded. Several species have been observed to give birth to twins and twins seem to be born in captivity more frequently than in the wild. A Grey seal in the Louisville Zoological Garden, in Kentucky, gave birth to twins (in each case a male and female set) in successive years. Even more remarkably, there was a Grey seal in Copenhagen Zoo that gave birth to triplets in 1977 and again in 1980. In both cases these were still births. Survival prospects for twins are poor. The seal's reproductive strategy is highly tuned to maximum investment in one pup, and the strain on the mother of having to raise two (or more) to nutritional independence would be great.

LACTATION

The pinnipeds show a wide variation in their pattern of lactation. The phocids have, in general, developed a much shorter lactation than might be expected in mammals of their size, while the otariids and the walrus have extended the period.

From the point of view of lactational strategies, the phocid seals fall into two groups: those that breed on ice and those that breed on land. Phocids have adopted an ice-breeding habit at least twice, and probably more often, in their evolutionary history. Ice has many advantages to a breeding seal; it provides a virtually limitless area for breeding; it is easier for a seal to move over than rock or sand; and it usually provides quick access to deep water. It has disadvantages too; ice affords little shelter; it is a significant heat-sink; and it is liable to break up. Ice-breeding seals meet these disadvantages by secreting a very rich milk, so that the pup soon builds up an insulating layer of blubber, and by abbreviating the lactation period, so that the pup becomes independent before there is much risk of the ice breaking up.

A Harp seal feeds its pup for only nine days, during which the pup's weight increases from an average of 10.8 kg (24 lb) at birth at a rate of 2.5 kg (5.5 lb) per day to reach an average of 34.4 kg (75.8 lb) at weaning (see Fig. 8.4). Obviously, such a rapid gain of weight requires a very rich milk, and the fat content of Harp seal milk increases from 23 per cent at the beginning of lactation to more than 40 per cent at the end. This is associated with a decrease in water content. Because females fast while lactating, this decrease in water content helps maintain the water balance of the mother. On the other hand, the extra water may be useful to the new-born pup which, until it has built up its blubber layer, needs to metabolize carbohydrate and protein to meet its energy demands. Later, the pup switches to a fat-dominated metabolism, which results in the production of more metabolic water.

The shortest of all lactations in the ice-breeding seals, and indeed in all mammals, is that of the Hooded seal. It has recently been shown that the Hooded seal pup is weaned between three and five days after birth (most at five days), during which time its weight increases from 22 kg (48.5 lb) at birth to 42.6 kg (93.9 lb) at weaning, a daily weight gain of about 7.1 kg (15.7 lb).

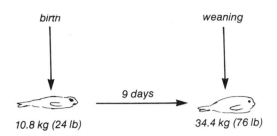

birth   weaning

9 days

10.8 kg (24 lb)   34.4 kg (76 lb)

Fig. 8.4   Growth in the Harp seal pup is astonishingly rapid.

Ringed seals, which are born in birth lairs on the fast ice, have more protection at birth and less need for an abbreviated lactation period. In their case, lactation lasts for about 42 days, though those born on stable ice have a longer nursing period and wean at a greater weight than those from less stable ice areas. These differences may affect the size of the adults.

The six land-breeding phocids (Harbour seal, Grey seal, the two elephant seals and the two monk seals) have different evolutionary histories. The Harbour seal and the Grey seal are believed to be rather recently derived from ice-breeding ancestors, while for the others there is no previous history of ice-breeding. The Hawaiian monk seal has a lactation period of about five to six weeks. The same, or slightly longer, is probably true for the Mediterranean monk seal. Reports of lactations as long as four months have not been substantiated.

Harbour seals are closely related to the ice-breeding Spotted seals but they have abandoned the ice-breeding habit, which has allowed them to extend their range to the south. Harbour seal pups, as we have seen, can swim with their mothers at the first tide. They are suckled at the water's edge for about four to six weeks, the mother and pup spending most of the time in the water, swimming together. The lactation period is longer than one might expect for a descendant of an ice-breeding ancestor, but Harbour seals have come to terms with terrestrial predators, notably Man, by producing highly precocious young and reducing the period needed to be spent ashore to suckle the young. Because of this, there has been no pressure to keep the lactation period short and the extended association between mother and pup, coupled with maternal care, may have survival value.

Grey seals show no such tendency. They still breed on ice in some parts of their range, but the great majority are land breeders. Lactation lasts 16 to 21 days, during which the pup's weight increases by 1.64 kg (3.6 lb) per day, while the mother loses 3.6 kg (7.9 lb) per day. The average maternal weight loss during lactation is 65 kg (143 lb), or 84 per cent of her stored energy reserves, while the pup gains 30 kg (66 lb). In energy terms, the mother uses 126 kilojoules per day (30,000 kcal) to maintain herself and produce milk. The pup stores 440 kj (10,500 kcal) per day but assimilates 146 kj (3,500 kcal) per day more for its own metabolism. To obtain this 586 kj (14,000 kcal) per day, the pup must receive about 711 kj (17,000 kcal) per day, equivalent to about

Harbour seal pups are very precocious and they can swim within an hour or so of birth, as must this one, which has been born on inter-tidal wrack.

3 litres (5½ UK/6¼ US pints) of milk (which can contain 52 per cent fat), since the efficiency of transfer of milk into stored or metabolizable energy is not 100 per cent.

The elephant seals are closely similar to Grey seals in their lactation patterns. Pups are suckled for 23 to 28 days with an average daily weight increase of 6.8 kg (15 lb) in the southern species. Fat content of the milk rises from about 12 per cent at birth to 40 per cent in the second week. Because of the huge fat store laid down, the young elephant seal can fast for eight to ten weeks, perfecting swimming skills, before having to search for its own food. Elephant seals are very gregarious and there is much interaction between the animals on the breeding beaches. Some newly weaned pups prolong the suckling period by stealing milk from other lactating females, or by being adopted by 'foster mothers'. This permits a pup to increase its weaning weight, which may give it a better chance of survival, or even a permanent size advantage as an adult. Male pups are most persistent and successful in milk stealing and exceptionally large weaners are almost always males. Males are suckled by their natural mothers for one day longer than females and their canine teeth erupt late, which may be an adaptation to facilitate milk stealing.

Milk stealing has been observed in other seals, but in most cases it seems of little advantage to the thieves. In Grey seals, it is associated with disturbance, and the pups that sucked from most cows did not thrive as well and spent less total time feeding than those which sucked from one cow only.

A Southern elephant seal pup feeds from its mother. It will be independent in about three weeks.

A Galapagos fur seal with her pup and a yearling she gave birth to the previous year.

Walrus milk contains about 24 per cent fat, but as we have seen, the lactation period is greatly extended, the pup receiving milk for about two years, though after the first six months it begins to do some feeding for itself. The sea lions and fur seals are a much more uniform group with regard to lactation patterns than are the phocids. After an initial period, when the mother stays with the pup continuously, feeding takes place in a series of episodes and usually lasts for the remainder of the summer or until the next pup is born. In the Antarctic fur seal, there are about 17 of these episodes following the initial six to eight day period with the pup, making up a total lactation period of 117 days. Male pups gain weight at 100 g (3.5 oz) per day, compared with only 82 g (2.9 oz) per day for females, resulting in weaning weights of 17 kg (37.5 lb) and 13.5 kg (29.8 lb) respectively.

Extension of the lactation period is commonplace in otariids. The most extreme case is seen in the Galapagos fur seal, whose young may be suckled until they are two or three years old. Most pups have begun foraging for themselves at a year old, but they will return to their mothers for milk feeds. Milk can still form a significant part of the diet of two-year-old seals. The presence of an unweaned yearling has a disastrous effect on the survival of a younger sibling.

When a pup is born, it almost always dies in the first month if its older sibling is a yearling, or in about 50 per cent of cases if it is a two-year-old. This habit clearly reduces the potential fecundity of the females, but must have survival value, so widespread is it among the otariids. Perhaps it is associated with the polygynous habit of otariids, where a size advantage in the males can increase their reproductive success very greatly. In the case of the Galapagos fur seal, it may be an adaptation to maximize reproductive output in an unpredictable environment.

LONGEVITY

In all pinnipeds, as in all mammals, mortality tends to be clustered at the beginning of the potential life-span and again (unsurprisingly) at its end. Accurate figures are difficult to obtain, but perinatal mortality seems to be highest in those seals (Grey seals, elephant seals and the otariids) that breed in crowded conditions. Pup mortality may reach more than 30 per cent on a crowded fur seal rookery.

Having survived the early weeks, pinnipeds are generally long-lived mammals. Since the age of seals can be accurately interpreted from ridges on the roots of their teeth or from incremental layers in the dentine and cementum, there are many records of very old seals. Probably most seals have effective life-spans in the wild of about 15 to 30 years. Some remarkable ages reached by seals in the wild are 29+ years for a female Crabeater, 43 years for a female Ringed seal, and 46 years for a female Grey seal (though this was a specimen with an ovarian tumour that had rendered her sterile). The tiny Baikal seal is reported to reach 52 and 56 years for males and females respectively, but I would like to see the teeth from which these determinations were made.

What causes death is not known, since most seals die at sea and their carcasses are lost. Senile females (i.e., those which have ceased to go through

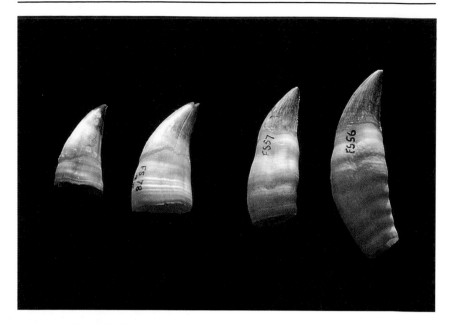

The age of otariids can be calculated by counting ridges on the roots of their canine teeth. From left to right, this series of Antarctic fur seal teeth are from animals one, two, four and six years old.

Age can also be determined from incremental layers revealed in stained sections of tooth root. This Crabeater seal was 26 years old.

the normal reproductive cycle) are very rare, except in association with pathological conditions of the reproductive tract. It is probable that an old female produces a pup as normal, rears it, but then on returning to the sea to feed for herself, fails to recover condition and dies at sea. The same probably happens to males, though at least in some fur seals it is apparent that some senile males survive after they have had their last season as breeding bulls. In the Antarctic fur seal, many such bulls haul out during the breeding season and die on the land behind the breeding beaches.

SOCIAL STRUCTURE

Seals are not particularly social animals. Some, like the Bearded seal, are solitary except during the breeding season. None shows the kind of highly structured society seen in, for example, African hunting dogs or meerkats. Outside the breeding season, some seals, such as Harbour seals, regularly occur in small groups of half a dozen to fifty or so. If one watches at a haul-out place of Harbour seals, one can soon see the advantage of this. While most of the seals in the group bask peacefully, snoring and snorting away, there are always one or two that are alert and watchful, peering about and scanning the horizon for possible danger. Because of this vigilance, it is almost impossible to approach a haul-out without warning the seals and the seals benefit because of the group structure.

Elephant seals are very gregarious during the moult. As we saw earlier, this is a device for conserving energy at a time when the superficial layers of the skin must be well supplied with blood, and hence warm, while the new hair grows. But the elephant seals merely lie about in heaps. There is no division of labour or hierarchical structure in these groups.

We do not really know enough about the feeding tactics of seals to say whether there is any co-operative feeding, as has been shown for humpback whales, for example. Humpback (and other baleen) whales may hunt in groups, several whales isolating a shoal of small fish or crustaceans by swimming round and setting up currents, or by blowing out bubbles that create an air curtain around the shoal. The concentrated fish or krill can then be engulfed by the whales. Sea lions and fur seals have often been observed feeding in groups and it seems at least possible that when doing so, they are co-operating so as to isolate shoals of prey.

The walrus is unique among pinnipeds in maintaining a long period of dependence of the young – two years. This is in contrast to some of the fur seals, where the only significant bond between mother and offspring is the milk provided. The walrus mother provides not only milk, but also protection. The social system in walrus groups is clearly complex, as the many dominance displays indicate, but it is as yet insufficiently studied for analysis.

Most social interactions between seals take place during the breeding season. Mother–pup relations and copulatory activity are basic social interactions, but the most complex social structures arise in those land-breeding pinnipeds that assemble in great numbers to breed.

No one who has seen a fur seal rookery or an elephant seal breeding beach at the height of the season can fail to be amazed at the activity, and wonder at the purpose. Why do such huge numbers of cows congregate in these ill-

Antarctic fur seals breed in very crowded colonies, but each bull controls a recognized space in the rookery.

tempered, squabbling groups? Why do the bulls compete so assiduously, and at such cost? Why are they so much larger than the females? What survival advantage can there be in the dead pups that litter the most crowded areas of the rookery at the end of the season?

The first convincing answers to these, and other, questions were given by an American seal biologist, George Bartholomew. Bartholomew wrote his doctoral thesis on the reproductive behaviour of the Northern elephant seal and this species very clearly demonstrates the general principles involved, not only in the social organization of the polygynous pinnipeds but of many other mammals as well.

First of all, why do seals congregate? Pinnipeds, as we noted earlier, have sacrificed mobility on land for superb performance in the sea. Gregarious breeding permits animals which are widely dispersed when feeding at sea to exploit especially advantageous sites – such as oceanic islands or protected beaches – where suitable terrain and the absence of terrestrial predators allow them to breed safely, despite their lack of terrestrial agility. There would have been especially strong selective pressure on species that fed far offshore to develop strong breeding-site fidelity to ensure that the sexes were reunited for breeding.

Their limited mobility ashore, combined with the need to come together for breeding, results in the formation of very dense breeding groups. The females lie in close proximity, though rarely in actual body contact, but the males are more widely spaced. This is because of their aggressive tendencies,

This rookery of Southern elephant seals at St Andrew's Bay, South Georgia, contained about 4,000 females and 400 males.

mediated by their sex hormones, chiefly testosterone, at this time.

Why are the bulls so much bigger than the cows? If the males are more widely spaced than the females (and if males are more or less equally numerous in the population as a whole, which is, in fact, the case), it follows that many of the males will be excluded from a position among the breeding females. These excluded, or 'marginal', males, because they are not with the females, are not in a position (literally!) to mate, and hence pass on their genes to subsequent generations. Those males that can keep their position among the females, either by dominating all the other males on their section of the beach, as in elephant seals, or by defending an exclusive territory, as in fur seals, are the ones that will pass on their genes. And the longer these males can stay among the females, the more matings they will enjoy. There will thus be a very strong selection for those characters that ensure the males are stronger (which usually means bigger) and which can stay longest on the beach before they must leave to feed again (and this also means bigger, since big males have more blubber reserves and the larger they are, the lower their weight-relative metabolic rate).

These characters that equip a bull with the means to establish himself among the females, and to defend his position in the face of the testosterone-induced aggressiveness of other bulls, are known as the epigamic characters. These are predominantly: large size; aggressiveness; big teeth; a protective shield of thickened skin (elephant seals) or mane of fur (fur seals and sea lions); special structures used in display or challenge, and so on. The males

Southern elephant seals fight fiercely for the opportunity to have a place on the beach and to mate with the females.

that develop these characters to the greatest extent will – provided also that they are sexually vigorous and fertile – pass on a quite disproportionate number of genes to the next generation. A really successful elephant seal on the shores of Año Nuevo Island, in California, may impregnate 100 females in a single season and four times that number in his lifetime. At best, a female can produce about 12 pups, so the potential reproductive success is tipped heavily towards the males.

These enormous selective pressures towards the development of large size, aggressiveness, etc. do not apply to the females. Their role, in the pattern of life, is to pass on genes by producing healthy pups. There is no special pressure for females to be especially large, or especially aggressive, though in fact elephant seal cows are very large (so as to be able to produce large pups) and pretty aggressive (so as to defend them). But the difference exists, and the sexual dimorphism in these polygynous seals is greater than anywhere else in the mammalian series. Because the seals are aquatic for most of their life, the restraint on upper-body size associated with mechanical properties and locomotion is absent, but male elephant seals may be approaching (or may already have reached) their upper limit if they are to move about within their harems.

But why is it better to breed in such crowded circumstances that 20 to 30 per cent of the pups are trampled or otherwise killed before they are weaned? Surely it would be better for a female to slip away to a quieter part of the beach to suckle her pup and eventually mate with one of the marginal males?

The disparity in size between adult males and females in the Southern elephant seal – sexual dimorphism – is greater than in any other mammal.

Obviously, the extent to which a bull tramples and kills pups which may be his own progeny reduces his reproductive efficiency, but because successful bulls are so highly fecund this is of much less importance to the bulls than it would be to the cows, who if they lose a pup, decrease their lifetime reproductive efficiency by about 10 per cent. However, a cow that slinks off to a quieter place to rear her pup in peace, more or less guarantees that she will mate with a bull who is less reproductively successful than the one in the thick of the breeding crowd. To the extent that this bull's lack of success is due to genetic factors, these will be passed on to his progeny. While this may not matter for female pups, his male offspring might be expected also to share his marginal status and hence impregnate a negligible proportion of females. Most, of course, would not impregnate any at all, and hence their gene lines would become extinct.

As Burney Le Boeuf has pointed out, the best reproductive strategy for a female is to locate herself where she will be mated by a dominant male. The 'marginal male effect' will ensure that gregariousness in females will be positively reinforced.

Of course, it is not as simple as all that; a logical consequence of the system described would lead to all the elephant seals, or all the fur seals, breeding in only a very few huge colonies. This has very nearly happened with fur seals on the Pribilofs, and with elephant seals in California, but physical limitations can often prevent colonies becoming too large. Small breeding groups do occur and in these the marginal male effect may be much less marked – often these colonies involve younger animals. In South Georgia, a young fur seal cow may move through the crowded beaches to give birth to her pup high up on the hill behind. She will soon be joined and eventually impregnated by a marginal male, which in this situation is almost certainly also a young seal. Young elephant seal cows in California have been shown to improve their chances of rearing their pups successfully by moving from the crowded beaches to start new colonies. But this applies only to first pups. Experienced mothers, who can protect their offspring better, are still better off breeding in the crowd where they are mated by a dominant bull.

The pressure to breed with the crowd in these animals makes the establishment of new colonies very difficult. Most populations of fur seals have been at one time or another radically reduced by hunting. The pattern of repopulation following the end of exploitation is constrained by the seals' reluctance to colonize new areas. On South Georgia, a relict population of fur seals survived on some inaccessible rocks at the west end of the main island. The present population has now recovered, probably to more than its pre-exploitation numbers, but the seals are still crowded together at the western end of the island, with some traditional breeding areas still unoccupied.

Of course, not all pinnipeds have followed this route. The ice-breeding seals, with the almost limitless extent of secure pack ice as their breeding grounds, remain dispersed breeders and there is in them no sign of the extreme sexual dimorphism seen in the elephant seals. On the other hand, the Grey seal, which rather recently in its evolutionary history was an ice-breeding seal, has adopted a terrestrial breeding habit, and it is showing a trend towards the elephant seal style. A big bull Grey seal is twice as heavy as a cow. Sheila Anderson and her colleagues, working at the large Grey seal breeding colony on North Rona, found that the three most successful bulls of 31 observed accounted for 35.6 per cent of all copulations. This is not as impressive as in elephant seals, but Grey seal cows are very much more dispersed than are elephant seal cows. Perhaps continuing evolutionary trends will result in Grey seals breeding in the same sort of assemblies as elephant seals.

Chapter 9
Seals and Hunters

SUBSISTENCE HUNTING

Because seals live in the sea, they possess characters that make them very attractive to hunters. In order to keep themselves warm, as we have seen, seals have developed a blubber layer, or dense waterproof fur. From earliest times, human communities wandering the barren shores of the Arctic, or paddling their canoes by the cold, wet forests of Tierra del Fuego, were to find these products essential for their cultures.

Seals and Stone Age Man

We cannot be sure how Stone Age humans used seals, but we do know from archaeological excavations that seals were at least significant in their life. The earliest seal-related relics from northern Europe come from the Aurignacian and Magdalenian sites in the Dordogne region of France, where seal jaws have been found. These places are currently some 200 km (125 miles) from the sea and they would have been further inland in Stone Age times, when sea levels were lower. In the Dordogne there are also some excellently drawn Upper Palaeolithic engravings – one on a bear's tooth and the other on a reindeer antler – that are easily recognizable as pictures of Grey seals. The antler shows a male and female Grey seal pursuing a salmon and it may indicate that seals were captured in estuaries when they congregated to feed on the salmon run, just as they do today (Fig. 9.1).

Elsewhere in Europe, definite indications of seal hunting have been found. At Norrekjöping, in southern Sweden, the skeleton of a young Ringed seal was found together with a bone harpoon head, while at Närpes, in Finland, a Harp seal skeleton was found, also in association with a harpoon head. One can envisage the wounded seal escaping when the harpoon line broke, only to succumb to its wounds, sink to the bottom and finally to be covered with silt and then discovered thousands of years later as workmen dug through the clay.

On the little Danish island of Hesselø, in the Kattegat, six wooden clubs were found in a bog, together with many bones and teeth, mostly of young Grey seals. It seems Hesslø was an important sealing station in Stone Age times. Hunters probably visited the island seasonally to kill weaned pups before they left for the sea.

Seals and the Inuit

Until a few generations ago, a Stone Age culture continued to exist in the Arctic. The Netsilik Inuit (or Eskimos, as they are often called) lived a life that was entirely dependent on marine products and particularly on seals. Their seal hunting was made possible by the development of the harpoon. Other native hunters to the south of the Netsilik could hunt deer with bows and arrows. A wounded animal on land could be pursued until it expired and

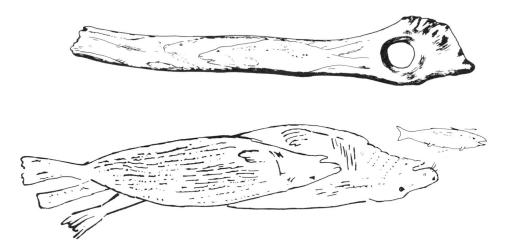

Fig. 9.1   The 'Montgaudier baton', a piece of reindeer antler engraved with a pair of Grey seals pursuing a salmon, from the Upper Palaeolithic in the Dordogne region of France. The baton is usually pictured as shown above, but the artist has shown the seals swimming on their backs, as they often do, as they follow the fish. The bull and cow Grey seal are very accurately depicted.

then be recovered; with a seal, it was essential to maintain a material link between the hunter and the quarry after it was struck, otherwise the wounded animal would almost certainly swim away or sink and be lost. The harpoon provided the means to strike from a distance, but at the same time, to stay in touch with the prey.

An Inuit harpoon consisted of a tip, or tokang, made of ivory or bone and provided with a sharp blade of slate or volcanic glass. This surmounted a walrus tusk balanced on an ivory socket, the qatirn, in turn attached by sinews to a wooden shaft. To the tokang was attached a line which was braced by a tab over a peg on the shaft. The whole thing was rigid until, on striking the target, the tokang slipped off the tusk and the tab came free of the peg. The shaft would then float free, to be recovered later, while the hunter kept hold of the line until the seal could be drawn close enough to be lanced and killed.

Such a harpoon was used for hunting from a kayak, mostly in the summer. In the winter and spring, a common method was to wait motionless at a Ringed seal breathing-hole until the seal surfaced to take a breath. This would be signalled to the hunter by laying a goose-down feather across a fish bone wedged in the breathing hole. Seeing the feather stir when the seal came up to breathe, the hunter would drive down his harpoon through the ice fragments in the hole and, if successful, drag out the seal, to be killed by a blow to the head from the hunter's hand. Anyone who has seen the impressive archive film of the Netsilik Inuit will recall the patient figure, crouched over the seal hole, harpoon at the ready, standing motionless on a seal skin to keep his feet from freezing, and wonder at the extraordinary patience of these people.

The capture of a seal, even a small Ringed seal, was a significant event.

Subsistence sealing on a small scale continued in Shetland until the 1970s. Here a Shetland hunter skins a Harbour seal pup.

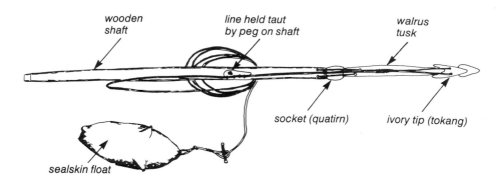

wooden shaft

line held taut by peg on shaft

walrus tusk

socket (quatirn)

ivory tip (tokang)

sealskin float

Fig. 9.2   An Inuit kayak harpoon. The tip, or 'tokang', comes loose from the tusk on which it is mounted when embedded in the prey and the shaft floats free, to be picked up later.

Here in one package was food (the liver would be eaten first), fuel for cookers and lamps, and clothing. However primitive Netsilik life might have seemed to the nineteenth-century whalers who first encountered them, it was actually a very sophisticated existence. Having available only a very limited range of resources, the Inuit had to provide themselves with technologically complicated tools, such as their harpoons and kayaks. To use these tools in the harsh environment they inhabited, they had to manufacture warm and waterproof clothing.

No Inuit could live alone, because hunting and manufacturing and maintaining the equipment and clothing used in hunting required the combined resources of a family. If a Netsilik wife was dependent on her husband for food, he was equally dependent on her for his clothing. Both were dependent on the seals. Food might have been obtained from fish and birds, but seal skins were needed for clothing and blubber lamps were essential during the long Arctic night, not only for the warmth they provided but also for the light they shed, without which it would have been impossible to make or repair skin clothing and the hunting equipment.

The Netsilik Inuit were particularly dependent on seals but almost all other communities where seals occurred made use of them. Native Americans on the California coast left the remains of Guadalupe fur seals in their middens. The Straandlopers of southern Africa did the same with Cape fur seals, as did other aboriginal peoples wherever coastal seal colonies occurred. These people seemed mostly hunter-gatherers, and seals would have formed only a small part of their food, though it has been claimed that the predecessors of the Yamana and Alacaluf peoples of the Beagle Channel 6,000 years ago obtained most of their calories and fats from the South American fur seals they killed. The Danish Stone Age people who killed the seals at Hesselø almost certainly had other means of support, since their sealing appears to have been very seasonal.

Seals and farmers

As groups became more settled in farming communities, sealing did not necessarily decline in importance. In the eighteenth century, Carolus Linnaeus noted examples of seal hunting by farmers in the diary of his journey in 1741 to Öland and Gothland. Nets might be set around an offshore rock on which seals were wont to bask. Such rocks were valued assets on a farm and if no suitable ones were naturally present, farmers would arrange stones in the water to attract the seals. Seals were trapped as well as netted. Their habit of hauling out on floating platforms made pitfall traps easy to use. Snag hooks were also employed. These were large hooks fastened to a rope encircling a seal rock just below the water. When the tide fell, the seals were scared off the rock and, with luck, would become hooked on the exposed barbs.

Subsistence seal hunting has continued among small farmers and crofter-fishers almost to the present day. In most cases, the product principally sought was the oil. Besides its use for illumination (seal-oil lamps were in use in Orkney up to the last century), seal oil was valued as a dressing for harness leather and as a medicinal draught. It could scarcely be surpassed as a means of getting energy into a poorly nourished frame! Seal meat, though palatable when from a young seal, does not seem to have been so favoured despite its potential value in the diet of a crofter who otherwise might have had red meat relatively rarely. In Catholic communities, however, it had a special value, as it could be consumed in Lent: seals, living in the sea, were clearly fish and not meat. A peculiar traditional use for seals in Scotland is (or was) the manufacture of sporrans from the skin of the Harbour seal.

Even where a community was very largely dependent on seals, as in the case of the Netsilik Inuit, these hunting operations did not pose any great threat to the seal populations. A balance between the hunter and the hunted was necessarily established, for if it were not, the human society depending on the seals was doomed. More dangers developed when farmers took up seal hunting. Not being greatly dependent on the seals, they might locally exterminate the population, yet still continue to live on their farm products. To a large extent, this is what in fact happened in the Baltic, aided by the widespread use of fire-arms. But in many places, seals continued to thrive, protected by their wariness or the inaccessibility of their breeding grounds.

COMMERCIAL SEALING – THE HARP SEAL HUNT

A change came when seal products began to be traded on a substantial scale. This was the beginning of commercial, as opposed to subsistence, sealing. Its roots can be traced back to the sixteenth century, when Basque fishermen were exploiting the plentiful cod stocks on the Grand Banks off Newfoundland to provide salted cod. They found that besides netting cod, they could also net Harp seals on their migrations through the Strait of Belle Isle, between Quebec and Newfoundland. As the region was settled throughout the succeeding centuries, seal netting became a significant industry. By the 1740s, substantial quantities of seal oil were being exported. In those years when the ice with the pupping Harp seals on it was carried close to shore, the settlers could move out on the floes to club the seals and make exceptionally large harvests.

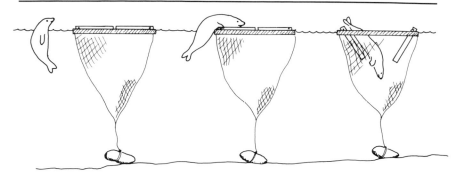

Fig. 9.3   A pitfall trap for seals of a sort seen by Linnaeus in Sweden in the eighteenth century.

It was inevitable that when the ice was not accessible from the land, boats would eventually be used. By the middle of the eighteenth century, shallops, about 10 m (33 ft) long and decked fore and aft with an open well, were used to reach the ice and carry away the skin and blubber – the 'sculp', as it was known – of the killed seals. From these developed the 30- or 40-tonne Newfoundland schooners that could work up to 160 km (100 miles) offshore in the spring. The sealing in the winter and spring proved a perfect complement to cod fishing in the summer. By the second quarter of the nineteenth century, 300 schooners were sailing to the sealing grounds and taking more than half a million seals (Harps and some Hoods) yearly.

The schooners severely reduced the available seals, but in 1863 steam-powered auxiliary vessels were introduced which could penetrate thicker ice. These 'wooden-walled steamers' were themselves supplanted by larger steel ships with ice-breaker bows in the early part of this century. Just before World War 1, there were nine steel ships and about a dozen of the old wooden-walls operating.

The depression between the Wars was a bad time for sealing. It corresponded with a vast over-production of whale oil in the Antarctic, and since seal and whale oil were used for the same purpose (by this time mostly for the production of margarine and other edible fats and oils), the market for seal oil collapsed.

Sealing recovered rapidly in a world of food shortages after World War 2, but by then Newfoundland vessels were being supplanted by modern Norwegian diesel-powered sealers, which effectively killed off the Newfoundland industry. Earlier than this, Norwegians had been exploiting Harps and Hoods in the Denmark Strait, and together with the Russians, in the White Sea, and they had considerable sealing experience. The Russians made a couple of expeditions to the north-west Atlantic sealing grounds, the last in 1963, but thereafter stayed in the White Sea.

Harp sealing (and the same applies to Hood sealing) was very simple. Seal pups ('white coats' in the case of new-born Harp seals, 'beaters' for weaned pups, or 'blue backs' in the case of Hood pups) were killed with a blow to the

Blood on the ice. Harp sealing attracted a great amount of media attention.

head; clubs were used by the Canadian sealers, while the Norwegians preferred an instrument like a small pickaxe on a long shaft, a *hakapık*. The carcase was then turned over and slit down the middle and the skin turned back, cutting the major arteries to the flippers. After the carcase had been allowed to bleed, the sculp was stripped off and brought back to the ship, where it was stored in chilled brine or treated with antioxidants to prevent the oil staining the fur yellow.

The carcase was left on the ice. Some Newfoundland hunters ('landsmen') would often remove the pup flippers and take them home for that local delicacy, flipper pie, but in general the carcase was not used.

Originally, the products of the seal hunt had been primarily the oil, with some leather. The entry of the Norwegians, with superior handling and storage methods, led to the development of a trade in furriers' skins. Seal skins became popular for trimming boots and après-ski gear. The best skins were used for coats and jackets and this put particular pressure on Hooded seals, since the blue-back furs were the most highly prized of all.

In the early 1950s, Canadian fisheries' scientists began to investigate the dynamics of the seal fishery. The first figure for pup production, 645,000, was little more than the catch, 456,000, which caused considerable concern. A Seal Assessment Group appointed by the government reported a decline in the Harp seal stock over the previous 15 years. To arrest this, the duration of the

Killing seals in a cavern. The early nineteenth-century southern fur sealers found many of their prey in caves, as this contemporary print shows.

hunting season was shortened and the killing of adults in the whelping patches prohibited.

A quota of 245,000 pups was introduced in 1971, but this was not reached, perhaps because of the scarcity of seals. The following year, the quota was reduced to 150,000 and reduced again to 127,000 in 1976.

However, further reviews by scientists indicated that the seal stocks were in much better shape than believed and the quota was increased to 160,000 in 1977 and 170,000 the following year. In 1982, it was set at 175,000 at which figure it remained until pup hunting was banned by the Canadian government in December 1987. In that year, the actual catch had been only 49,000 pups, well below the quota. The reason for this was not the lack of seals, but the prohibition in 1983 by the European Economic Community (the principal market for the dressed skins) of the importation of products from pup Harp and Hooded seals. This was a direct consequence of the intervention of animal-protection groups and I shall come back to this in Chapter 11.

Hunting of moulting or moulted pups ('ragged jackets' and 'beaters') is still permitted and it is carried on, though on a markedly reduced scale, by the 'landsmen' who go out on to the ice when it comes close to shore, just as the settlers did in the eighteenth century. Norwegians take Harp seals in the

Denmark Strait and Russians harvest them in the White Sea, but the market is comparatively small. Harp seals are now very abundant in the North Atlantic and Norwegian fishermen, in particular, complain of this, but there is little likelihood that the populations will ever again be reduced by large-scale hunting.

COMMERCIAL SEALING – FUR SEALS

Fur seals have been exploited in all their haunts for the sake of their skins, but the principal and longest-lasting hunt was that for the Northern fur seal in the cold waters of the Bering Sea. The Northern fur seal was first described by Georg Steller in 1742, at which time a few skins from Kamchatka were being sold to Russian fur traders. It was the discovery of the huge rookeries in the Pribilofs, St George Island in 1786 and St Paul the following year, that started mass harvesting.

Between 1786 and 1867, perhaps 2.5 million skins were taken from the Pribilofs, though no precise records of the early years were kept. The Pribilofs had been uninhabited when discovered, but the Russian overseers imported native peoples from the Aleutian Islands to kill the seals and salt the skins. By 1834, the Russians realized that the herd was declining, despite closed seasons in 1806 and 1807. The killing of females was forbidden and restrictions on the killing of males introduced. On the Pribilofs, the non-breeding, juvenile male fur seals – the bachelors – hauled out in special areas during the breeding season, so it was relatively easy to regulate the harvest in this way.

By the time of the purchase of Alaska by the US in 1867, the Pribilof fur seal population numbered between 2 and 2.5 million and it was sustaining an annual harvest of several thousand young males each year. For the first two years under American control, sealing got out of hand, the kill reaching 329,000 in 1869. In that year, however, the Pribilofs were declared a special reservation for the seals and the sealing rights were vested in the Alaska Commercial Company, which paid a rental and tax on each skin procured by the US government. The killing of females and males younger than one year was prohibited and a yearly quota of 100,000 set, though this was never achieved by the end of the company's lease, in 1889.

With a new lessee, the North America Commercial Company, new regulations were introduced. The quota was set year by year and lay mostly in the range 15,000 to 30,000. By this time, however, a new development in sealing had arrived. Throughout the breeding season, the seas around the Pribilofs were dotted with seals coming and going from the islands, or resting at the surface of the water. These seals were easy targets for men armed with shotguns who operated from small schooners or rowing-boats. Beyond the three-mile limit were international waters in those days, and the American authorities were powerless to control this increasing toll on the fur-seal stocks. To make matters worse, the majority of the seals killed were lactating females, since these needed to make frequent feeding trips to sea while they reared their pups. The loss of the mothers inevitably meant that the pups starved as well.

Most of these pelagic sealers were Canadians and the US entered into negotiations with Great Britain (representing Canada) and a treaty was concluded in 1892 in Paris which banned sealing within 60 miles of the

A pod of Northern fur seal bachelors about to be 'knocked down'.

Pribilofs, or any pelagic sealing from 1 May to 31 July. Unfortunately, this treaty was ineffective, since it covered neither the whole area of operations nor the whole season and, like many fisheries conventions, was very difficult to enforce. Additionally, Japan, which was not a signatory to the treaty, had entered the field.

Pelagic sealing continued until the density of seals was so reduced that it became economically scarcely worthwhile. By 1912, the Pribilof herd had been reduced to its lowest level – about 300,000 seals. In 1911, a new treaty was drawn up, the North Pacific Fur Seal Convention, which involved all those nations with interests in fur sealing in that region. The two primary operators onshore were the Americans on the Pribilofs and the Russians on Robben Island and the Commander Islands. The catch at these places was to be divided according to a complicated formula that allocated a proportion of the skins harvested to Canada and Japan, in return for which they would give up pelagic sealing.

Under the 1911 Convention, the seals had a chance to recover. Sealing was banned on the Pribilofs from 1912 to 1917 and thereafter annual quotas were set, initially 35,000 until 1920, then 30,000 until 1923, when it was reduced to 25,800. After 1924, quotas were not set, the kill being limited by the availability of male seals of a specified size in the limited season.

Sealing on the Pribilofs under American control continued in much the same manner as under the Russians. The actual operations were carried out by the Aleuts, of whom a sizable community now lived on the islands. It was this more-or-less captive labour-force that allowed sealing to be carried on

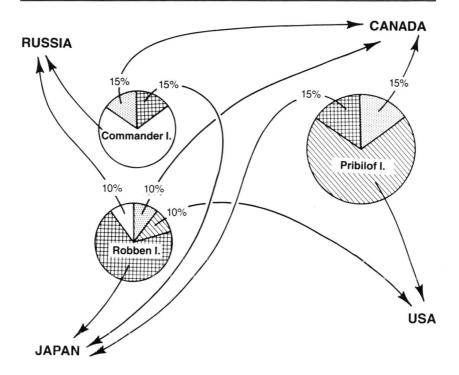

Fig. 9.4   The division of catch of Northern fur seals as agreed under the North Pacific Fur Seal Convention.

profitably for as long as it did. Work started very early in the cool of the morning, when a sealing crew would travel by truck to the bachelor hauling grounds. From 20 to 50 men would cautiously cut off a group of several hundreds or thousands of bachelors from the rest of the seals and drive them to the killing field. Here, the herd would be rested to cool off, and then small groups, or pods, would be separated. Any seals outside the permitted length limits were allowed to escape, but the remainder were killed by a blow to the head from a club, after which each seal was slit open, cut around the flippers, head and tail, and turned over to bleed. The dead seals were skinned by pinning the head to the ground with a large fork and ripping off the skin with tongs, thus avoiding knife cuts in the pelt.

The skins were then taken by truck to the village processing plant, washed, deblubbered and brined. The salted skins were dispatched to a processing factory in St Louis, where they were dehaired to expose the soft underfur, tanned and dyed. The carcasses, meanwhile, had been gathered up and taken to a reduction plant to be converted into meat meal for animal food. The Aleuts used significant quantities of carcasses for their own food.

The whole operation was overseen by American managers and scientists, some of them, such as Victor Scheffer, world-famous wildlife biologists. The American scientific management of the Pribilof fur seal herd had rightly been

Aleuts skinning Northern fur seal bachelors on the Pribilofs.

an object of admiration by other wildlife biologists. Colin Bertram wrote in 1950: 'One can give no higher praise than sincerely to hope that planning and agreement for the future may be as beneficent and rational as has been the administration and conservation of the herd during the last forty years'.

Unfortunately, it was almost from this time that things started to go wrong for the Pribilof fur seal herd. From averages of over 50,000 seals per year between 1951 and 1965, the catch fell to about half this in 1976 to 1979. In 1956 a commercial catch of females had been begun, in the expectation that reducing the density of the breeding animals would enhance the survival of the young. The commercial harvest of females ended in 1968, by which time about 300,000 females had been killed, but none of the beneficial effects of this strategy had been realized. In 1973 St George Island was declared a research sanctuary and harvesting suspended (apart from a small kill of 300 to 400 for subsistence purposes by the Aleuts).

From the mid-1970s to the early 1980s, the fur seal population declined at between 4 to 8 per cent a year. It was thought that some of this decline could have been caused by mortality resulting from entanglement in marine debris – net fragments and packing bands – and this mortality for pups in their first year may have exceeded 14 per cent in the late 1970s and early 1980s.

The Fur Seal Convention lapsed in 1984 and thereafter commercial harvesting of fur seals ceased (they are protected under the US Marine Mammal Protection Act), apart from a small native subsistence harvest – 1,676 in 1992.

The decline and subsequent ending of the Pribilof fur seal harvest was the result of many factors. Inappropriate management techniques and additional mortality resulting from entanglement in marine debris and drift nets were two such factors. Another was a change in fashion (seal becoming less popular than mink), which made the industry less profitable. But pre-eminent was a change in public attitudes which made the killing of fur seals, like Harp seals, for their skins, unacceptable to a large segment of the public and resulted in the passing in the United States of the Marine Mammal Protection Act.

It was not only in the North Pacific that fur seals were exploited. Wherever they occurred, the seals were hunted. The oldest industries were established in South Africa from about 1610 and in Uruguay even earlier, shortly after the European discovery of the country in 1515. Both these hunts continue to this day. Initially, these hunts were for oil and hides and were relatively small-scale affairs. Large-scale fur sealing began in the Southern Hemisphere in 1775, when a group of four New England oil merchants fitted out 16 vessels to go whaling in the South Atlantic and take seals on the Falkland Islands.

It was in the same year, 1775, that Captain Cook discovered South Georgia, and commented in his account that the beaches swarmed with seals. They soon swarmed with sealers. The first recorded sealing visit to South Georgia was in 1786. Sealing there reached a peak in 1800–01, when 17 British and American vessels took 112,000 skins of the Antarctic fur seal. By 1822 James Weddell calculated that 1,200,000 furs had been taken at South Georgia and its seals were nearly extinct.

Other southern sealing grounds were soon opened up. By the late 1770s, British vessels were combing the beaches and rocks round Tierra del Fuego and moving on into the Pacific. The huge herds of fur seals on the Juan Fernandez Islands were soon under attack. One ship alone, the *Eliza* from New York, took 38,000 skins direct to Canton and sold them for $16,000. Sealing on the California coast for Guadalupe fur seals was first recorded in 1805, but these skins, together with those of the Galapagos fur seal, were not as highly valued as skins from colder regions.

Returning to the Atlantic sector, in 1819 the South Shetland Islands were discovered and in only three seasons, the fur seals there had been almost completely exterminated. James Weddell calculated that 320,000 had been taken there during 1821 and 1822.

Because fur seals were hunted so relentlessly, the search for new grounds was continuous. Seals were taken on Tristan da Cunha, Gough Island and the Prince Edward Islands, and then further into the Indian Ocean, at the Crozets, Amsterdam Island, and Kerguelen and Heard Island. The Bass Strait colonies of Australian fur seals, and the New Zealand fur seal colonies around the south of that country and finally at Macquarie Island, were all visited and stripped of their seals.

The sealers were indiscriminate in their activities. All the seals on the beach were killed: the younger ones and the females for their fur and the old bulls for their leather. Often more seals would be killed than there was salt available for preserving the skins. A sad story is told of the *Pegasus* which took 100,000 skins from the Antipodes Islands, but had insufficient salt for them. On the voyage home, the skins heated and on arriving in London had to be dug out of the hold and sold as manure. The early practice of the sealers had been to dry the skins and carry them to China. Here, the principal product may have been not the furred skin, but felt, made by shaving the guard hairs and fur from the skin and pressing them together. Later, a process was developed in London for removing the guard hairs, leaving the underfur exposed. This could then be straightened and dyed, to produce the seal skin of the furrier. For this, salted skins were required, since the hide of a dried pelt might not be sufficiently well preserved for tanning.

Life on a sealer was hard. Although seals were initially abundant, the terrain at most rookeries was extremely rugged and landing through the surf of oceanic islands was dangerous. Even if lives were not lost, as they not infrequently were, it was no sinecure to be landed on a Subantarctic island beach, wet to the skin, for a day's sealing.

Parties were often left ashore with a few provisions, to kill seals and salt the skins until their parent vessel returned for them. Writing in the 1870s, Captain Althearn tells a friend about to set off for the Bounty Rocks what to do should he have the fortune to discover an undisturbed rookery:

> If you got out there early and saw a great show of seals, I should get as many on board as I could without running any risk of not getting back in time. I would leave on the rocks all the men I thought would blab; go to the most convenient port, ship my skins, get what I needed [more salt] and go back to the rocks, and finish up the season and go to Valparaiso without touching at New Zealand, and I should expect to have another season without company.

Many men were left on the rocks, and sometimes their ships failed to return for them. One group, left on the Snares Islands in 1810, was not picked up until 1817!

By 1830, almost all the sealing grounds had been visited and stripped of their seals. However, usually not all the seals were taken and often there was a slow recovery. At South Georgia, for example, after the near-extermination recorded by Weddell in 1821, a few skins were taken in 1838–39 and again in the 1870s. The last recorded catch was in 1908, when the New Bedford brig *Daisy* took 170 skins.

Southern Hemisphere fur sealing died out everywhere but in Uruguay and South Africa, initially because of the lack of seals. By the time the stocks had recovered, as they did at almost all sites, the seals had been protected and the market had collapsed, as it did for Northern fur seals. The South African industry has continued, but more as a fisheries protection measure (see Chapter 10) than as a commercial undertaking. In Uruguay, a small local market sustains a minor industry.

COMMERCIAL SEALING – ELEPHANT OILING

While the Southern Hemisphere sealers sought for fur seals, they could always get some sort of cargo by slaughtering elephant seals and boiling their blubber for oil. Elephant oiling, as this was known, was carried on at nearly all the fur seal locations and a few other places besides. Little equipment was needed, other than cast-iron trypots identical to those used by the whalers of those days, and barrels to hold the oil. The small seals were killed with a club and the big bulls with a lance or a musket ball. As in fur sealing, shallops (light boats brought down in frame and erected at the sealing grounds) were used to take sealing parties around the islands and bring back the catch. Alternatively, parties might be put ashore to kill seals and be picked up later.

Once a seal was killed, the skin was stripped off and the blubber removed in segments. These were then minced into fine strips and boiled out in the pots, either on the sealing vessel or ashore. For fuel, the boiled-out scraps of blubber, 'fritters', were used, though it was rumoured that the fire might be initially lighted with a fat penguin or two. At several places around South Georgia, for instance, one can find the trypots used by the sealers, together with bundles of oak barrel staves and iron hoops, now indicated only by circles of rust in the soil.

Elephant seals were never so radically reduced as the fur seals, but by the end of the nineteenth century the price of oil was depressed, first by the development of petroleum and kerosene for lighting, and subsequently by competition with whale oil produced by the developing Antarctic whaling industry. Elephant sealing in this form died out soon after the turn of the century, save for one remarkable old skipper. Benjamin Cleveland, who took the last cargo of fur seals from South Georgia in his brig the *Daisy*, stayed on as the last of the old elephant oilers. He combined elephant oiling with hunting whales in a small way and made his last trip after elephant seals in 1921, when he visited Kerguelen.

But elephant oiling had a longer history and a modern development. When the Norwegian whaling pioneer, C.A. Larsen, established the first Antarctic whaling station at Grytviken in South Georgia in 1904, he noted the abundance of elephant seals there and in 1910 he was granted a licence by the British authorities to take them. This was on very different terms from those assumed by Cleveland and his like. The coast of South Georgia was divided into four sealing divisions, of which only three could be worked in any one year and the catch was restricted to adult males. Not more than 2,000 could be taken each year from each division.

Techniques differed markedly from those used by the old sealers. Modern elephant oiling was run as an ancillary industry to the whaling shore factory. Seal boats (obsolete whalecatchers of between 80 and 250 tonnes) were sent out from the whaling station. A gang of nine men was sent ashore in a pram. One man, the beater, selected a bull and drove it to the water's edge by striking it over the head with a metal tube about 2 m (6½ ft) long. It was not necessary to hit the seal heavily; even light blows on the top of the head – an area very vulnerable in the course of normal seal fighting – would drive a big bull. On arriving at the water's edge, the seal was shot in the head and then stabbed in the heart to bleed. Next, one of three flensers would cut the seal along the centre of the back, around the head and tail, and around the fore flippers. Two flaps of skin and blubber together were then flensed away from the sides of the seal. At this stage, three hookers would join the flenser, and with long iron hooks roll the carcase away from the blubber while the flenser (often joined by a companion at this stage) freed the carcase with long sweeps of his knife. Finally, when the carcase had been rolled free, a rope strop was passed through the almost circular sheet of blubber, which was then floated off into the sea, to be towed out to the sealer and stowed in its hold.

It sounds a very simple operation and in good conditions could take no

Elephant sealing on South Georgia in 1958. An old trypot from the previous century lies on the beach; at the water's edge a group of sealers flense a bull elephant seal.

more than five to ten minutes, but conditions rarely were good. Rough seas and ice on the beach made it very much more difficult and the sealers were always exposed to attacks from cows, anxious to protect their pups. The sealers showed great ingenuity in overcoming difficulties, but at the best it was a cold, wet job.

On arrival at the whaling station, the cargo of skins was unloaded and, after mincing in a mechanical hogger, boiled up under steam pressure exactly as for whale blubber. No attempt was made to separate the skin from the blubber: all was chopped and boiled together. The average seal produced about a third of a tonne of high-quality oil, all but indistinguishable from whale oil, and used for the same purpose – mainly margarine.

The original quota – 6,000 a year – had been chosen arbitrarily, but it was an excellent guess. Unfortunately, the authorities were tempted to raise this quota in the late 1940s to 9,000. This was more than the stock could bear and the population declined. However, following a careful analysis of the population by Dick Laws, who was to become the UK's leading seal biologist, a management plan was developed. Laws based his plan on calculations of growth and survival made possible by his discovery that seals could be aged by counting patterns of rings in the dentine, revealed by cross-sectioning the teeth. It was a coincidence that, at the same time Laws was doing his research in South Georgia, Vic Scheffer in the Pribilofs had made the same discovery: this time using cementum ridges on the roots of fur seal teeth.

Laws recommended quotas for South Georgia, based on the stock in the different divisions – but totalling 6,000 – which were designed to bring the average age of the kill to about 7.5 years, this being the age at which the combination of growth and mortality would result in the highest production. To monitor the progress of this plan, the sealers were required to collect a lower canine tooth from every twentieth seal killed. These teeth were later polished and examined to determine the trend in the average age, and the quota adjusted accordingly.

Laws' management plan was highly successful and oil production from the South Georgia herd increased from the mid-1950s as the average age of seals killed went up. By 1961 it had reached 7.7 years and the herd was providing a maximum sustainable yield, in this case about 6 per cent of the standing crop each year.

The elephant seals at South Georgia were a good example of a rationally managed natural resource. Their basic pinniped characteristics had, in a way, pre-adapted them for this role. Because they were naturally highly poly-gynous, there was an available surplus of bulls that could be harvested without risking a drop in the impregnation rate; because of their great sexual dimorphism, there was no difficulty in distinguishing the harvestable males from the strictly protected females; and their great absolute size meant that the sealers were handling economically sized packages of the desired product.

Sealing at South Georgia, unlike whaling, was rationally managed and sustainable. However, when the whaling industry collapsed in 1964, because of gross overexploitation, the sealing industry which was intimately tied to it, also ceased. The elephant seals now live in peace.

In this chapter I have reviewed four important industries based on pinnipeds. There are others: for example, Caspian seals are harvested for blubber and fur, and Weddell seals were once taken extensively in the Antarctic to feed sledge dogs. Walruses have been hunted since prehistoric times and their tusks are still taken by native hunters for carving. Besides oil, skins and ivory, pinnipeds provide another commercial product: the oriental medicine market values highly 'trimmings' from seals. A set of trimmings comprises the penis, with its baculum, the testes and the whiskers. These were once sold from the Pribilofs, obtained from either Northern fur seals or Steller sea lions. Now the supply comes mainly from Cape fur seals.

Sealing industries, though not yet dead, have passed their peak. In many areas, seals are strictly protected, though native subsistence hunts may be allowed. In most other regions, sealing is regulated. Today the greatest threats to seals come from factors other than hunting. I shall examine some of these in the next chapter.

Chapter 10
Seals and Fisheries

However much they are loved by the general public, seals are not usually popular with fishermen. Seals and sea lions are claimed to affect fisheries adversely in three ways: firstly, and usually most conspicuously, by damaging fishing gear and captive fish; secondly, and perhaps most seriously, by eating fish which might otherwise have been taken in the fishery; and finally, though not significantly on a global scale, by acting as the definitive host of parasites which spend the larval stage in food fish. Let me examine these three categories.

DAMAGE TO GEAR AND CAUGHT FISH

Damage to fishing nets most often happens with what are called 'fixed engines'. These are usually netting cages, erected in the sea or a river where local conditions cause fish to follow a restricted course. Salmon, for example, must return to rivers to spawn, and salmon fishermen set bag nets along the coast near the estuary where the salmon are migrating towards the river. The bag net consists of a series of netting pens, each leading into the other through funnel-shaped cheeks containing a narrow door. Leading out from the bag is a long panel of netting – the leader – which intercepts the fish and guides them to the first of the doors. The fish swim through the doors and finally accumulate in the last pen, the fish court.

Nets like these can be very effective in catching salmon and at the end of a day's fishing the fish court can be teeming with a crowd of ripe salmon. Not surprisingly, these nets attract seals. A seal snapping at the captive salmon through the meshes of the net can damage many fish and, as salmon is a luxury dish, marked fish are generally a good deal less valuable than perfect specimens. An even worse situation arises if a seal follows the fish down the leader and into the fish court. Here the seal is trapped and in its struggles to escape, it may tear the net, allowing the captive fish to escape and putting the net out of commission until it is repaired.

In Scotland, where net fishing for salmon is an important local industry, seal damage was once very significant. However, the replacement of tarred hemp by synthetic fibres (which are stronger and more elastic) for making the nets, and the fitting of guards to the doors, which allow the passage of salmon but not seals, has lessened the damage. It is still significant, however, and where seals are numerous, it is usual to set the nets where a watch can be kept from the cliff top by a net skipper armed with a rifle. Probably not many seals are shot by the net skippers, but firing at them may remove the occasional rogue animals, for it seems that most of these attacks are the work of individual seals which have adopted the behaviour pattern of feeding at nets.

In the Maritime Provinces of Canada, trap nets – unlike bag nets which are anchored to the shore – float freely in the sea, and are set for herring and

The sight of a seal chewing a fish is likely to arouse strong feelings in fishermen.

mackerel. Seals enter these by sliding over the float lines at the top of the nets. A seal swimming about inside the net may drive out fish already caught and may deter other fish from entering the net.

In recent years the practice of farming salmon by rearing the young fish in netting cages suspended in the sea has become widespread. Many sheltered fjords in Norway or sea lochs in Scotland contain these salmon pens. Like a bag or trap net, the pen attracts seals, which attempt to break through the netting to get at the fish. Seals are only rarely successful in this, though when they are, the results can be disastrous for the salmon farmer, since several thousand fish may be released and lost. A Shetland salmon farmer reported that in one night's attack a single seal had 'decimated' his crop, destroying up to 13,000 salmon worth around £20 apiece (*The Times*, 2 March 1989). It is hard to believe that a single seal had actually destroyed this number of salmon (or that they were worth £20 apiece to the producer), but it is possible that this was close to the number of fish liberated.

Besides actual damage or loss of fish, the presence of a seal around a pen is claimed to have a bad effect on the trapped fish. Most salmon farmers now enclose their rearing pens in an outer wall of stout netting which keeps seals (and otters) at a distance.

In Tasmania, similar cages are used for rearing salmon and rainbow trout and, as in the Northern Hemisphere, these are sometimes visited by seals. Fish are damaged and nets holed, though only rarely to the extent that

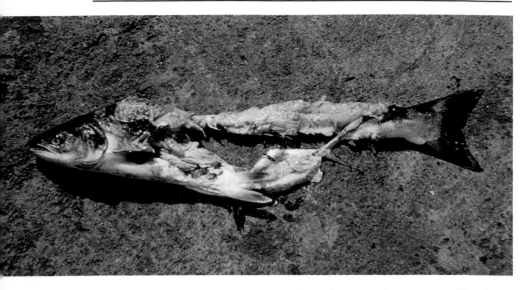

A salmon partly eaten by a seal, recovered from a bag net on the east coast of Scotland.

substantial losses of fish result. Even so, one producer claimed to have lost more than A$500,000 worth of fish in a year. Most of these attacks are caused by Australian fur seals, though occasionally Leopard seals are involved: perhaps the only instance where an Antarctic seal impacts on a commercial fishery. In a year-long study, 35 dead seals were examined at Tasmanian fish farms – 33 Australian fur seals and two Leopard seals. Interestingly, all were males.

Drift-net fishermen can also be troubled by seals. In the North Sea it was once common for shoals of herring to be caught in floating panels of netting suspended in the sea. The herring swam into the meshes of the net and were trapped there by their gills. Seals would often attack the gilled fish, biting off their heads or bodies (depending on from which side of the net the seal approached). The loss of the fish eaten was probably negligible in terms of the total catch, but the fishermen claimed that the seal snapping at the net would shake free many more fish than were devoured. I vividly recall an outing on a herring drifter from Lowestoft, in East Anglia, where at one stage the crew were attempting to haul in a net while in the water a Harbour seal was vigorously tugging in the opposite direction!

Drift nets are also used to take salmon and seal damage to these may at times be severe. In one sample of 286 salmon caught in Scottish drift nets, 70 (24.5 per cent) had been damaged by seals. In the next chapter I shall have more to say about drift nets, but from the opposite viewpoint – as a danger to seals and other marine life.

Long-lining can also be affected by seals, which eat the baits from the hooks or the hooked fish themselves. Bennet Rae, a Scottish fisheries biologist with a peculiar aversion for seals, gave an account of a seal which had stripped every hook on a long-line up to the one on which it was itself caught and drowned.

In some places, removing baits from hooks or traps may be a significant cause of damage to a fishery, but it is not usually possible to pin this on seals. In eastern Canada, seals are claimed to break into lobster-pots to steal baits, releasing lobsters already caught and, of course, making it unlikely that the pot will catch further lobsters. In Orkney, on the other hand, many of the lobster fishermen favour seals since they eat octopus, which themselves prey on lobsters.

Off southern Africa, the resident Cape fur seals are a substantial problem to fisheries. Purse-seine vessels fishing for anchovy, pilchard or horse mackerel, are plagued by these seals which disturb fish shoals or fish within nets. A purse seine consists of a wall of netting suspended in the water. This is deployed to surround a shoal of fish. When the net has encircled the shoal, the bottom of the net is drawn together, or 'pursed', and the fish are trapped. Large numbers of fur seals, up to 500, may gather as the net is pursed, and jump over the float line into the bag. Here, in full view of the fishermen, the seals feed on the catch. Worse than this, by depressing the float line as they move over it, the seals allow large quantities of fish to escape. According to the skippers, however, the main damage is done before the pursing is complete. The presence of the seals causes the fish to dive rapidly and thus escape being trapped as the net is pursed.

Fishing operations can be impeded in other ways also. Seals may get caught in the fish pump (used to remove the fish from the net) and die. Peter Shaugnessy recounts how on one occasion three fur seals clambered up a net and climbed aboard the fishing vessel. Two of them were chased overboard, but the third could not be removed until the vessel reached port. One can imagine the embarrassment of having a large and active fur seal loose on the factory deck!

Cape fur seals also follow bottom trawlers fishing for hake to pluck fish from the meshes of the net. Fish in a trawl are less accessible than those in a seine and so the seals present fewer problems, unless they get trapped in the trawl and are delivered live on the factory deck.

Another factor involved in fisheries damage by seals is damage to gear. Torn nets may not fish so efficiently, or indeed, at all, in the case of a bag or trap net with a large hole in it. Although repairs may not be expensive, the time lost in recovering a net, repairing it and setting it again, may be significant in a seasonal fishery where most of the catch is taken in a few weeks. Many salmon fishermen believe that fish will avoid a net which has previously contained a seal. Since salmon are known to have an extraordinarily sensitive olfactory sense (they locate their natal streams by smell) and since most seals have a strong odour, even to the relatively insensitive human nose, this seems not unlikely. But it is difficult for a netsman to know whether his net is failing to catch fish because a seal has been in it, or for some other reason. Very often the temptation will be to blame the seal.

Perhaps understandably, fishermen can be enraged simply by seeing seals feeding on fish. An inshore fisherman watching a Harbour seal devouring a fat sea trout off Blakeney Harbour in Norfolk was convinced that had the seal not been there, he would certainly have caught the trout, though in fact sea trout rarely figured in his catch. At the mouths of the salmon rivers on the north-west coast of North America, sea lions and Harbour seals congregate during the run to feed on the fish. Again the presumption is made that the fish eaten would otherwise have figured in the catch if the seals had not been there, and the fishermen feel aggrieved.

DAMAGE TO FISH STOCKS

Close encounters with seals provoke the most immediate reactions. More thoughtful fishermen, however, realize that seals eat fish, and where there are large numbers of seals, large amounts of fish are being consumed and hence their potential catches are reduced. This is the aspect of seal damage that most often concerns governments. Although the apparent logic of this argument seems irrefutable, it is surprisingly difficult to demonstrate in practice. Ray Beverton, one of England's leading fisheries biologists, noted that the only really convincing case of this sort of which he was aware was the exceptional one of a population of freshwater Harbour seals living in the Lower Seal Lake in Ungava, Quebec, which had depleted the population of lake trout (*Savelinus namaycush*) in the lake. The fish showed all the characteristic signs of gross over-exploitation (i.e., high mortality, reduced age at maturity, accelerated growth-rate and high specific fecundity), compared with other populations living in lakes where no seals occurred.

The conditions in Lower Seal Lake were very simple. In the oceans they will always be more complicated, and in order to make any sense of them at all, we need to simplify them. Beverton did this by means of a series of simple models. In the first, it is postulated that the seals and the fishery both exploit a single species of fish (we will call this the target fish). This is an unlikely situation, for the fishery is likely to target many species and the seals may switch from prey to prey as availability changes. Furthermore, the target fish are likely to have other predators, such as sea-birds or porpoises. Or again, the target fish population may be preyed upon by other fish, the predator fish, which in turn may be eaten by the seals or caught by the fishermen. If the seals preferentially feed on the predator fish, they may actually benefit the target fish stock. Indeed, if the seals fed exclusively on the predator fish, while the fishery concentrated exclusively on the target fish, then the effect of the seals on the fishery would be beneficial. If the converse were true, with the fishery catching the predator fish and the seals eating their prey exclusively, the outcome for the fishery could be severe, even though the seals did not destroy any of the predator fish.

In all these cases, which are very simplified, the effects of the seals will be different, ranging from beneficial to adverse, with the latter predominating. Fisheries biologists try to calculate the magnitude of the effect of seal predation on fish stocks. To do this they need four sets of data: the size and composition of the population of seals concerned; the qualitative and quantitative composition of their diet; their daily food requirement, adjusted for season, age class, etc; and their feeding locations and how these correspond with the fishery concerned. None of these data are easy to obtain, but considerable efforts have been made to provide them for some seal–fishery interactions.

Fisheries biologists are usually concerned with calculating the possible increase in commercial catches should seal predation be reduced. The ratio of the change of commercial catch to the change of seal consumption, R, depends (in a simple analysis) on the relative magnitudes of the fishing mortality, F, and the natural mortality (excluding seal predation) of the fish stock, M, and it is not affected by their absolute values, or by the rate of predation by the seals.

$$R = F/(F + M)$$

From this model we find that the benefit to the fishery from a reduction in seal predation increases as the fishing intensity (F) increases and also as predation intensity increases, particularly when fishing intensity is high. Also the relative gain to the fishery is greater when the seal predation starts earlier in the life of the target fish than does the fishing mortality (i.e., the seals are eating fish smaller than the commercial catch).

The theoretical gain to the fishery may be either greater or less than the quantity of fish removed by the seals, depending on the relative rates of fishing, seal-induced and natural mortality, and on the ages at which the fish become susceptible to fishing and seal mortality.

Models such as this can be applied only if certain assumptions are made. These include:

- that a change in the rate of seal predation would not change the natural mortality of the fish;
- that the seal predation is spread evenly over the whole of the fish population;
- that the seal predation rate is independent of the fish density;
- that fish growth and recruitment rate are not density dependent.

In practice, these assumptions are not often valid and this, coupled with the imprecision of the data used, makes the application of such models a rather unscientific process. However, even with all its faults, it is difficult to deny the general applicability of the model that in areas of high seal density, reduction of seal numbers would result in an increase of fish landed. This, of course, may not be simply related to the value of the catch, the feature which is usually of greatest interest to the fishermen. One economist has even argued that not only the price per tonne landed might fall if landings increased – because of ordinary supply and demand – but so too might the gross return to the industry. Most fishermen might be sceptical of this and eager to take the risk.

SEALS AS PARASITE HOSTS

Pinnipeds, in common with all other wild mammals, harbour a variety of internal parasites. Conspicuous among these are nematodes, or round worms, that live in the stomach, lungs and other viscera, and cestodes (tapeworms) and acanthocephalans (hookworms) usually found further down the gut. For the most part, the seal or sea lion lives happily with its internal fauna, though some individuals are found with what seem to be excessive parasite burdens.

Three roundworms are very commonly found in the stomach of many different pinnipeds. These are *Contracaecum osculatum*, *Pseudoterranova* (= *Porrocaecum*, = *Terranova*, = *Phocanema*) *decipiens* and *Anisakis similis*. The first of these worms is usually the most abundant. The larvae of *Contracaecum* live in cephalopods and are of no importance to fisheries. This is very much not the case with *Pseudoterranova*, the notorious codworm. On both sides of the North Atlantic, codworm causes a serious problem to fisheries.

The life cycle of *Pseudoterranova* begins when the adult worms in the stomach of the seal (or sea lion, or walrus) shed their eggs. These are passed out with the faeces of the pinniped, hatch within 10 to 60 days, and the resulting first-stage larvae are eaten by benthic crustacea and establish themselves in their bodies. These in turn are eaten by a second invertebrate host, which may be various sorts of crustacean, or a polychaete worm or nudibranch mollusc. Should these infected organisms be eaten by a demersal fish, the liberated larvae bore their way through the gut wall and encyst in the mesenteries of the muscles of the abdominal cavity. Here, the larvae remain until their host is eaten. If the host's stomach is a suitable environment, the larvae are liberated and mature into egg-laying adults, completing the cycle.

Pseudoterranova seems to have a particular preference for cod and, to a lesser extent, other gadoid fish, such as haddock and saithe, as hosts for the final-stage larva (or perhaps these fish, because of their economic importance, are better sampled). For a definitive host, it seems to prefer the Grey seal.

When cod is gutted for sale, the codworm larvae in the mesenteries are discarded, but any that have encysted in the body wall – the 'flaps', as this part of the fillet is known – are quite conspicuous. They are yellowish or pink and stand out well against the white cod flesh. Mostly they are overlooked, but if the fish has not been iced or frozen, they are capable of a little languorous wriggling, which can distress a sensitive cook. Codworm are of little actual danger to humans, since they are killed by even the lightest

An opened stomach from a Grey seal, showing the nematode worms that infest nearly all seals. Most of these worms are *Contracaecum*, which pose no problems, either to seals or fisheries; but some are *Pseudoterranova*, the larvae of which are codworm.

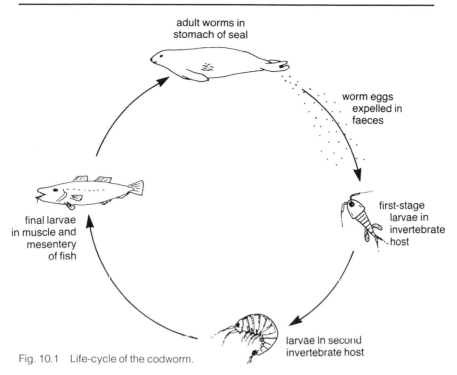

adult worms in
stomach of seal

worm eggs
expelled in
faeces

first-stage
larvae in
invertebrate
host

final larvae
in muscle and
mesentery
of fish

larvae in second
invertebrate host

Fig. 10.1   Life-cycle of the codworm.

cooking or by freezing, but in Japan, where eating raw fish is common, there have been cases of infection by codworm.

The problem from the fisheries point of view is that cod infected with codworm are not only less marketable, but may prejudice the consumer against further purchases of fish. Because of this, it is necessary to candle cod fillets from areas where infection rates are high and remove the worms by hand – a tedious process. Interestingly, large dried cod from the Grand Banks that were infected with codworm ('pearly cod') were at one time said to be preferred on the Portuguese market for making the traditional dish, *bacalhau*.

The discovery that seals, and particularly Grey seals, were the definitive hosts of codworm led to demands in Canada, the UK and Norway for the control of the seals as a means of reducing infection rates. There is, however, no clear relationship between the abundance of definitive hosts and the proportion of fish infected. In the central North Sea, the proportion of infected cod rose from 4 per cent in 1956–61 to 47 per cent in 1966–70, which paralleled an increase in Grey seal numbers. Since then, although the seals have continued to increase, there has been no corresponding trend in codworm.

The third common stomach nematode, *Anisakis simplex*, is the herring worm, the larvae of which are found in herring. This is perhaps more potentially dangerous to humans in the West, since the practice of eating raw or only very lightly salted herring is common in the Netherlands and neighbouring coastal communities. However, seals seem to be less involved in the transmission of this parasite, whose principal definitive host appears to be small cetaceans.

SEAL CONTROL – THE FISHERMEN'S RESPONSE

Fishermen who feel strongly that their livelihood is being endangered by seals are likely to try to do something about it. The remedies they can employ, however, are limited. I have mentioned already how salmon net owners in Scotland station net skippers on cliffs to shoot at seals in the water. Many other fishermen who encounter seals carry rifles with them with which to pot at seals, even such rare species as the Mediterranean monk seal. However, seals in the water are difficult to shoot from a boat and any reduction in the number of seals encountered is more likely to be caused by the seals learning to be wary of boats than by a real reduction in seal populations. Dynamite charges tossed over into the water to disable (and certainly discourage) seals have been used off the Pacific coast of North America, but it is not known whether this form of deterrence is economically worthwhile.

Poison was used to kill Grey seals at salmon at nets in Scotland. A kelt (a spawned-out salmon) was packed with strychnine and hung on the side of a net to be taken by a maurauding seal. The method was claimed to be successful, in that a seal which regularly raided nets could be killed in this way, but strychnine causes an agonizing death and the method was subsequently declared illegal.

Attempts to reduce seal damage by killing seals at nets or in their vicinity do not seem to have been very successful in general. Active discouragement has also been widely experimented with. People have tried using underwater fireworks, arc-discharge transducers (which produce a sharp 'crack' underwater) and even recordings of killer whale vocalizations. None of these has proved very successful.

In one series of experiments with Cape fur seals off South Africa, it was found that Thunderflash and Beluga firecrackers were effective in making seals dive, but they did not cause them to move away from the vessel. In the 1970s, one of the skippers concerned was using 5,000 firecrackers in a season and the manufacturers produced 248,000 between 1973 and 1975. Their use was prohibited in 1976 on the grounds that they had no adequate effect on the seals and they were extremely harmful to shoals of pelagic fish. Both these reasons were queried by the scientists who conducted the experiments.

Recorded Killer whale vocalizations had been shown to have a strong deterrent effect on Grey whales and belugas, and these also were tried off South Africa. Playing the recordings had a noticeable effect on the fur seals. They dived and remained submerged for 15 to 30 seconds. They then rose and looked at the ship playing the recordings, before resuming their previous behaviour of floating in the water or swimming slowly at the surface. None fled.

Other experiments with different species of pinnipeds have shown similar negative results. Seals respond strongly to the presence of Killer whales in the water, usually by hauling out if that is possible, but they seem to be able to distinguish the real thing from the recordings (which is perhaps not surprising, in view of the seal's auditory sensitivity). An added risk of using sound signals as a seal deterrent around nets or rearing cages in the absence of any supporting negative stimulus is that the seals may not only become habituated to the device, they may actually learn to recognize it as a signal that potential food is in the neighbourhood. From being a warning device, the signal becomes a dinner bell.

SEAL CONTROL – THE GOVERNMENT RESPONSE

When fishermen are sufficiently distressed, governments, or their fisheries departments, may take action to attempt to alleviate the problem by reducing the population of seals. There are two ways of doing this: by introducing a bounty system, or by direct culling of seals.

Bounty schemes have operated in the Wash in the UK, in Norway, Sweden, Denmark, Ireland and in Canada. Such schemes are more likely to be successful in areas where the carrying of firearms is customary. The Canadian scheme was instituted in the Maritimes in 1927 and lasted till 1976. It was very successful in reducing the local populations of Harbour seals. Initially the bounty was paid on production of the snout of the seal, but this was not very easily identifiable and hunters would at times substitute other bits and pieces (including the occasional porcupine scrotum!). To avoid this, in 1949 the hunters were required to produce the jaw of the animal killed. Jaws were easily identifiable as being from seals, but the authorities were surprised to receive a substantial numbers of jaws which proved to be from Grey seals, a species which at that time was not known to be abundant in Canada. In 1976 the bounty was switched from Harbour seals to Grey seals and from then until 1983 bounty was paid on 5,751 Grey seals, though it was believed that the number actually killed may have been twice as great.

Another means of government control of seal numbers has been the encouragement, or even sponsorship, of commercial seal hunting. In South Africa, the culling of Cape fur seals is justified largely on the grounds of fisheries protection. In the UK, Grey seal pup hunting in the Orkneys was licensed by the Department of Agriculture and Fisheries for Scotland (DAFS) as a means of controlling increasing seal numbers in response to complaints from fishermen.

A Consultative Committee set up in 1959 had recommended in 1963 that the Grey seal stock be reduced by 25 per cent of its 1961 value in the Orkneys. It was proposed that this reduction could be achieved by allowing private hunters to cull weaned pups, whose skins could then be sold to defray the costs of the operations and yield a profit. An annual quota of 750 was set, though this was done in the knowledge that this number would be insufficient to achieve the result desired.

The small industry thus established was modestly profitable. Most of the hunting was done by a couple of hunters from Glasgow (both of them zoology graduates!) who purchased two small islands in Orkney for their operations. Interestingly, this had the direct result of establishing a parallel industry based on Harbour seals in the Wash, East Anglia. At this time (the early 1960s), Harbour seals, unlike Grey seals, were not legally protected and in fact were bountied in the Wash.

Despite the pup cull, the Grey seal population in the north of Scotland continued to increase. The quota was raised from 750 pups to 1,000 in 1971, but this had little effect, except to outrage those who felt that the killing of baby seals was wrong. Grey seal numbers in Scottish waters increased from about 35,000 in the mid-1960s to about 60,000 in 1978. DAFS calculated that the amount of fish consumed by these seals had an estimated value of between £15 million and £20 million.

This loss was regarded as intolerable and a decision was taken to reduce stocks to their mid-1960s' level by killing 900 cows and their pups together with another 4,000 moulted pups in each of the six years 1977–82. Pup culling alone was rejected because it had been shown that the equilibrium obtained by killing only pups was unstable and the six-year lag that must elapse between killing the pups and observing the effect of this on the population could leave the stock vulnerable to unforeseen environmental hazards.

This ambitious policy was introduced in 1977, when a Norwegian sealing vessel was chartered to carry out the cull. The Norwegian sealers found work on the storm-swept Scottish islands very different from the calm seas of the pack ice of the north-west Atlantic Harp-sealing grounds. The season's work resulted in a kill of only 394 pups and 286 cows.

The policy collapsed when public opposition caused a political reversal, but it seems unlikely that it could ever have succeeded in the form in which it was mounted. The Grey seal population in Scotland continued to increase and fishermen continue to complain, but it is likely that the major problem they face is not the abundance of the seals but the excessive harvesting by the fishing industry. Were all the seals to be removed, it is likely that fishing effort would increase until stocks were reduced to or below their present levels. Fisheries biologists seem unable to persuade governments to adopt and enforce sustainable fishing regimes.

Chapter 11
Seals and Life in the Modern World

INTRODUCTION

For millenia, seals have had to contend with the pressure from hunters and the anger of fishermen. As we have seen, both these factors continue to affect the life of seals. The past few decades, however, have seen other interactions between human activities and seals which may ultimately have just as significant consequences for the latter. There has also been an important change in attitudes to seals and marine mammals in general among some influential sectors of public opinion. In this chapter I shall examine these factors.

INCIDENTAL TAKE IN FISHING NETS

Since the time of Aristotle, seals have become entangled in fishing nets and many have drowned. The problem became greatly exacerbated, however, when synthetic fibres replaced natural fibres, such as cotton or hemp, in the manufacture of nets. In the late 1970s, a new form of fishing – oceanic drift-net fishing – began on a large scale. Oceanic drift nets are made up from segments of fine, almost invisible, nylon netting about 50 m (164 ft) long and 10 m (33 ft) deep. Along the top of the net is a line of floats and the bottom is weighted to make it hang vertically in the water. These segments are strung together to make floating curtains which can be up to 60 km (37 miles) long. At the peak fishing season in the North Pacific, fishing vessels from Japan, Taiwan and South Korea deployed as much as 40,000 km (25,000 miles) of these nets nightly.

Drift nets are set for species such as salmon, tuna or some squid, but they are liable to catch everything in their path: turtles, sea-birds and marine mammals, including in the Pacific Northern fur seals and occasional elephant seals. Similar activities impacted New Zealand fur seals in the South Pacific.

However recent intergovernmental agreements restricting the use of large-scale drift nets on the high seas in the Pacific has greatly reduced mortality from this. In other areas, the danger of drift nets to marine life generally has resulted in restrictions on their use. The European Community has banned the use of drift nets more than 2.5 km (1½ miles) long in its waters. Unfortunately, the advantages of this ban have been largely nullified by the exemption from it granted to the largest users, the French tuna fishermen. They continue to operate 5 km (3 mile) nets under a phase-out period.

Even if oceanic drift nets are adequately controlled, seals will probably continue to die in smaller-scale nets. Off the coast of California, for example, gill- and trammel-netters frequently catch marine mammals, with Harbour seals appearing as the most frequent species, at one Harbour seal for every 712 m (2,300 ft) of nets hauled. Arctic trawlers occasionally haul up to find a drowned Ringed seal in the cod end.

ENTANGLEMENT WITH MARINE DEBRIS

With the introduction of synthetic fibres, the life of fishing nets became greatly extended. Eventually, however, nets do wear out, or are damaged and discarded. Traditionally, the way to dispose of unwanted things at sea has been to throw them 'over the wall'. Damaged nets are added to nets lost in storms or by some other mischance, and float in the ocean until eventually they wash up on a beach somewhere. As they float, these 'ghost nets' can continue to catch or entangle marine organisms, including seals. Mortality resulting from entanglement is now considered a significant threat to marine mammals, particularly in the north Pacific.

It has been shown that entanglement with even small pieces of netting can seriously impede swimming. A sea lion encumbered with a piece of trawl netting only 1.4 by 5 m (5 by 16 ft) and weighing 580 g (20 lb) was found to have its drag force increased nearly five times when swimming at 2 m/sec (6.6 ft/sec). Such an extra load on the seal's energy demand is bound to decrease its chance of survival, especially in the critical first winter.

Other forms of synthetic debris, particularly packing bands, can impose hazards. Hard nylon packing bands are used to hold together bales of

Marine debris causes much suffering to seals. This bull Antarctic fur seal has a piece of netting round its shoulders which has cut into the hide.

A young Antarctic fur seal girdled with a fragment of fish net. If this is not removed, it will cut into the skin of the seal, eventually causing death.

cardboard boxes on factory trawlers, for example. When the bales are undone to take out the boxes, the intact bands may be thrown into the sea, where they float at the surface. These seem to have an irresistible attraction, particularly though not exclusively, to otariids. At South Georgia, Antarctic fur seals are often seen with a packing band encircling their shoulders. It seems probable that these fur seals were in the habit of diving through the band in play, but continued to do this until finally they grew too large for the band to slip off. As a seal with a band round it continues to grow, the band cuts into its hide, creating an open wound that may encircle the whole of its body. There is no escape for a banded seal (unless a well-intentioned biologist takes the risk of capturing it and cutting the band – a very risky procedure) and so severe a lesion must significantly reduce the victim's chances of survival. Phocid seals, with the exception of monk seals, seem much less likely to become entangled with this sort of debris, but plastic waste in the sea remains a significant threat to many pinniped populations.

Current regulations for vessels of flag states that are members of MARPOL (the International Convention for the Prevention of Pollution from Ships) prohibit disposing of any plastic waste at sea, but it is difficult to enforce the provisions of the convention, and seals and other marine mammals are still becoming entangled.

This bull Antarctic fur seal swam into a hard nylon packing band when younger. As it has grown, the band has cut through the hide, right round the bull's shoulders.

It is less usual for phocid seals to become entangled in debris, but this female Southern elephant seal on South Georgia has a hard nylon packing band round her neck.

POLLUTION AND SEALS

The oceans are the ultimate sink for all the liquid wastes discharged into rivers or running off the land. Because of their vast extent, they have considerable power to dilute and buffer substances that are toxic, but in regions where the discharges are high, or where mixing is limited, concentrations of pollutants can occur which affect marine life. Many of these substances are not readily metabolized and hence pass through the food-chain, a process known as bioaccumulation. Seals, being top predators, are likely to accumulate the greatest proportion of such substances in their tissues.

Mercury is an example of a substance not metabolized. Mercury is an important industrial chemical, with uses in dyestuffs and fungicides, for example. High concentrations of mercury were first found in the liver and kidneys of seals from Lake Saimaa, in Finland, perhaps derived from effluents from paper mills in the vicinity. Subsequently, mercury has been found in many seals, though it was not clear that the seals were suffering any pathological symptoms as a result of this.

Mercury in fish (in which it is widespread) occurs in the highly toxic alkyl mercury form, mostly methyl mercury. However the proportion of alkyl mercury in seal livers is low, and it seems likely that seals have a mechanism for demethylating organic mercury. Since high levels of mercury appear to occur quite naturally in predator fish, such as swordfish, it is not surprising that seals which feed on fish should have evolved a mechanism for protecting themselves from the dangers of organic mercury compounds.

Such an evolutionary mechanism has had no chance to develop for compounds which have been only recently created. Chemists are constantly developing new substances, some of which are put into industrial production and made in huge quanitities. If the new compounds are stable and are not metabolized by naturally occurring organisms, they will persist in the environment. This may be seen as an advantage by their developers and users, but it can have dire consequences for ecosystems.

The organochlorines are one class of compounds that have presented special problems. The first of these to attract attention was the insecticide DDT, widely used in the closing years of World War 2 as a means of combating insect-born disease. Subsequently, it became popular as a cheap and effective agricultural insecticide and now DDT and its degradation products, DDE and TDE, are widespread throughout the world. Another important class of contaminants are the polychlorinated biphenyls, or PCBs. These very stable compounds found many uses in industry, from paints and lubricants to transformer dielectric fluids. They seemed ideal from an industrial view; no one realized their biological activity.

DDT residues were detected in Harbour seals from Holland in the early 1960s. Since then, they and other organochlorine compounds, such as dieldrin (another organochlorine insecticide) and PCBs, have been found in seals from many areas. Organochlorines are fat-soluble substances and hence accumulate in the blubber of seals, where concentrations of several hundred parts per million wet weight can occur.

At first, the damage caused by these contaminants was not obvious. Some seals with high concentrations of organochlorines appeared to be perfectly healthy. In the late 1960s, an epidemic of spontaneous abortions appeared in

California sea lions. High concentrations of DDT and PCBs were found in affected animals, but there were other tissue imbalances of mercury, selenium and cadmium, while some of the affected sea lions carried a virus similar to vesicular exanthema of swine, and others were infected with leptospirosis. Probably there was an inter-relationship of disease agents and environmental contaminants which gave rise to the abortions.

More conclusive evidence for the role of organochlorines in seal pathology came from a study of Ringed seals in the Bothnian Bay (the northern part of the Baltic Sea) by a Finnish biologist, Eero Helle, and his colleagues. Here the population of Ringed seals had been declining for several years. The examination of seals caught in fishing nets showed that about 40 per cent of females in the sample had pathological changes in their uterine horns, whereby the lumen of the uterus was greatly reduced – a condition known as stenosis. The females with stenosis, or complete occlusions of the uterus, had significantly higher concentrations of DDT and PCBs than other females. Helle concluded that since equally high levels of DDT had been recorded from California sea lions that were breeding normally, the condition was caused by the PCBs.

It was not until the 1980s that a controlled experiment was to be done on the effects on seals of organochlorines at dose rates which actually occurred in the environment. Peter Reijnders of the Dutch Research Institute for Nature Management was concerned by the steady decline of Habour seals in the Dutch Wadden Sea, an area much affected by industrial discharges from rivers draining the industrial heart of Europe. Particularly worrying was the

These seals at a research station in Holland look perfectly healthy, but they are not producing pups. The fish they receive is caught in the Wadden Sea and carries a high burden of organochlorine compounds, including PCBs and DDT residues.

decline in pups, for without recruitment the population could not maintain itself, let alone recover.

Reijnders set up a long-term experiment with two groups of seals, each of 12 females, kept in large pens provided with running sea water and a haul-out area. One group was fed on fish from the Wadden Sea, the other on fish caught out in the north-east Atlantic. The diets were nutritionally comparable (though the fish species composition was different) but they had different contents of DDT (actually the break-down product DDE) and PCBs, the Wadden Sea fish containing about seven times as much organochlorine as the Atlantic fish.

The two groups' reproductive success differed markedly. The 12 seals fed on Atlantic fish produced 10 healthy pups, while the twelve receiving the Wadden Sea fish produced only 4! Reijnders concluded that the PCBs coming from the Rhine and spreading into the western part of the Wadden Sea, where pup production declined sharply, were responsible for this, rather than the DDE or any other pollutant, since it was in this area that the decline in pups was most marked.

The actual mode of operation of the PCBS is not clear, but it seems most likely to be interference with the steroid hormone balance, causing failure of implantation or early resorption of the embryo, perhaps followed by pathological changes in the uterus.

It is not only in industrial areas that pollutants are found in seals. In the mid-1960s, DDT and its break-down products were found in the Antarctic in Crabeater seals and DDT, PCBs and chlordane compounds in Weddell seals.

Even in the Antarctic, remote from industrialization, the scene is not so pristine as it appears. Organochlorine pollutants have been found in the blubber of Crabeater seals.

Although some of these pollutants may have been introduced to the Antarctic by local activities (for example, the operation of research stations), it is possible that the main route may be via the atmosphere, implying world-wide contamination.

Pollutants are now universal in our world. The risks from persistent compounds are recognized and in many countries stringent control measures operate. However, this is not universal and in any case it will be many years before existing contamination of areas such as the Baltic disappears, even if discharges are halted. It seems that the adverse effects of a polluted diet are to some extent reversible, so if clean-up campaigns can be instituted at the source of discharges, there may be some recovery of seals and other marine mammals.

Oil pollution

With vast quantities of petroleum products being transported every day around the world, it is inevitable that small spillages occur almost constantly and occasional big ones catch the headlines depressingly frequently. The damage most associated in people's minds with oil spills, besides the aesthetic offence of oil-encrusted beaches, is the heavy mortality caused to sea-birds. Birds which come in contact with floating oil have their plumage saturated by it, are unable to fly and eventually die of hypothermia or poisoning from the toxic fractions of oil swallowed while preening. Seals can be affected in much the same way, though they seem a good deal more resistant to oil than birds.

Initial observations on oil and seals seemed reassuring. Petroleum is, after all, a naturally occurring substance and more gets into the marine system through natural seeps than through spillages. On San Miguel Island, on the Santa Barbara Channel side, the rocks are covered with smears of crude oil. These are not the results of pollution, but natural seeps. They seem not to deter a local colony of Harbour seals at all, which continue to bask on the oil-stained beach. Oil can even attract seals. On South Georgia, Southern elephant seals are often found basking in spills of heavy fuel oil (the residue left after the lighter fractions have been distilled). Here, the seals seem to appreciate the warmth generated by the sun on the intensely black oil spill. The seals apparently suffer no injury from their coating of oil.

A blow-out of a production well in the Santa Barbara Channel in 1969 caused a good deal of contamination in the elephant seal rookery on San Miguel and over 100 pups were coated with oil. However, follow-up studies failed to show that these suffered any significant consequences from their oiling. Studies on Grey seals showed that mothers were able to contact and feed their pups successfully, even if the latter were severely oiled. Attempts to clean oiled pups by well-meaning human observers probably do more harm than good.

The wreck of the supertanker *Arrow* off the Newfoundland coast in 1969 gave rise to reports that seals were suffering considerable pain from the contact of oil with their eyes, ears, noses and throats, and that suffocation by oil was a prime cause of death. This report, and others, stimulated laboratory studies into the effect of oil on seals. Ringed seals and Harp seals in outdoor pens were exposed to a floating layer of light crude oil, or had it painted on them with a brush. It was found that after 24-hours' exposure to the oil, the eyes of the

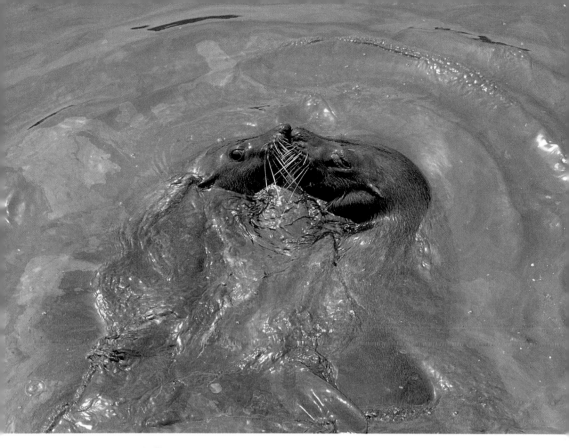

These young male Cape fur seals play happily in Cape Town docks, oblivious of the oily film that covers the water.

seals were severely inflamed, but they recovered quickly when placed in clean water.

On the other hand, when the experiments were repeated indoors, at a higher temperature, the seals quickly died on exposure to the oil. Although the experimenters attributed these deaths to the stress of captivity, it now seems more likely that the seals had been poisoned by inhaling the lighter components of the oil which, in the enclosed experiment laboratory, could not dissipate.

On 24 March 1989, the tanker *Exxon Valdez* ran aground on a shoal in Prince William Sound, Alaska, spilling its cargo of 38,000 tonnes of crude oil. Because of the enclosed nature of the area where the spill took place and the calm sea conditions, the oil took a long time to break up. Initial concern was directed to sea-birds and sea otters, but it soon became apparent that seals also had been affected.

The local population of Harbour seals was exposed to the oil both in the water and when they hauled out. Seals made no effort to move away from the spill and soon became coated with oil. Five weeks after the spill, 80 per cent of the seals seen in areas affected were heavily oiled, though this had fallen to 20 per cent by September. In the first few months after the spill, 18 Harbour seals (13 of them pups) were found dead (or died later in captivity). Necropsies of three of these suggested damage to the brain tissue that was consistent with poisoning from inhaling light oil fractions. The behaviour of living hauled-out seals seemed also to be affected: they became lethargic, which could be the result of hydrocarbon intoxication, a response similar to solvent abuse.

The comparatively small number of seal deaths recorded is only one aspect of the incident. Probably others drowned and were not recorded. Pup mortality seems to have been greater in 1989 in oiled areas and by 1992 there were still 35 per cent fewer seals in oiled areas than in 1988 (though there were 18 per cent fewer in unoiled areas also). Researchers calculated that there were about 350 fewer seals in Prince William Sound as a result of the *Exxon Valdez* spill, but some of this may have been accounted for by displacement resulting from the high level of disturbance after the spill in this normally secluded area. What the chronic effects of the incident are is not known. In 1991, hunters from a nearby village reported seeing blind seals, and seals with ulcers and sores, but it is not possible to associate these observations with the oil spill.

Some of the impact to the environment and wildlife resulted from the clean-up operations, rather than the spill itself. During the clean-up, two seals died from injuries that might have been caused by collision with a boat; a pup was hit in the face by an outboard propeller while people were trying to 'rescue' it, and a seal giving birth was scared into the water by an animal-rescue crew.

A much larger spill occurred in January 1993 when the tankler *Brear* ran aground on the south-east corner of Shetland, spilling 45,000 tonnes of light crude oil. However, in this very exposed area, the violent winter storms soon dispersed the oil. Although there is a Grey seal haul out within a mile of the spill, no seal casualties were recorded. It was noted that many of the seals appeared to be suffering from respiratory symptoms, but these could not be associated with certainty with the spill.

Seal and disease – is there a link with pollutants?

When, in the spring of 1988, reports of dead and dying seals around the North Sea began to accumulate, many people supposed that this was a result of chronic pollution of this enclosed sea. The first signs were of premature births of Harbour seal pups in the Kattegat and soon there were reports of sick seals on both the Danish and Swedish coasts. The seals were lethargic, had runny noses and struggled for breath. When dead seals were examined, it was found that their lungs were very congested and that there were signs of interstitial emphysema. The immediate cause of death was pulmonary oedema, the seeping of fluid into the lungs.

The disease spread rapidly from its start in May in the Kattegat, around Denmark and along the German and Dutch North Sea coast. By the end of July, there were large numbers of dead Harbour Seals at their breeding grounds off north Norfolk and in the Wash. By September, nearly 15,000 Harbour seals had died around the North Sea. Grey seals were also affected, but much less severely than Harbour seals. By the beginning of 1989, over 17,000 Harbour seals had died in Europe from what became generally known as 'seal plague'.

A great deal of veterinary effort went into tracking down the causative agent of this epizootic (the animal equivalent of a human epidemic). It soon became

At an oil spill from a storage tank on South Georgia, a female Southern elephant seal basks in the sun. The sun's radiation warms the black oil on the ground, and it may be this that attracts the seals.

This young Harbour seal was a casualty from the *Exxon Valdez* oil spill.

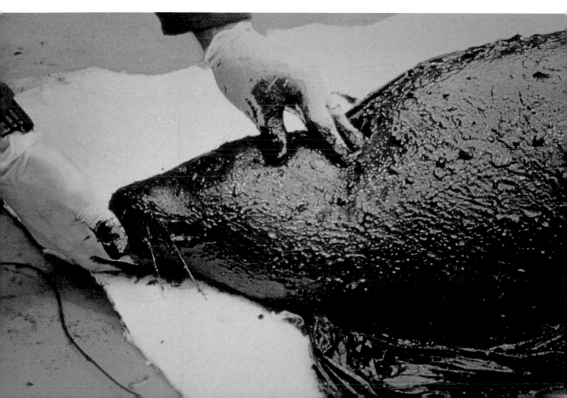

apparent that it was a newly discovered virus. It belonged to a family of morbilliviruses, which included, besides the virus affecting the seals, the viruses associated with rinderpest of cattle, human measles and canine distemper. Because of the similarity of the symptoms with the latter, the new virus was named phocine distemper virus, or PDV.

While the news of seal deaths, and many harrowing pictures, filled the newspapers and television channels, the media were quick to lay the blame at the door of pollution of the North Sea. An algal bloom and widespread reproductive failure of sea-birds in Shetland were said to be associated with the seal deaths and to result from the same cause.

It was plain to most seal biologists that the seal plague was a straightforward epizootic and the research of the virologists supported this view, but this was not necessarily evidence that the condition had nothing to do with pollution. John Harwood, head of the Sea Mammal Research Unit in England, and Peter Reijnders, the Dutchman who had done the work on pollutants and reproductive success in Harbour seals, examined this possibility. They pointed out that seals accumulate organochlorines in their blubber which are released when the seals mobilize their energy reserves at times of stress. At the breeding season, when the blubber is being used to

Seal deaths around the North Sea to the end of September 1988.

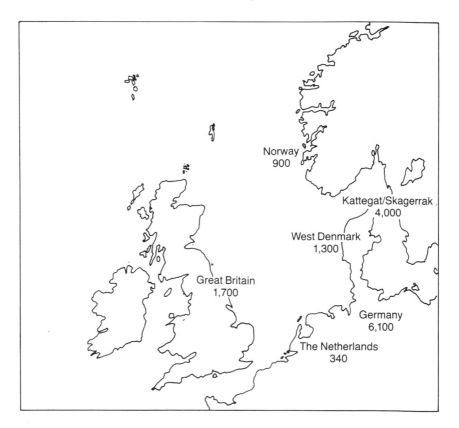

produce milk, for example, PCBs and pesticide residues, which are known to suppress the immune system of mammals in the laboratory, are released into the blood and this might render the seals more susceptible to infection. They concluded that in this way it was possible that pollution might have contributed to the severity of the epizootic, but it could not be held directly responsible.

Some cases of seal plague cropped up the following year, in 1989, but the epizootic seems now to have burnt itself out, and many surviving seals have high levels of PDV antibodies in their blood. The origin of the disease is still not known, but it seems possible that it may have been present at a low level among Harp seals, which had been extending their range in 1988 down the coast of Norway. Encountering Harbour seals with no natural immunity, the Harp seals passed on the disease which rapidly spread around the colonies in the North Sea.

Most wild animal populations live more or less in balance with their normal diseases. Some perish, the remainder develop immunity, until after a long period without the active disease, immunity declines and the stock becomes susceptible again when an outbreak is likely if the causative agent is introduced into the population. Another, less common, reason for a sudden severe outbreak of disease is if the causative agent mutates so that an existing immunity is rendered ineffective. What happened in the case of the seal plague is not certain, since screening of the population prior to the outbreak had not been done. Seal populations are subject to a host of diseases, some caused by viruses – such as PDV, or San Miguel Sea lion Virus, SMSV, or an influenza virus – some by bacteria, including strains of *Staphylococcus*, *Streptococcus*, *Corynebacteria* and *Salmonella*. However, there is no evidence that these diseases are any more or less affected by pollutants in the environment than is seal plague.

A NEW LOOK AT SEALS

For centuries people had generally been either indifferent to seals or regarded them as pests to be killed or products to be harvested. That changed in the 1960s, when the actuality of the north-west Atlantic seal hunt was brought by means of television into the living-rooms of a huge audience. A film company in Canada produced a film of Harp seal hunting around the Magdalen Islands that was syndicated on television. The beauty of the quiet splendour of the pack and the appealing dark-eyed, white-coated pups contrasted sharply with crimson blood on the ice and the harsh reality of slaughter and pelting. There were suggestions that some of the excesses of the film had been set up by the director, but whether or not the scenes shown were authentic was irrelevant. People unfamiliar with any form of animal slaughter were appalled at what they saw. Killing by clubbing was to them more repulsive than killing with a captive-bolt pistol in an abattoir and the fact that the animals killed were only a few days old made it even worse. There were widespread accusations that pups were skinned alive. This may have occurred on some occasions – some sealers might have been sadistic beasts – but, generally, in their own interests the sealers would make the sure the animals were dead before beginning skinning. Observers on the ice misled the public by reporting that the seals' hearts continued to beat even after skinning was complete and assuming that this meant the seals were still alive. Careful experiments in Norway showed that although a blow on the head brought an instantaneous end to all brain activity – the animals were 'brain-dead' – respiratory activity was observed up to 15 minutes later and the heart might continue to beat for between 30 and 56 minutes.

There had been protests about the Harp sealing before, but it was when television broadcast the scene widely over North America and Europe that action began to be taken. Attention first was concentrated on killing methods. Canada and Norway both introduced more stringent regulations on the implements or weapons to be used for killing seals. Humane society officers offered the use of pistols for killing pups without explaining why it was more humane to shoot seals than to kill them with a club. A dispassionate observer might suggest that the suffering of a seal pup on the ice, whose life was suddenly ended with a blow to the head from a club or a hakapik, was substantially less than that of a sheep or a steer transported hundreds of miles from its home to be held in lairage at an abattoir before being taken into a killing chamber and shot or electrically stunned. However, the argument was not really about suffering. It was about the ethics of killing seals at all. The fact that the seal products – fur and leather – were for a luxury trade made it even less acceptable. Fading film stars visited the ice and burnt their fur coats, rejecting the blood-stained luxuries.

In 1968, the International Fund for Animal Welfare, IFAW, was established with the expressed intention of ending the commercial exploitation of seals. Greenpeace adopted the anti-sealing campaign in 1976. Greenpeace's very effective organization kept the matter in the public eye. It concentrated its activities in Europe, where, in 1982, the European Parliament banned trade in products derived from young Harp and Hooded seals. This ban, enforced by the European Commission, largely destroyed the market for the sealers (see Chapter 9). Greenpeace and IFAW had largely achieved the end they desired, though at the cost of employment and subsistence for some fishing communities and Inuit peoples in Canada, since public revulsion at Harp sealing reflected on all seal products.

The campaign was often alleged to be based on conservation. It was not. Harp seals represented a depleted but not in any way endangered species and quota controls could have maintained the population in a steady state. Conservation interests would better have looked at the general exploitation of the North Atlantic, rather than the seal hunt. But there is inevitably less concern for fish than for cuddly seal pups. For most people nowadays, there is a deep feeling that it is wrong to bash the heads of baby seals. Victor Scheffer, now the doyen of North American seal biologists, agrees with this view and admits that it is an emotional one and claims that sentiment is a valid reason for saving marine mammals.

Whether or not one takes the view that sealing is inherently bad, or that a sustainable use of a living resource is justifiable, there is no doubt that the campaign against sealing has brought the general issue of wildlife protection to the attention of a wide public and this may be to the benefit of species and ecosystems far more endangered than the seals of the north-west Atlantic ever were.

216

We cannot be certain what the future holds for pinnipeds, but by controlling our own activities we can help to make the world safer for this young Antarctic fur seal.

THE FUTURE FOR PINNIPEDS

The world is changing rapidly today and few of these changes are in the best interests of wildlife. The greatest threat to the environment is the inexorable increase of the human population. More people require more space, more crops, more fuel wood, more everything, and this inevitably means that habitats available for wildlife are shrinking. Marine mammals are less affected by this process of habitat destruction than are terrestrial ones. Mankind has so far made few spatial demands on the ocean and none at all in the Antarctic, where more than half the world's pinnipeds live. Seals may suffer as fisheries expand and deplete stocks, but it is likely that even when it is no longer worthwhile to send out trawlers or seiners, seals and sea lions, albeit in reduced populations, will be able to find a living. A more serious threat than over-fishing may result indirectly from the thinning of the ozone layer in the stratosophere by man-made chemicals, such as the chlorofluorocarbons, or CFCs. The increased ultraviolet B radiation reaching the earth's surface as a result of this is known to be biologically damaging. As it penetrates water quite readily, it could have a serious effect on the productivity of the seas, particularly at high latitudes, and thereby affect the food sources of seals. Pinnipeds themselves are unlikely to be directly affected by increased UV-B radiation since their skins are deeply pigmented, the radiation will not penetrate deep enough to cause damage.

Subsistence hunting of seals is not currently intensive and it is likely to decline further as native people become more urbanized – a trend which seems unlikely to be reversed. Sport hunting of seals is likewise very limited and will probably disappear where it is not already banned.

Seals are probably better off than most large mammals in the struggle for survival in the coming century. They have earned public sympathy in a way that no other mammals, except the whales and the giant panda, have done. I hope that these inherently attractive and fascinating animals will continue to hold public interest; by so doing, they will ensure their future and help to protect that of other wildlife as well. If this book helps to sustain and develop an interest in the seals, sea lions and walruses of the world, it will have been worthwhile.

Further Reading

Here are some of the books I have found useful as sources for information about seals. This alphabetical list is not exhaustive, of course, and new books about seals seem to come out frequently.

Beddington, John, Beverton, Ray and Lavigne, David (1985), *Marine Mammals and Fisheries*, George Allen & Unwin, London. (An authoritative multi-author account of the subject.)

Busch, Briton Cooper (1985) *The War Against the Seals: A history of the North American Seal Fishery*, McGill-Queen's University Press, Kingston and Montreal. (A very comprehensive account of seal hunting from America.)

Fay, Francis (1982) *Ecology and Biology of the Pacific Walrus*, Odobenus rosmarus divergens *Illiger*, US Department of the Interior, Fish and Wildlife Service, North American Fauna no, 74. (A complete account by the acknowledged expert).

Gentry, Roger and Kooyman, Gerald, eds, (1986), *Fur Seals: Maternal Strategies on Land and at Sea*, Princetown University Press, Princetown. (A multi-author account relying heavily on the use of time–depth recorders.)

Howell, Brazier (1970) *Aquatic Mammals: Their Adaptations to Life in the Water*, Dover Publications, New York. (A classic account, first published in 1930, that really relates the anatomy of aquatic mammals to their life.)

King, Judith (1983) *Seals of the World*, British Museum (Natural History), Oxford University Press. (A comprehensive work by the foremost museum worker on seals in the UK.)

Lavigne, David and Kovacs, Kit (1988), *Harps and Hoods; Ice-breeding Seals of the Northwest Atlantic*, University of Waterloo Press. (The best up-to-date account of Harp and Hood seals and the sealing controversy written by experts.)

Lentifer, Jack, ed., *Selected Marine Mammals of Alaska*, Marine Mammal Commission, Washington. (A good account of research and management of seals and whales in Alaska.)

Lister-Kay, John (1979) *Seal Cull: the Grey Seal Controversy*, Penguin Books, Harmondsworth. (A good dispassionate account of seal culling in Scotland.)

Macdonald, David, ed. (1984) *The Encyclopaedia of Mammals*, Vol. 1, pp. 238–291, Seals and Sea lions, ed. Nigel Bonner (A well-illustrated account by several experts.)

Martin, Richard (1977) *Mammals of the Seas*, Batsford, London.

Reeves, Randall, Stewart, Brent and Leatherwood, Stephen (1992) *The Sierra Club Handbook of Seals and Sirenians*, Sierra Club Books, San Francisco. (A recent account of all the species, presented as a field-guide.)

Reinjders, Peter, et al. (1993) *Seals, Fur Seals, Sea Lions and Walrus*, IUCN/SSC Seal Specialist Group Status Survey and Conservation Action Plan, IUCN, Gland, Switzerland. (An up-to-date survey of the current status of all pinnipeds.)

Ridgway, Sam and Harrison, Richard (1981) *Handbook of Marine Mammals*, Vol. 1 *The Walrus, Sea Lions, Fur Seals and Sea Otter*; Vol. 2 *Seals*, Academic Press, London and New York. (A technical account, largely anatomically based.)

Riedman, Marianne (1990) *The Pinnipeds: Seals, Sea Lions and Walruses*, University of California Press, Berkeley/Los Angeles & Oxford. (A modern account of the biology of pinnipeds with much material about cetacea as well.)

Scheffer, Victor (1970) *The Year of the Seal*, Scribner's Sons, New York. (A beautifully written account of a year in the life of a Northern fur seal, by a biologist who knows this species better than any other.)

And finally, two of my own books:

Seals and Man: A Study of Interactions (1982), University of Washington Press, Seattle and London. (A concise account of seals and their interactions with mankind since prehistoric times.)

The Natural History of Seals (1989), Christopher Helm, London. (An account of phocid seals.)

Index

DATE			